The NORTHDALE later became the KYLEMOUNT.

Also in this Series___ _ _ _ _ _ _.

Estuary & River Ferries of South West England.
by Martin Langley & Edwina Small.   *ISBN 0 905184 08 4.   148 pages.*
   The many creeks and rivers of the area had rowing and sailing ferries which were later replaced by paddle and screw steamers or steam chain ferries in a number of cases. Full histories of some 139 ferries are supported by sketch maps, plans and photographs from the River Severn in the north to the River Stour, Christchurch and Poole in the south.

The Steam Collier Fleets
by J. A. MacRae & C. V. Waine.   *ISBN 0 905184 12 2.   226 pages.*
   This book was begun by Captain Jim MacRae aboard the Thames up-river collier **Hackney.** On his retirement he continued the project with Charles Waine to produce a companion volume to 'Steam Coasters & Short Sea Traders'. With the untimely death of Captain MacRae it was left to Dr. Waine to complete the project containing some 20 years research covering over 800 owners and 1200 steam colliers. It contains a full history of the coastal and continental colliers of the British Isles and the harbours built to serve them illustrated with 93 ship plans and coloured profiles, 55 photos, some in colour and 53 sketches, harbour maps and charts.

Steam Coasters & Short Sea Traders.
by C. V. Waine.   *ISBN 0 905184 04 1.   157 pages.*
   The history of the British steam coaster covering, building, repairing, engines, early designs, Clyde 'puffers' and the various engines-aft types, including the big east coast colliers. Also covered are those with engines amidships and coastal tankers. An account of the various owners, their fleets and trades is also given, with 68 plans and 29 colour profiles selected with the modelmaker in mind plus 89 black and white sketches and photos.

British Steam Tugs.
by P. N. Thomas.   *ISBN 0 905184 07 6.   222 pages.*
   The history covers early tugs, wood, iron and steel paddle tugs; harbour seeking and coastal screw tugs and ocean tugs. Thames craft, tenders and passenger carrying tugs, naval and wartime tugs. Tug owners and builders. Tug construction, engines and deck gear. Over 1000 steam tugs, 100 builders and 400 owners are covered. The plans from 1833 to 1956 will be of interest to modelmakers. More than 90 photographs, sketches, funnel colours and 29 colour profiles.

GLEN HELEN (see page 11).

s/s 165.

GENERAL ARRANGEMENT

Dim^{ns} 130'-0" x 23'-0" x 10'-6 MOULDED

SCALE ¼ ONE FOOT

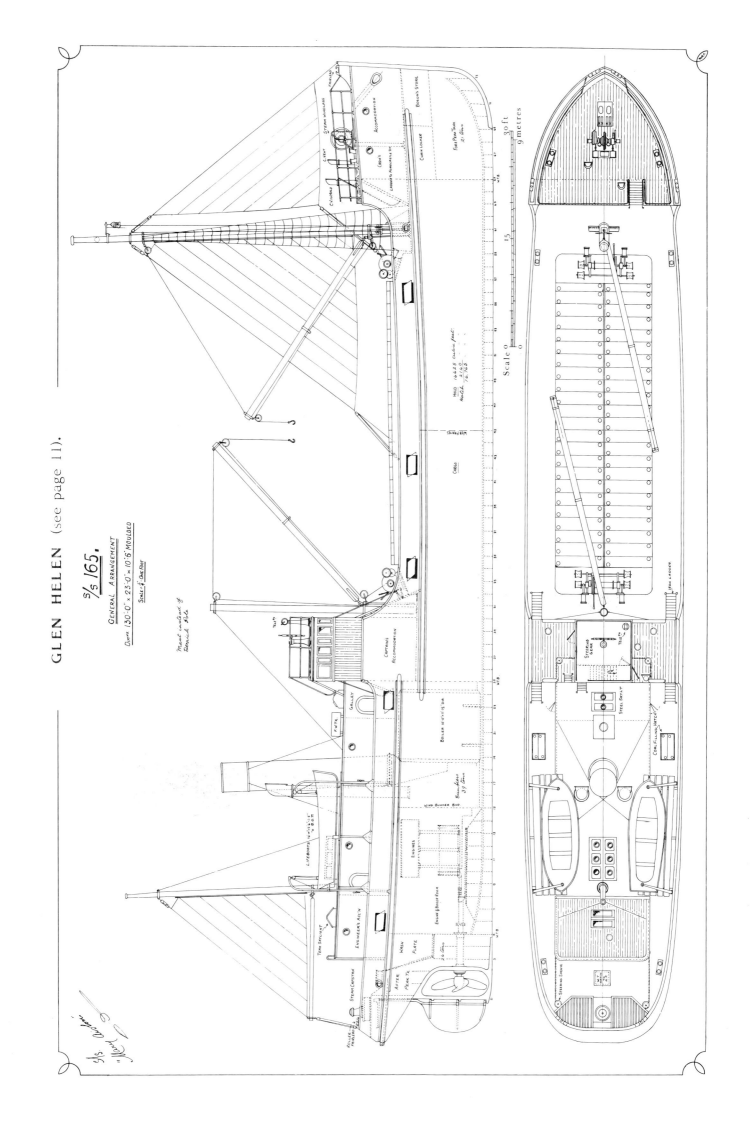

The WYTHBURN approaching Preston.

Plate 2

Old Time

Steam Coasting

Owen G. Spargo & Thomas H. Thomason

"Elizabetta."

Illustrated by C. V. Waine

WAINE Research Publications

To: The Coasting Sailor.

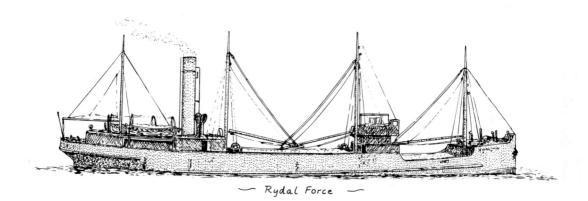

— Rydal Force —

© The Authors.

Published by:

Waine Research,
Mount Pleasant,
Beamish Lane,
Albrighton,
Nr. Wolverhampton

First Published 1982

Reprinted 1991.

ISBN 0 905184 05 X.

Printed & Bound in England.

Contents

For ease of reference, figure numbers and plate
numbers correspond with page numbers.

Foreword

6. s.s. DUNVEGAN (ex. SPRAY).

The first book in this series, 'Steam Coasters & Short Sea Traders', is about the building, design, owners and trades of the small steam tramps.

This new book, 'Old Time Steam Coasting', gives an eye-witness account of what it was like to go to sea in these small vessels in all weathers from the crews' point of view. Conditions in coasters were spartan and required a special breed of men. Two of these coasting men, Captain Owen G. Spargo and Thomas H. Thomason give their accounts of their time in steam coasting during the 1920s and 1930s. Throughout the narratives the effects of the depression of the period can be seen, with owners economising in every way possible. This usually meant seamen and firemen being laid off whenever the ship was idle or sometimes even loading over the weekend in Liverpool. If the vessel was to lay up, then the whole crew were paid off. As the crews' agreements of the period allowed owners to sign them on and off at will and as there were generally more coasters than cargoes, owners who did not save in every way possible soon went out of business. Conditions were often slightly better in ships belonging to merchants or companies not primarily engaged in shipping since they were more interested in having a ship handy to move their cargoes than their ship making a profit, which was essential to shipowners if they were to repair or replace their ships.

The great coasting collier fleets were controlled mainly from East coast ports, but it was on the West coast where the steam coasters and short sea traders were largely based, especially the Mersey Ports. Many were owned in Ireland too.

In the first part of the book Captain Spargo concentrates on the smaller coasters, particularly those of Monroe Brothers who had moved to Liverpool at the end of the first world war when they had purchased the bulk of Joseph Monks' fleet. At first they concentrated on the Irish trade but at the latter end of the 1920s they began to purchase larger coasters which were placed in the short sea trades culminating in the purchase of STAGHOUND and TEST which were chartered to Cunard for their regular Channel Islands' service.

In the second part Mr. Thomason describes his 12 years in W. S. Kennaugh & Co.'s STANLEY FORCE. The STANLEY FORCE was one of the smaller vessels in their fleet which was engaged in the short sea tramping trades. The company was originally established in 1883 in Whitehaven and moved to Liverpool in the 1890s to become one of the leading owners of short sea traders. The history of the fleet has been covered in detail by R. S. Fenton in a Monograph published by the World Ship Society.

Thanks are also due to John Clarkson and E. N. Taylor for the photographs and P. N. Thomas who provided plans of some of the vessels. Finally we all extend our thanks to Mrs. Sheila Muir who typed the final script.

Charles V. Waine, Ph. D.,

Albrighton, 1982.

1.

Where it all Started.

7. Garston Old Dock around the turn of the century.

Owen G. Spargo

Garston, once a small village about 5 miles higher up the River Mersey than Liverpool, now absorbed into and part of Liverpool, had at the latter part of last century a population of about 1,200 people. It was a hive of industry having salt works, copper rolling mills, tannery, ship building yard and dry dock, engineering works, steel and iron works, iron foundry, bobbin works, saw mill, two sail makers, several ship chandlers, tin and copper smiths, and many others.

There was also one tidal dock, with four coal tips from which were shipped large quantities of coal for use in bunkering the large liners at Liverpool, also for export to Ireland, other English Ports and to bunkering stations all over the world. There were also large quantities of minerals imported, such as nitrates from Chile, copper ore, iron ore and pyrites from Spain, Portugal and the Mediterranean. Slates came from Portmadoc, flintstones for the potteries from France, large amounts of sawn timber and matches from the Baltic. Lumber arrived in large American and Canadian fore and aft schooners some of them with as many as five masts such as the JANE PALMER, PRYDWEN and many others from Canada. And last but by no means least, about a dozen small Breton Ketches and schooners would arrive in their season with a cargo of onions made up in 'strings' or bunches. The crews of these vessels would go around the countryside selling the onions, carrying them suspended from either end of a pole carried on their shoulders. Very few of them would speak English but they could all speak Welsh and took their wares into Wales. Our local term for them was 'Johnny Onions'. Their cargo being sold, they would then buy a cargo of coal with the proceeds, which they would load and return to Brittany. This trade carried on until well into the 1920s.

Towards the end of the last century the London and North Western Railway Company purchased the Garston Dock Estate with certain reservations of which more later. They soon decided that the quay space of one dock was insufficient for the amount of trade, and built another larger dock at the North end of the Old Dock and called it the North Dock. They later built yet another still larger dock with a lock at the South end of the Old Dock, on the site of what had been two small inlets called the Salt Dock and Rock Salt Dock and called it the Stalbridge Dock. Until then with the North and Old Docks only having one set of dock gates, traffic was restricted to about two hours before, until High Water, but now with the new Stalbridge Locks they were able to deal with traffic from three hours before, until three hours after High Water and did handle a large amount of ships.

I do not remember the North Dock being built, but I do very clearly remember the Stalbridge Dock being opened and as I was about four then, I think it would have been about 1909. I remember the place being all decorated with bunting and all the ships dressed with flags for the occasion, and the London and North Western Railway Company's steam Hopper "D" with her well (hold) decked over with boards to accommodate the V.I.Ps and Captain J. Atherton in command, steaming through a ribbon stretched across the lock entrance to open the dock, the place was crowded with onlookers.

The three docks were linked by communication passages with draw bridges worked by hydraulic power, so that ships could go from one dock to the other at all times. These communication passages were also fitted with double dock gates, so that by closing the appropriate gates different levels of water could be maintained in any dock at any time and often were. It was an extremely well thought out piece of engineering and dock system which has always paid well, even until the present day.

It seems that the reservation which the London and North Western Railway Company inherited with their purchase of the Garston Dock Estate, concerned the Dock dues paid by ships using the Old Dock in which apparently the original Lady owner retained some interest. The dues were not allowed to be increased on ships using the Old Dock, and consequently, because the dues were less in the Old Dock, all the coasters and schooners 'booked' in to the Old Dock, if they locked in or out through Stalbridge Dock or entered through the North Dock then they had to pay the higher dues. Although it only amounted to coppers, money was in short supply. The dodges that were used to get around these were too numerous to mention and would fill a book on their own.

It was into this environment that I was born. My father who had spent many years at sea in the big deep water sailing ships and also Portmadoc schooners, had run away to sea before he was twelve and was in Australia when he was twelve. My maternal grandfather was from Portmadoc and had owned and sailed as Master of his own schooners before settling in Garston. My grandmother and mother had sailed with him on occasions. My father had given up the sea and taken on this job as lock gateman, which was regarded as a very secure job by the sea-going people. At that time we lived in a company's tied house on the Dock Road within fifty yards of the dock, one of a dozen or so similar houses all occupied by lock gatemen, all of whom were ex-seamen, mostly, sailing ship men. They all had fairly large families, mostly boys, and almost all of us went to sea when we left school at fourteen, and a large majority succeeded in obtaining their Masters certificate and gaining command.

As children we would play on the Docks, and in return for pumping out some of the old schooners or flats and running errands for their Masters we would be rewarded by the loan of their small boat which they always kept tied up under their stern, we very soon learned to scull and not surprisingly we all became very efficient boatmen.

In the middle of the North and Stalbridge Docks were two mooring buoys where ships would moor whilst awaiting a berth to discharge or load. In the evenings when we could borrow a boat we would earn a few coppers ferrying the crews to and from the shore.

When one of the sailing ships, including the schooners was docking we boys, at the least excuse (and most of us had either a relative or friend in many of them) would jump on board of them and pull on ropes and generally help on deck. They were probably glad of our help because everything was done by manual labour. After the sailing ship was securely moored, very often some crew member would organise a race for us to 'cap the truck', that was we would race up the rigging, and swarm up the topmast stays, and arriving at the mast head, take off our cap and put it on the 'truck' (top) of the mast, the winner probably getting a penny for doing so. I remember on one occasion I was engaged in one of these races, and my father who was standing at our front door saw me, he called my mother. She watched with horror whilst my father admired my prowess, my mother had different ideas and told me so in no uncertain terms when I returned home.

During the 1914/1918 war, the steam coasters and schooners, in fact all sailing ships, being so defenceless suffered badly from the German submarines, who found them an easy target. When they tried to avoid the submarines by keeping in shallow water where the submarines could not submerge they found these waters infested with mines which were equally dangerous. So the Government started to arm and equip them with defensive armament mostly in the form of 'smoke boxes', a device in the form of a wooden box, which when ignited and thrown over board would form a 'smoke screen' behind which the 'victim' was supposed to make his escape. Many ships were also fitted with a six pounder gun which was also placed aft, because armaments were only allowed to be sited where they would be in a defensive position when the 'victim' would be running away from the aggressor. Had they been mounted where they could aim ahead of the ship, they would have been in an aggressive position, and Merchant ships were supposed to be non-combatants (what a joke). Schooners also came in for defensive armament, some were converted into decoy or "Q" ships. The MARY B. MITCHELL and HELIGOLAND being two instances while others were just defensively armed. I remember one wooden schooner the BLACK CAT having a six pounder gun mounted on her at Garston and when she sailed a few practice rounds were fired whilst she was proceeding down the Garston channel. They shook her so much that it loosened the

9. MARY B. MITCHELL.

oakum in her seams and she started to leak and had to be beached and re-caulked. On one occasion a small steam coaster called ACME had smoke boxes stowed near her galley funnel. Whilst she was loading coal at one of the coal tips, one of the smoke boxes caught fire, this in turn set off the remainder and we had an exciting few hours until the smoke cleared. The submarines did not get it all their own way with the coasters and several of them successfully fought the submarines off. The Monks' coaster ELIZABETTA (3), was one of them, for which her Master, Captain Lewis (senior) received the D.S.C. also Lloyds silver medal. The Wigan Coal and Iron Company's steam coaster BALNIEL also sank a submarine by ramming it for which her master was decorated and the ship carried a well polished brass star on her all black funnel in recognition of the feat.

There were several regular traders using Garston. Elders and Fyffes had bi-weekly arrivals and sailings with bananas from the West Indies and Canary Islands, the Hutchison Line (later Moss Hutchison) had a regular trade to Rouen, Nantes, Bordeaux, Bayonne, Lisbon and Oporto with general cargo with steam coaster-type ships such as CHLORIS, MEMPHIS, THETIS, BUSIRIS, FLORIS, PARIS, etc. and the ARDENZA which they bought from Stevens of Leith. The ARDENZA was a steam coaster type ship of about 900 tons with engines amidships and two hatches forward and one hatch aft. Prior to Hutchisons buying her she had been boot-legging (engaged in the illicit liquor trade) on the American coast during the prohibition period in the U.S.A. When Hutchisons bought her she had just spent eight months at sea, being bunkered and provisioned at sea. Her master, Captain John MacAllister had graduated from the forecastle to obtain his foreign going Master's certificate required in that trade and had been Master with Hutchisons for years, during which time he had only spent four hours sheltering from bad weather, and that was only to renew the hatch tarpaulins which had been washed off in a gale. He was a very experienced seaman, and 'knew all the answers'; a hard driver both of ship and men. I made two voyages with him and got on very well with him, which was the exception rather than the rule. The house flag of the Hutchison line was interesting in that it consisted of the French national tri-coloured flag with a thistle on the white portion. The story went that the company were allowed to deface the French flag in recognition of some service they had rendered to France in the dim past, at sometime during the French revolution. Hutchison's ships had an all black funnel; they were run on "foreign going ship" lines and were reported to be "Good feeders", they were smart clean well kept ships.

The Co-operative Wholesale Society also had two ships on an alternate regular weekly service with general cargo to and from Rouen, their names were FRATERNITY and NEW PIONEER. They were both ships with engines amidships, two holds, two hatches. They had a black funnel with a white band, the FRATERNITY had a black letter "F" on the white band of her funnel, and the NEW PIONEER carried the letters "NP" in black on the white band of her funnel. Being on a regular trade and free from dirty cargoes, also having the advantage of duty free goods, they were considered by the seafaring fraternity as one of the best jobs obtainable. The Masters of them fully realising this, exploited it to their fullest advantage, and despite their advantages, the turn round of crew in them was considerable. The Captain of one of them had at one time been Captain of Thomas Lipton's famous yacht SHAMROCK, he probably thought that he was still in her. Like the ARDENZA and Hutchison's ships they were driven to their utmost and maintained a tight schedule.

The coasters arrived and sailed, no time being wasted in loading and despatching them. In what little leisure time crews had they would frequent the local hostelry, the various countrymen having their favourites and after the public houses closed, they would wend their erratic way back to their ships, often stopping in groups to exercise their vocal chords in a bit of a sing song, each in their own National language. In the case of the Welsh and Spanish

(Basque) crews in particular, this singing could often be of good quality and very entertaining. Occasionally there was a fracas between them, but as they were mostly too drunk to harm each other, it was soon over, and by next morning forgotten. Generally speaking all the seamen were very friendly to each other, everything ran smoothly and bitter feelings were unknown.

Unfortunately many men returning to their ships the worse for drink fell between the quay and the ship or between the ships and lost their lives, some times their bodies would be recovered with the use of a grapnel, generally the following day (I personally helped to retrieve several by this method), if this failed, they would either 'surface' on their own in the customary 9-10 days, or be picked up in the grab of one of the three steam grab hopper dredgers (RHYL, NORTH WESTERN and B). On one occasion I was joining my ship at 5 a.m. on a winter's morning and passing the steam grab dredger RHYL which was dredging a berth that had just been vacated by a French barque which had laid there for a long time. The Rhyl had picked up a body in one of her grabs and had hove alongside the quay to land it, the corpse had a rope fastened around its neck at the other end of which was a weight, the grab had caught hold of the rope; it was landed within feet of where I was walking. The police and the ambulance crew arrived and took it away. Incidents like this, together with the advice of old sailors of 'one hand for yourself and the other for the ship' taught us to be careful when playing around the dock. We could all swim like fish, but swimming in the docks was frowned upon by the dock police so we generally swam on the foreshore.

It was in this environment that I was born, so what more natural than that I should turn to the sea for work when I was ready. The day after I left school at the age of 14 saw me on my way down the Mersey on a small ketch called TRYFAN as Cook and Ordinary Seaman. She only carried two men and a boy and very often only two men. We took a cargo of coal to a small creek in Caernarvonshire and returned light to the Mersey. My wages were £2 a month, but as I was only away for a fortnight I only earned £1. The Captain and Mate were elderly Welsh men, neither of whom spoke much English; they were very kind to me. When I arrived back I heard that a Scandinavian iron schooner called ETHEL wanted hands, so I went aboard of her and got a job as Ordinary Seaman at £3 a month and spent a month or two chipping and red leading and overhauling her before taking her to Clover's dry dock, Birkenhead. Whilst we were in dry dock, I got word of an Ordinary Seaman's job going in one of the London and North Western Railway Company's steam dredgers. I applied for the job and got it, and said Goodbye to ETHEL.

The job in the steam dredger was quite a good job with about double the money I had been earning hereto. We were doing tidal work and I was home more or less every night and every weekend. I gained a great deal of experience whilst I was in them, one of which I still vividly remember. The high light in the Garston dredgers was to go to Holyhead for their annual overhaul and dry docking, where the London and North Western Railway Company had their own large dry dock and engine repair works. It was on a passage from Garston to Holyhead for overhaul, whilst I was serving on their self-propelled bucket dredger CREWE that we were caught in bad weather and lay hove to for a day before running before the sea up the Welshman's Channel (entrance to the River Dee) and anchoring in Hilbre Island anchorage. The motion of that ship during that passage had to be seen to be believed, still she must have been a well-built ship to have come through it without any trouble. Of course in those days we did not have the advantage of the weather forecasts that we have today, and the weather lore of the old skippers did not always come up to expectations, although they were generally fairly accurate in their predictions. They were well out on that occasion.

The life in the Dredgers was quite good, but it was a 'dead end job' with no hope of promotion, because to rise to an Able Seaman I would have to be a qualified Able Seaman, and to qualify I would have to serve for three years in a sea going ship, and as the service in the dredgers only qualified as part time, I decided to look for a ship where my service would count as qualifying time both for an Able Seaman and also as time for an officer's certificate. I was fortunate in obtaining a berth in a steam coaster called GLEN HELEN.

10. NEW PIONEER.

2.

"Glen Helen."

Owen G. Spargo

11. GLEN HELEN.

The GLEN HELEN was the first steam coaster I served in. I joined her as Ordinary Seaman on 12 March 1921. She was a sturdy little vessel of about 300 tons and had originally been called the MARY AISTON and had originated from Crabtree's Yard at Great Yarmouth in 1918. She was now owned by Wilson Brothers (Bobbin) Co. Ltd., King Street, Garston, Liverpool, who had a factory there and as the name would suggest, made wood bobbins for the Lancashire cotton mills. They also made wood soles for clogs, and employed quite a number of men and women. At that time they also owned a very similar ship called GLENCONA and a few years later had another similar ship built which they named GLEN MARY.

The GLEN HELEN carried cargoes of household coal from Garston to the small ports in Ireland. Wicklow, Bray, Wexford, Dundalk, Drogheda and Waterford were favourites, and she loaded cargoes of beech logs back to Garston where the timber was used in their factory. Occasionally we would go to remote lochs in the Hebrides such as Inner Loch Sween also Loch Broom, where we would anchor as close as possible to where the trees were being cut. The GLEN HELEN had one hold with one long hatch with a mast and derrick at either end. She also had a third (Mizzen) mast which carried a boom and mizzen tri-sail. With her long hatch and derricks at each end she was ideally suited for carrying timber and when the hold was full, also carried a good cargo on deck and on top of the hatch.

On approaching the site where the timber was being felled, both anchors were let go in a splayed fashion, and the ship's stern allowed to drift towards the shore, mooring wires were then run from the stern and made fast to the stumps of trees which had been felled and around the trunks of some of the larger trees still standing. The stern ropes were then hove tight with the capstan, and the anchor chains slacked until the ship was moored at right angles to the shore with her stern no more than 80 feet off. The shore which consisted of rock, was steep-to and sloped upwards from about a foot at the waters edge, it was heavily wooded with beech trees, which ran back further than we could see, because they towered high above us. These trees were being felled and rolled into the water, from where we ferried them with one of our lifeboats, to the ship's side where they were slung and hoisted on board with the ship's winches and derricks after the men in the lifeboat were well clear.

The derricks were rigged in 'yard arm' style, that is one derrick was guyed out over the rail at almost 90 degrees, this being known as the yard arm derrick, whilst the other derrick was plumbed over centre line of the hatch, this was known as the standing derrick. The derrick guys were set tight and an extra length of wire rope set up alongside them to act as a 'preventer guy' (Plate 19). If we had any exceptionally heavy logs, then an extra 'preventer' stay was fixed to the mast. With extra heavy logs, the yard arm method was also dispensed with and both derricks were plumbed in the centre line position over the hatch and the unison hooks disconnected and the log slung at both ends, each derrick taking an end, and then 'skull-dragging' the log over the rail and eventually man handling it into position.

When the derricks were guyed in the 'Yard arm' position, the (hook) ends of their winch runners would be joined together by what was known as 'union gear' that is two steel swivels joined together by a steel link, one runner would be shackled to each swivel and a cargo hook would be shackled to the link. To load the after end of the hold and hatch, the forward derrick would

Shackles &c.

be the 'yard arm' derrick and the after derrick the 'standing derrick'. The log would be lifted from the water by the yard arm derrick, the standing derrick at the same time taking in the slack on its runner. When the log came above the level of the rail with the yard arm derrick, we would then heave in on the standing derrick at the same time slacking gently on the yard arm derrick until the standing derrick took the full weight and the log would be plumb over the hatch and could be lowered into position as required. If it was too heavy to be positioned manually then a 'bull rope', a manilla rope about 3" circumference, would be passed through a lead block, and one end made fast to the log and the other end taken to the windlass and the log hove into the position desired. To load the forward end of the hold and hatch the derricks would just be reversed, the after derrick becoming the yard arm and the forward derrick the standing derrick.

We used wire 'snotter' slings for the logs which we made ourselves. They consisted of a piece of wire rope with a 'soft' eye (loop) spliced in each end. The log was slung by the simple method of passing the bight of the sling under the end of the log and then working the sling along the log to near the middle then passing one eye of the snotter through its other eye and on to the hook of the derrick. When the runner was hove tight, the sling automatically tightened and gripped the log. The roughness of the bark on the log prevented it from slipping, but if the bark was removed then an extra round turn would be taken with the sling to prevent it slipping. No steadying lines were used to control the logs. If one got wild then it was just lowered and steadied; otherwise they were just handled manually except when it was needed to stow one at some distance then the 'bull rope' would be used. No dunnage was used and the logs were just jammed against each other. During the loading the crew would be stationed, one at each winch, and one, maybe two, in the boat. The lumberjacks who had felled the trees would be rolling the trees into the water and some of them stowing the cargo in the hold, and maybe one or two of them assisting the boatman, it was a case of everybody pulling his weight.

The derricks were rigged to lift two tons, but by doubling up the runners, stays and topping lifts, we used to lift much more and when the logs were very heavy we used both derricks together. It must have been a hit and miss method of arriving at the weight of the logs, and it appeared that if the winches would not lift them, then they were too heavy. I never even saw a log being left behind because it was too heavy, neither do I recollect any serious accident due to overloading the derricks. So everything ran smoothly. Loading was started at daybreak and continued until dark, with two one-hour breaks for meals (no mid-morning or mid-afternoon tea break), it was very hard work but everybody gave of their best, and we worked away quite happily, no overtime was paid or expected. Loading had generally run into the third day by the time a full cargo had been stowed.

The GLEN HELEN carried a crew of nine which was a big crew for a ship of her size at that period, and probably because the firm did not depend on the ship's earnings, they did not try to economise, yet she must have shown a profit because they quickly increased their fleet to three ships, one of which they had built for them. They were managed by Messrs. E. W. Turner of Garston and Captain Turner, the principal of that firm, was a very widely experienced old sea dog, and if he could not make a ship pay, then there was not much hope for anyone else.

The crew consisted of master, mate, chief and second engineer (the second engineer was the chief engineer's son and about a year older than me, so we soon chummed up together), two able seamen, one ordinary seaman and two firemen. The sailors and firemen lived in a common forecastle at deck level under the forecastle head and being at deck level it was considered to be one of the élite of forecastles. It was not divided and had four two-tiered bunks, two on each side of the ship. In the centre was a deal table (scrubbed white) and two wood forms for use as seats at the table, whilst a plank of wood running the length of the bunks at the level of the lower bunks, served as seats for the occupants, also each occupant was provided with a locker about 18 inches square to hold his food and eating utensils. The forecastle was heated by a round slow-combustion coal burning stove about three feet high by 15 inches diameter (called a bogey) which, when well stoked, and with the forecastle door kept closed, made the place reasonably warm and with a bit of manipulation could be made up to remain alight for four hours. Unfortunately these stoves, which were common to most coasters, created fumes in enclosed spaces and accidents were frequent on their account.

Each crew member provided his own bed and bedding, also eating and cooking utensils and of course food. His mattress, made of Hessian, a 6 foot by 3 foot sack filled with straw was known as a 'donkey's breakfast'. These could be bought from the local ship chandler for 2/6d. The bunks themselves were made of wood, with solid bottoms and the donkey's breakfast was laid directly on the wooden bunk boards. Not the most inviting of beds, but when

A 'snotter'

the donkey's breakfast was new and one was tired, it was heaven. However, after a few weeks the straw either cracked or compressed and disappeared and any bit of comfort in them vanished. The more experienced 'weekly boatmen' carried their own bed-tick and bought a 'cock' of straw from a farmer or the local corn merchant for about 1/- or 1/6 which made a donkey's breakfast twice as thick as those supplied by the ship chandler. The term 'weekly boatman' was a description given mostly by 'deep watermen' referring to the fact that coasting men received a weekly wage whereas the foreign going men were paid a monthly wage.

Glen Helen

Lighting was by two paraffin lamps and although there was reasonable light from the two portholes in the ship's side when at sea, when the ship was in port, the side nearest to the quay was invariably obscured by the quay and if another ship was laying alongside, then the natural light was obliterated and the paraffin lamps were going day and night with their attendant fumes.

Sanitary arrangements although rather crude were better than the average coaster of that period. Each man was provided with a galvanised bucket (the officers were provided with an enamel one) for washing and bathing purposes, there was neither wash room nor bath room. Outside the forecastle on the same deck were two small rooms about four feet square; the one on the port side was the 'lamp locker' and had storage for the paraffin oil and navigation lamps (which were also paraffin). The room on the starboard side was the W.C. which held one pan, the flushing arrangement was by draw bucket (a bucket with a rope lanyard attached to the handle with which to draw water from the sea).

At the outer end of the soil pipe was a flap valve which was supposed to stop sea water coming in when the ship was pitching; unfortunately this did not always work. When the ship was pitching in a sea way, a gush of water used to come up the pan like a pressure hose, and one had to be either a contortionist or good acrobat to use it in such conditions. To get a bath one used to stand the bucket in the W.C. pan and bath standing on the floor, when after soaping oneself well down, we emptied the remainder in the bucket over our heads, the water then drained through scuppers on the floor at deck level and thence on to the deck whence it drained overboard through the main scuppers. We were fortunate in having a water tank with drinking water outside the forecastle door, so we did not have to go aft for water. Cooking was done in the galley which was aft, food being then carried forward to the forecastle to be eaten, and was very often lost overboard in transit during bad weather, or was cool if not cold by the time it reached the forecastle.

A fry-up in the frying pan could be made in an emergency on the bogey but this was frowned upon by the other occupants on account of the fumes and smell. A favourite dish made in these circumstances was 'panacutty' which was made by putting a couple of rashers of bacon in a frying pan together with a sliced onion and thinly sliced potatoes, and plenty of salt and pepper and about half a cup of water and covering the pan with a lid or in most cases an inverted tin plate, and the whole put on top of the bogey to boil. As the bogey was not fitted with rails it had to be held in position whilst it cooked which took about a quarter of an hour. The criterion being that when the potatoes were soft it was ready and was turned out on to the now hot covering plate and with a couple of rounds of bread and butter and pint mug of strong sweet tea, made a substantial and filling meal.

Part of my duties as Ordinary Seaman was to cook for the Captain and Mate and to have the kettle boiling ready for when I called the men at seven o'clock, if work on the cargo was not starting before 8 am. I was up at 6 am., to light the galley fire and cook breakfast for the Captain, Mate and myself for 7.30 am., and to call the men to have their breakfast and be ready to start work at 8 am. If the mate did not hear me on deck at a few minutes after 6 am., he was very soon after me in no uncertain manner. I think he must have slept like a bird with one eye open, or perhaps he could not sleep, scheming up how much work he could get out of the men the following day and more than likely the Captain slept with one eye open watching him!

The Captain and Mate belonged to Runcorn and were typical Mersey sailing flat men, and like all up-river men, very clean and they kept their ship and accommodation, as much as was possible, spotless. The homes of the Runcorn and Widnes barge men at that time were renowned for their cleanliness. They were both very widely experienced coasting men and very good seamen. Occasionally when we were lying in a tier waiting to load we would get a sly little jibe from other weekly boatmen who would enquire as to 'where we had stabled our horses.' This probably being a reference to our Widnes and Runcorn crew and their association with barges in general and horse-drawn narrowboats in particular.

As soon as breakfast was over, I had to clear up and prepare the dinner and be out on deck by 10 am. to work with the men, and leave the dinner on

Timber hitch

the stove cooking. The work consisted of chipping, painting or splicing and general maintenance and if the crew were driving the winches, then to relieve them on the winches when necessary, which was all very good experience for me, and I enjoyed it. There was never a dull moment and our attention was not distracted by transistor radios which of course were not heard of at that time.

The Captain and Mate lived in accommodation under the bridge, which consisted of a room each on either side of a shared saloon which was done-out in varnished pitch-pine and looked very attractive. It was approached by a stairway from the back of the wheelhouse, which held the steam steering gear (rod and chain). On top of the wheelhouse was an extension from the steam steering gear in the form of a wheel and pedestal, also binnacle and compass, and engine room telegraph. This steering position was only used when manoeuvring in port, the steam steering being converted to hand gear at sea, which led to better steering and also saved bunkers (and kept the sailors' muscles loose)! The cabin and wheelhouse were kept immaculate in spite of the coal cargoes we carried. At the foot of the stairs to the saloon there was a small W.C. This was flushed from a small tank on the bridge deck above it (very posh); the only draw-back was that I had to fill this tank every other day with a draw bucket!

The Captain and Mate also had collapsible wash basins, but the water had to be carried to them (in a bucket) and after use they tipped and drained into a receptacle underneath. Then this was generally used to flush the toilet, which delayed filling the tank a little.

The Engineers (both shovel engineers) lived in separate rooms opening off the engine room which were very warm, if comfortable small rooms. They also had wash basins which they rarely used preferring to wash and bath in the engine room where they had a plentiful supply of warm soft condensed water from the exhaust steam tank. This tank into which ran all the drains from the various pumps, etc. was a good source of condensed water, unfit for drinking, but very soft and excellent for washing. This tank was referred to in all coasters as 'the old man', so that if you were sent for a bucket of water from the Old Man, you would certainly be on the wrong track if you went to the Captain for it! He was also known to the crew as the 'Old Man' even if he was a young man!

GLEN HELEN was what we considered in those days a 'good job', a very good job. The discharging of the coal and loading of timber cargoes and vice versa, together, used to take an average of three days so that we were sure of two free nights although work on the cargo rarely stopped before 7 pm. I very soon got acquainted with, and made friends with, the people in the Irish ports, many of whom I knew from my schooner days and my chum and I took the opportunity of going to a ceiledh (or 'caley' as they pronounced it) whenever one offered. It was a real Irish dance and very good fun. Unfortunately, the political troubles were still on in Ireland and there was curfew in many places and more often than not we failed to get back before curfew and were picked up on our way back to the ship by the military. If we told a convincing story, they might take us back to the ship and leave us with a caution, but if they were 'meanies' they would round a few more up with us and we would spend a few hours in the 'cop shop', before being escorted back to the ship and threatened as to what would happen to us next time we were caught.

There was never any question of drink involved, for my part I did not earn enough to drink. My wage was £2 per week plus two shillings and sixpence war risk money (the war risk money was at that time still being paid on account of the risk from mines after the 1914-1918 war). It amounted to ten shillings per month on foreign going ships and two shillings and sixpence per week on Home Trade ships. After my National Insurance was deducted, and I had paid for my food, generally about 10/- and 15/- per week and sent a few shillings home, I did not have much left to waste on drink. We fed very well, on good plain food often supplemented with a rabbit trapped locally or an occasional pheasant found wandering and lovely fresh-caught fish bought from the local fishing boats for next to nothing. Our Chief Engineer who had been a gamekeeper, and his son, the second engineer, were also able to make many appreciable contributions to our larder due to their previous experience on the land.

The GLEN HELEN with her three masts and one long hatch between the fore and main masts, two derricks, a steam windlass, two steam winches, also a steam capstan aft (a very handy piece of machinery), and steam steering gear, was fairly up-to-date as far as coasters went at that time. We steered from the wheelhouse which was dry and warm and we were not exposed to the weather during the watch and so were very comfortable. I was very sorry to leave when she was laid up owing to a coal strike and all the crew paid off. So I received my introduction to the dole, where like many thousands more, I received the large amount of eighteen shillings (90p) a week to live on.

3.

"Braebeg."

Owen G. Spargo

15. The St. TUDWAL when new.
The BRAEBEG was similar.

The coal strike was eventually settled and with the GLEN HELEN still laid up, along came another little ship looking for a deck hand and I was able to secure a temporary berth in a steam coaster called BRAEBEG. She was a very different type of ship, she was made of iron and built in 1878 so she was 43 years old when I joined her, a fairly mature ship by any standard. Her name was originally TELEPHONE. She was a very small ship and sat low in the water; she had a raised forecastle head (about 3'6") and raised after deck (about 3'0"), she had two hatches to one hold, two masts and two winches placed one each side of the foremast serving the hatches. The winch also drove the windlass, which was on the forecastle head, by means of a 'messenger', a continuous chain worked like a pulley and belt. She did not have a capstan aft. She had wood decks all over which were not on top of iron or steel as in some later ships. Her fore deck had bulwarks about 3'0" high, whilst her hatch coamings were about 18" high with round corners. She had hand rails on her forecastle head and around the after deck from the bridge to stern.

Her rather short counter stern was very low in the water when she was loaded, her stern only being about 4'0" above the water and yet in bad weather I never saw her put water on her after deck. I was later in another very old ship with a similar stern, the S/S ADAM SMITH and I noticed the same thing about her also. Both were very good sea boats despite their small freeboard. She had old fashioned 'stock' anchors and a radial davit with a fish-tackle to lift the anchor overboard before anchoring and to lift it back on board for lashing and stowing on the forecastle head when on passage. She also had a full suit of sails, fore staysail, main and mizzen tri-sails, which were used whenever possible, and on one occasion when we were bound from Irvine to Waterford, we sailed her from the Clyde to the Tuskar lighthouse off the S.E, coast of Ireland, whilst the engineers repaired the main engine which had broken down, and she sailed very well.

She was owned then by Mr. Murphy, a coal merchant of Bridge Street, Waterford, Ireland, who also at that time owned some other very old steam coasters. 'They were THE LADY BELLE (17), NORSMAN and St. TUDWAL. He also owned two topsail schooners. The names of which slip my mind just now, but I remember they had green topsides. Mr. Murphy kept all these ships fully employed; mostly with his own cargoes and shipped black oats in bulk outwards. They also ran outside cargoes and the BRAEBEG had taken a cargo from Limerick to Jersey and had also carried china clay from the Cornish ports to Runcorn and Lancaster, so she was doing some brave runs for a small ship. Mr. Murphy's ships ran successfully until after he died when they were all sold, THE LADY BELLE running for many years afterwards with coal to Dungarvan. The St. TUDWAL (15), afterwards had many owners and on one occasion when her owner failed, she was auctioned in Boston, Lincolnshire, in seaworthy condition and fit for trading for £140, at the same time a lovely old Irish schooner the IRISH MINSTREL built of bog oak in Dundalk went for £45. She was cut down and worked on the Mersey for many years afterwards as a dumb barge.

BRAEBEG had a low bridge (painted white) with a pitch-pine wheelhouse (scraped and varnished) abaft the main hatch. In the wing of the bridge was the ship's bell, highly polished and suspended in a very ornate cast iron stand in the form of two dolphins. The name TELEPHONE was inscribed on the bell and the tongue had a plaited bell rope which was an exhibit of seamanship and was painted white with two turks-head knots on it painted green. It was a real show piece, but a bit of a nuisance at sea when the bell rang with every roll of the ship and we had to muzzle it by lashing the tongue.

Abaft the bridge and on the same level was a small boat deck, on top of the engine room casing. The boat deck had one pair of radial davits at each side in which were carried the two lifeboats; one of which had a transom stern, and was presumably intended to be also used as a working boat. These transom sterned boats were common to most coasters and I think would have originally been carried on deck. It was made use of quite often for running buoy ropes when loading coal in ports where this was the practice, and also as duty boat when the ship was moored on the buoys awaiting a berth. It was also used as a mooring boat when the ship had to moor on buoys. The boatman's work being done by the deck hands and the ability to scull and handle a boat and run ropes was a very necessary requirement for a coasting sailor, and I know of occasions when a sailor has lost his life in this operation, either by the boat being crushed by the ship or being caught by the propellor when running the stern rope.

Under the bridge was the Captain's cabin and toilet, small but quite comfortable, whilst the mate and two engineers had accommodation below decks right aft. The two sailors and one fireman lived forward in the forecastle. Although she was a very small ship, Mr. Murphy kept her well manned with a crew of seven. I was to sail in very much larger ships in later years with a much smaller crew. She was a happy ship, with a mixed crew of English, Welsh and Irish who all got on very well together.

We also took cargoes from the Bristol Channel ports of Burry Port, Llanelly, Briton Ferry and the river berth of Pill, which is just outside Queen Alexandra Dock in Newport. Pill was a tricky berth, for one thing there was a very large rise and fall of tide, one of the largest in the world, and the moorings had to be carefully attended to until the ship took the ground in the berth where she would remain aground over the low water. It was a bad berth due to the fact that it sucked; that is the ship would fail to float on the rising tide and would be held by the suction of the mud in which she was lying. This could lead to a serious situation if not dealt with promptly.

There were many methods of doing this; one was to pass a wire rope or chain underneath the ship before she took the ground, and then to work the rope or chain back and forth when the water returned to allow it to get underneath and release her. Another method was to drop the anchor and heave it up and down, and yet another was to take a big hammer aloft and strike the truck of the mast. This was a favourite ruse on board the smaller sailing craft whose masts were stepped in the Keelson, as was the BRAEBEG's well scraped, oiled and varnished pitch-pine mast. The most successful method was to give a few turns with the main engine and even this could be slow, and when the ship freed herself she would rise like a cork out of a bottle and very often break the moorings doing so. The danger of using the main engine method was that the condenser would choke itself up with mud and would not function and lead to all kinds of resultant complications, so this method was frowned upon and only used as a last resort.

The engine room and stokehold were combined. The main engine was a compound and was I suppose, a very superior and up-to-date engine when it was built, since it had a condenser at the back of it with circulating air, boiler feed and bilge pumps all working off a rocking shaft connected to the main engine crossheads. Reversing was by a large lever on the same principle as a steam winch. Although the main engine was small, it required two men to work it on account of its layout. The independent general service pump was an upright tandem pump with a large heavy flywheel which had to be given half a turn or so to start it and was the only one I was ever shipmates with. She also had a steam injector for putting feed water into the boiler and a steam ejector which would pump out the engine room bilges. The ejector in particular being a very useful piece of equipment, which although used extensively in steam trawlers was not very common in coasters.

The steam for the main engine room came direct to the main engine from the top of the boiler through the main steam pipe (a copper pipe about 6" diameter) which had a large upright expansion bend to allow for metal expansion and also to prevent water getting into the engine by priming, and priming was a serious and not uncommon happening in bad weather in many steam coasters. The stop valve on the boiler top was the only steam valve to the main engine and as the breadth of the stokehold lay between the boiler and engine, it was some distance, thus the main stop valve spindle was fitted with a toothed sprocket, and a larger wheel and sprocket was on the main engine, the two were connected with a chain similar to a bicycle chain and this operated the valve. Little mishaps like the chain coming off the gear wheel were not uncommon. Reversing was achieved by lifting a very large lever, but des-

Turks Head.

17. THE LADY BELLE.

Braebeg

pite these 'Heath Robinson' and antiquated ideas, she ran quite well and could slip along at eight knots without much difficulty.

Bunkers were carried in side pockets in the space between the ship's side and the boiler and would carry I suppose about 30 tons between them. They were filled through round holes in the deck at either side about three feet in diameter, which were covered and sealed when full by a cast iron cover which screwed into place to secure it and then lay flush with the deck, the edge of the cover was then plastered heavily with tallow to keep the sea water out. Lighting was by paraffin lamps with cheap paraffin lamps and duck lamps for the accommodation and engine room. When, as was often the case, the paraffin ran out, then lighting was achieved with tallow candles mostly left by trimmers loading coal cargoes and saved for such contingencies.

Fresh water for drinking purposes was stored in a 200 gallon tank situated against the bulkhead in the forehold, and water was obtained from the tank by a very old fashioned vertical hand pump with leather valves. Whether it was fitted with a non-return valve at the foot or if they were invented at that time I would not know, but we always had to retain sufficient water to prime the pump because it continuously lost suction, then whatever fluid was available had to be used. This could be cold tea and if that was not available, then water from the drains of the winches or main engine. As in the process of priming the pump, a considerable amount of the primer reached the tank, by the time the water was getting low in the tank, it was beginning to mature and the tea began to take on a purple hue, but as we were often glad of a drink of anything hot and wet we overlooked this.

The forecastle where we lived was about three feet down from the foredeck and despite the fact that the step was only one foot high above the deck I never saw water come over the step or heavy water come over the forecastle head. The anchor cable was stored in two wooden lockers about 3'6" high, one at each side of the after end of the forecastle, the anchor cable passed directly from the windlass into the forecastle where it had to be dragged about eight feet to the lockers. The bight of the cable from the windlass spurling pipes was lashed up to the deck head when the anchor was not in use. When heaving the anchor up especially if anchored in mud, a lot of mud remained on the cable and was carried to the chain locker, so that letting go or heaving up the anchor became a major exercise, for when letting go the anchor, the cable would be flying around the forecastle like a wild snake and mud brought in from previous anchorings was flying all around the forecastle, so all the beds and floors were covered as much as possible and then it was a case of all hands on deck because it was very dangerous to remain inside.

As customary, a galvanised bucket was provided for ablutions, and a kettle and frying pan for cooking purposes. We had a small coal burning stove, with two cooking rings and providing everybody did not want to use it at the same time, we managed to do our cooking independent of the galley and being an Irish ship with a number of Irishmen in the crew, potatoes boiled in their jackets was a popular and cheap dish. The W.C. which was situated just outside the forecastle on deck was of the customary draw bucket system and served as a bathroom when not otherwise occupied.

The hand steering gear was of the rod and chain variety to a wheel in the wheelhouse and she had a tiller on the rudder head (not a quadrant). Although she was only a small ship it could be very heavy in bad weather, and on occasions would keep two of us fully occupied to steer her when loaded as she would kick very heavily and we had to rig relieving tackles to ease the strain on the wheel, chains and the helmsman's arms (see page 75). When light ship, in common with many of the older coasters she would steer herself. I have seen them run for hours without moving the wheel more than a spoke or two when the weather was fine, on which occasions a becket (a sliprope lashing) would be put on the wheel to prevent it from moving and the mate would make the most of the opportunity to get the ship painted up. While the

Bollards.

sailors would be painting about the decks he would be painting about the bridge with an occasional lookout for traffic and a glance at the compass.

She had a bar keel and like many other coasters I served in with bar keels was very easy on herself in a seaway and a good sea boat. She was one of the few coasters whose mast passed through the deck and was stepped in the keelson in the hold and had wood wedges and a canvas mast coat around it at deck level. Whilst in the ship I assisted the mate in making a new canvas mast coat for the foremast. I was to be proud of what I learned from him doing this job in later years, when I made mast coats for the telescopic topmasts in very big ships when the art of sailmaking was starting to become a forgotten art. This and very many other things that I learned in steam coasters were to become more than useful to me in later years.

My sojourn in BRAEBEG ended after a couple of months when the chap that I relieved returned to claim his job. He was a relative of the Captain and had been employed in the winter in-shore herring fishing while he had been off.

Although work was not too plentiful, it then being the Christmas period, there was work to be found if you looked for it and this often meant several miles of walking daily, prior to Christmas. There was always the chance that some English or Welsh sailors would leave to spend his Christmas at home with his family, or as we used to say to get his stocking filled. Once Christmas was over then the Scotsmen used to get homesick and had their turn and would go through hell or high water to let their Hogmanay in.

The coasting shipowner of the period was quick to exploit the seasonal advantages due to the fact that Christmas day was not a holiday in Scotland and New Year's day not being a holiday in England. Because the Articles (crew agreement) stated that New Year's day, Good Friday, Easter Monday, Christmas day and Boxing day were to be treated as holidays in ports where they were recognised as such, the owner in his consideration for the crews would make sure his ships were in Scottish ports for Christmas. If he was one of the more generous shipowners he would supply a turkey for the crew's Christmas dinner and then do his damnedest to make sure his ship was either at sea or in a Scottish port over the holidays where Christmas was not recognised and so the crew were kept working over both holidays. No extra payment was given for work done on holidays regardless of where the ship was. At sea everybody including the master worked watches, four hours on and four hours off, a total of twelve hours a day (without meal breaks) and if the ship had entered and left port once or twice during the week, another 20 hours could very easily be added to this amount and 100 hours was more often the rule than the exception. Leave and holidays were unheard of; if you wanted leave you got it 'off pay' and with no guarantee of returning to your job, and there were plenty of men on the dole, desperately needing work and ready to take your place.

18. The BIRMINGHAM was built in 1855 by C. & W. Earle at Hull. She was modernised over the years and even had an enclosed wheelhouse fitted eventually.

Plate 19 · GLEN HELEN loading a cargo of beech logs for her owners.

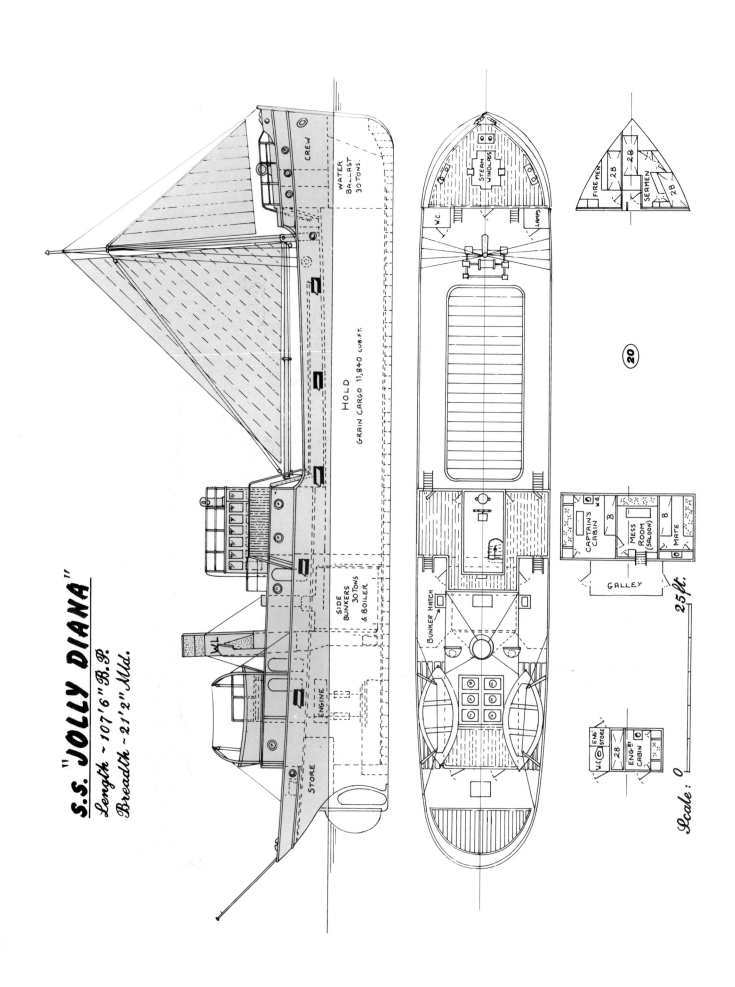

S.S. "JOLLY DIANA"

Length ~ 107'6" B.P.
Breadth ~ 21'2" Mld.

CREW

WATER BALLAST 30 TONS.

HOLD

GRAIN CARGO 11,840 CUB. FT.

SIDE BUNKERS 30 TONS & BOILER

ENGINE

STORE

WL

STEAM WINDLASS

W.C.

LAMPS

BUNKER HATCH

FIRE MEN 2B 2B SEAMEN 2B

20

CAPTAIN'S CABIN B W.B.

MESS ROOM (SALOON) B MATE

GALLEY

ENG'r STORE W.C. 2B ENG'rs CABIN

Scale: 0   25 ft.

4.

21. JOLLY CHRISTINE.

'Jolly' Voyaging.

Owen G. Spargo

The local Penzance paper of the 8th of January 1923 read; 'The s/s JOLLY DIANA arrived yesterday with a cargo of cement from London. This vessel had an exciting voyage. She was due to arrive at Penzance last Wednesday, but owing to the gale was delayed for four days. She left London on the 31st of December 1922, and only got as far as Beachy Head when the gale came on. The wind was blowing strongly from the West. The waves were mountainous and broke all over the ship. For eight solid hours the sea was one mass of foam. Nearing Weymouth the bilges of the ship became choked and the vessel was compelled to put into Weymouth. Three days elapsed before it was considered advisable to resume the voyage. Even then the voyage was very unpleasant in such a small craft.

The Trinity boat MERMAID is still unable to effect relief of the Wolf Rock Lighthouse owing to unfavourable weather......'

I had joined the s/s JOLLY DIANA on the 29th of December 1922 as she lay in the Britannia dry dock, one of two small dry docks in North Woolwich, London which is now filled in. They were close to a tier of buoys which were generally occupied by a fleet of sprit-sail barges, which the London river men called 'starvation tier', because it was here that their craft laid whilst awaiting a cargo, and as they mostly worked on a share basis, they were not earning money and consequently were feeling the pinch.

The JOLLY DIANA had just been purchased from Walford Lines by a Captain Walter Cowley in partnership with other Manxmen. He was working her round to the West coast with a view to trading mainly to the Isle of Man with coal, and some coal merchants had an interest in her. She carried a crew of six which consisted of Master, Mate (Walter junior, the Captain's son), two Engineers who did their own stoking as no firemen were carried, and two Able Seamen of which I was one. Captain Cowley had apparently owned ships before and had owned a schooner called the ESTHER. He had also been Master of a small steam coaster called SARAH BLANCHE, he might even have been part owner. He was a typical schooner man and without doubt a very good seaman, but very religious to the point of fanaticism. He ruled his son (Walty the mate) with a rod of iron and never gave him a minutes' peace. Walter junior was a very quiet, sociable and likeable young man who would dodge into the forecastle whenever he got the chance to get out of his father's way. Immediately his father missed him, he would come on to the bridge and roar 'WALTY' and poor Walty would run to him at the double.

If we had a night in port he would be sure to have us out at some time to tighten or slacken moorings or adjust ladder or gangway or some other trivial thing, for which no extra payment was made. Had he been paying overtime, I very much doubt that he would have been as keen, but then in that case, I suppose Walty would have got the full share. As it was, he had to do his full share of the work, the 'Ould Man' as young Walty described him to us, worked us every minute that he could and never seemed satisfied. On one occasion he bought a coil of four and a half inch manilla rope and it was a real pantomime opening it up and splicing eyes in it. I had opened up and spliced many coils of rope, some much larger, by myself on many previous occasions, but this was to the 'ould man' an 'all hands' job. The coil had to be rigged up on a turn-table to unroll it, then stretched along the quay to take the turns out of it, then cut into four equal lengths of 30 fathoms and an eye splice made in the ends of each length. The eye splices when finished, had to be hove tight before cutting off the surplus ends which did not have to exceed four inches, and which were carefully gathered up and teased out and kept for cleaning the brass work in conjunction with bath brick and colza oil.

Thames Barges.

He would never sail on a Sunday, and if we were ready to sail, he would lay over until after midnight on Sunday night. On one occasion we were in Belfast over Sunday and I went ashore to buy the Sunday papers, When I returned my colleague was sitting on a bollard on the fore-deck washing his clothes in a bucket. I sat down nearby to read the paper and was commenting on some of the articles in the paper, when the 'ould man' appeared on the bridge, dressed up ready to go to church. He went almost purple when he saw us and told my colleague that "he would not have washing done on board his ship on Sunday the Sabbath". My colleague replied that we did not get time to wash our clothes during the week, and in any case, cleanliness was next to Godliness. Some altercation followed, the outcome of which was that we were to be given Saturday morning off whenever possible to wash our clothes and clean our accommodation in the future, which was a big concession, he then turned on me and told me that he did not approve of the devil's pictures as he called the Sunday papers on board of his ship on the sabbath either, so both of us stood corrected. Between being hazed and lectured by this character, my colleague and I were anything but enhanced with him or his ship.

When I joined the JOLLY DIANA I had just paid off the s/s JOLLY MARIE which was another of Walford's ships, whose predominantly Cockney crew were anything but pious. With the remainder of the crew of the JOLLY DIANA living in the Isle of Man, the 'ould man' could envisage that with me living on board in the Isle of Man, he would have a free night watchman whilst the ship lay there over night, which was the lines upon which most of the coasting ship owners thought. They rarely had a full crew from one place, because if the ship was in a home port, all the locals would be at home whenever possible.

From London we went down river and loaded a cargo of cement in bags at one of the cement wharves in the Swanscombe/Greenhithe area. It was raining and snowing and blowing a gale of wind intermittently during the loading, and it was a case of open up the hatch to load, and close the hatch for rain every few minutes. Loading was carried out day and night at the cement wharves, the dockers working in shifts. We worked a continuous shift and by the time we were loaded completely, we were glad to get the hatches on and battened down ready for sea. Whilst we were battening down the hatch, the Captain stood on the bridge carefully scrutinising our every move and made my colleague withdraw one of the wooden hatch wedges which he had inserted with the grain of the wood the wrong way and put it in correctly. Fortunately I had been well schooled in this procedure so I took care that he did not get a chance to fault me, but we were to be thankful for his thoroughness in making his ship seaworthy later.

We left Greenhithe on New Years Eve and proceeded down river during the daylight. As I had been sailing on the London trade for some time with crews containing ex-sailing barge men, I had learned a lot of local knowledge from them. It was very soon apparent to me that Captain Cowley was not very well acquainted with the Thames estuary. As was customary with steam coasters, he was not employing a pilot and was doing the pilotage himself and not making a very brilliant job of it. I think he must have sensed that I had seen through him. When he got into a bit of a 'ravel', he promptly turned round and gave poor 'Walty' the rounds of the kitchen which was hardly the way to treat the mate in front of the crew. Walty was very passive and took it all without wincing. We passed through the Downs and the Straits of Dover as the New Year commenced and wished each other a Happy New Year and drank our health in a hot cup of tea, the last cup of hot tea we were to drink for some time. Shortly afterwards we ran into bad weather but kept plugging at it; the JOLLY DIANA was a very good little sea boat and was probably making some headway, although she shipped some very heavy water. The weather soon increased to a severe gale by which time we were unable to get forward to our accommodation and spent our 'watch below' sleeping as well as we could on the hard steel gratings of the fiddley over the boiler which was very hot but dry.

The two engineers because they had to do their own firing, were now both on watch together because the main engine was racing heavily each time the propellor came out of the water and one of them had to stand by the throttle which was an instant shut-off steam valve and was used to prevent the main engine damaging itself when racing. This had to be seen to be believed, and it could only be a credit to the men that made these steam engines that they did not shake themselves to pieces. The engineers were glad of our assistance, when we were off watch, to pull up the ashes for them and dump them overboard. Very soon as the weather got worse, it was a case of heaving the ashes up and dumping them over the engine room door-step where they were instantly washed away by the seas that we were shipping.

After a while the water in the stokehold bilges increased, then the main engine bilge pump, which was continually pumping the bilges when the main engine was working, became choked. The auxiliary bilge pump was brought into

Fid & Splice in
the making.

use and this also became choked. The engineers did all they possibly could to clear the pumps but to no avail and very soon the water was above the stoke-hold plates and washing back and forth as the ship pitched and rolled, washing the small coal and the ashes into the bilges which were common with the engine room. Soon the water was splashing into the ash pits, enveloping the place in stinking steam. By now the main engine cranks were turning in the water and throwing it across the engine room. The only light was from two duck lamps which gave off a lot of smoke. It was a very sorry sight and obviously the situation had become serious.

The Captain took the wheel and bridge and everybody shared in trying to clear the water from the engine space. We rigged the emergency hand pump, but this proved useless; the suction to this was also choked. So while the two engineers tried to clear the pumps, the Mate and my colleague and I filled ash buckets with water from the bilges and hove it up using the hand ash winch which was situated in one of the ventilators and emptied the water out of the engine room door. When the bucket was entering the ventilator it would invariably catch on the edge of the ventilator and some of the contents would be emptied on whoever was working underneath it.

The ship had long since refused to steer and we could barely keep sufficient steam with the coal being wet. Meanwhile the Captain was at the wheel by himself singing hymns. 'Nearer my God to Thee', 'Eternal Father strong to save', 'Abide with me' etc., whilst whenever the ship gave an extra heavy roll and upset the water from the ash bucket upon whoever was underneath them filling them, the language from that individual was anything but pious, and generally with advice to tell the 'old gentleman' to keep his 'so and so etc.', ship steady. If any prayers were said in the engine room, they were silent ones, neither was there any panic. We were all aware of the situation we were in and we all worked together to save the ship.

There was a method of pumping the bilges, which was only used in an emergency as a last resort, that was to use what was called the bilge injection which meant that instead of using sea water to circulate through the condenser, the sea water was shut off and the bilge water pumped through and outboard in its place. It was definitely an emergency measure because if the condenser got choked it could cause more serious complications. The Chief Engineer after consultation with the Captain had decided to do this and he had probably persuaded the Captain to try and get the ship into port. So the bilge injection was opened and the sea injection closed, this worked for a few minutes and the water went down some inches and stopped. Then the condenser started to run hot, so the injection had to be put back to sea water. At first nothing happened, then sea water got through and after a while the condenser cooled down, in the meantime the Engineer had taken a hammer and chisel and cut first the auxiliary bilge pump suction pipe which was lead, below the level of the water, but this pipe was blocked solid so this availed us nothing. He then cut the bilge injection suction which was also a lead pipe below the engine room plates and then changed over from the sea injection. This time we were able to pump the water through the condenser, get the water level down until it was just below the plates and control it. At the same time we were continuing to bail out the stokehold with ash buckets and after a while were able to raise more steam and get the engine turning a bit faster. Many hours after we limped into Weymouth, where we all set to bailing the engine room out by hand and cleaning out the bilges which were full of coal and ashes to the level of the plates for the entire length of the boiler and engine space.

It took us three days and nights of continuous work with very little sleep to clear the bilges and get the water out, after which the pipes which had been cut were removed by the ship's engineers and taken ashore and repaired and then replaced. By this time the weather having now improved, we resumed our passage to Penzance, where we duly arrived as the newspaper stated. After discharging our cement cargo we went light ship to Swansea, where we loaded a cargo of coal for Belfast where after a fine passage we arrived on a Saturday evening and had a comparatively free Sunday except for the incident I have already mentioned.

From Belfast we went to Killyleagh in Strangford Lough and loaded a cargo of potatoes for Liverpool. After discharging the potatoes we went light ship to Garston to load coal for the Isle of Man. I had by this time received an offer of a berth in the JOLLY CHRISTINE another of Walford's steam coasters, and which I quickly accepted. I left the JOLLY DIANA in Garston, where the 'ould man' would not pay me my wages until midnight claiming my day ended then. So I never reached the Isle of Man in the JOLLY DIANA which was renamed shortly after the MONAS BELLE. Captain Cowley handed over command to his son Walty who ran her successfully until she had an accident and grounded in the Solway Firth. I believe she was refloated and what happened after that I do not know, but Walty eventually turned up as a dock gate-man in Liverpool where he remained for many years. As the newspaper stated, we had an exciting voyage.

"Kilmarnock."

24. The KILMARNOCK.

Owen G. Spargo

New Year 1924 found me out of a berth, when along came a steamer called KILMARNOCK requiring an Able Seaman. Fortunately I was at hand, and I was lucky in obtaining the job, because work was scarce. Many ships were laying up and those that did manage to keep running would do a couple of voyages before laying up and paying off their crews.

The KILMARNOCK was a steam coaster or about 600 tons deadweight, and was one of the numerous 'KIL' class ships which had been built for the Royal Navy during the 1914/1918 war for use in coastal patrol and convoy escort duties. They were a curious shape, inasmuch that the bow and stern looked alike, the funnel and bridge were amidships and they also had a deck-house abaft the funnel which could easily be mistaken for the bridge which was forward of the funnel. The idea I was told was to confuse the enemy as to which direction they were going (25).

In the case of the KILMARNOCK she had a good many alterations; she had been built up forward, and a raised forecastle head added (24). She had two holds and two hatches, with boiler, engines, bunker and accommodation between them. Her forward hatch coamings had been lengthened and heightened, a cargo winch put on her forecastle head to serve the fore hold and another winch at the after end of the mid-ship house to serve the after hold, each winch being paired with a mast and derrick. A small platform right aft served as a cover for the quadrant and had on it a steam capstan and also served as the poop and rope grating. She had athwart-ship hatch beams and fore and aft hatches, and from a sailor's point of view was what they would term a 'heavy job' on deck. The layout of a similar ship, the KILDAVIN is shown on page 27.

She had one Scotch boiler, (when the Navy owned her it was said that she had two boilers). The boiler had three furnaces and a Howden forced draught fan for them. Her boiler tubes were fitted with retorts which were twisted lengths of steel the length and breadth of the boiler tubes, which were supposed to diffuse the flame and do other magic things to keep steam. Unfortunately when the firemen needed to clean the tubes and this was frequently, the retorts all had to be taken out, and then after the tubes had been swept, replaced. As each tube held one of these retorts, it made tube cleaning a long and heavy job. She also had vertical uptake tubes through which the smoke passed after going through the horizontal tubes. These uptake tubes were a continual source of trouble and would block up with soot which would then catch fire, and it was not uncommon to see the funnel red hot almost to the top.

She had a very good triple expansion main engine with 'double balancing' cranks and the auxiliary pumps were independent of the main engine. She did not have a generator so lighting throughout was by paraffin lamps. She was painted 'Admiralty grey' of which paint there was several hundredweights on board having probably come over with her from the Navy. This paint was dubbed 'crab fat' by the seamen of that time probably due to its resemblance to mercurial ointment which was for a very different purpose. Her deck houses and bridge were painted white, and the funnel then red with a black top. It was later changed to all black because we were unable to keep the red paint on it with the tubes going on fire regularly. Some time later, being unable to keep even black paint on it, we experimented with a mixture of colza oil, paraffin oil, black lead and tallow, which at least kept it a dark if not entirely black colour.

She was quite a smart looking ship and then owned by a Mr. Robert Leeson who had offices in Oriel Chambers, Water Street, Liverpool. He had acquired her for £4,000, but it was not his first venture in ship owning and he had at one time owned ships under the name of Donnelly and Leeson of Dublin and amongst others owned at different times the SAMOA, BIRMINGHAM (18), ADAM SMITH, and others. He kept her well manned, with a crew of 14, which was: Master, Mate, Bosun, two Able Seamen, two Ordinary Seamen, Chief and 2nd Engineers, one Donkeyman, three Firemen, and a Cook/Steward. The Bosun acted as Second Mate and kept the Captain's watch at sea together with 1 AB and 1 OS, whilst the Mate kept the opposite watch with the remaining AB and OS. The Donkeyman (a name I have been told originated from the man who attended the small boiler in the old sailing ships which supplied steam to drive the pumps and winches for setting sails and working cargo, and doing the 'donkey' or unskilled work previously done manually, hence 'donkey boiler' and the 'donkey man', the man who looked after it) was on watch with the Chief Engineer. The latter intended to keep his watch in bed, and leave the donkeyman to carry on alone, but later events were to upset his calculations on that score, as the boiler problems got progressively worse, the Engineers were spending as much time in the stokehold as the firemen, sometimes much more.

The KILMARNOCK was built with fine lines, similar to a steam trawler and I was told had a deep bar keel, and could not take the ground for fear of capsizing. A 'floating clause' was inserted in all her charter parties, that is, she had to be guaranteed to be afloat at all times in whatever berth she was allotted to. This restricted her trading to the deep water ports. Also she was deep draughted for her tonnage, being about 16 or 17 feet loaded, and being excluded from shallow water ports by her draught, she did not appear to be a very good business proposition, but I supposed Mr. Leeson knew his own mind best; but he certainly inherited plenty of worries with her. She was reputed to have a good turn of speed, and probably did have when the Navy owned her, because she then had, I believe, two boilers, but somewhere along the line between the Navy and Mr. Leeson acquiring her, one boiler had been removed, and the remaining boiler was not sufficient to maintain the amount of steam the machinery required, although she was reputed to have made a passage from Garston to Dublin in 8 hours (an average of 15 knots) but I think favourable tides would have been a large factor on that occasion.

The sailors and firemen lived in separate forecastles below the main deck right forward, whilst the Bosun had a small room on deck under the forecastle head above them on the Port side and the Donkeyman had a similar room on the starboard side. The Captain, Mate, Engineers and Cook/Steward lived in accommodation amidships, where there was also a comfortable saloon (probably originally the ward room) and at the after end a reasonable galley, with a coal burning 'Trawler' brand stove. A very good make of stove with two ovens which could dispose of a hundredweight of coal in 24 hours very easily. Access to the main deck fore and aft from amidships was by watertight (Navy type) doors which had a high step and could be closed and secured so that water could not enter by them. There were also ladders from the amidship deck to the main deck fore and aft.

She had just docked in Garston when I boarded her to ask for the job, and was laying alongside a coaster called the FULAGAR which had been built, I believe, by Cammell Laird & Co., of Birkenhead to try out a new diesel engine that they had invented and called Fulagar, after which they had named the ship. The FULAGAR was not entirely a motor ship, having a coal fired steam boiler, also steam winches, steam windlass and steam steering gear. She was of all-welded construction and must have been one of, if not the first all-welded ship. Brocklebank Line were tied up in that venture and I believe that engine was installed in one of their ships later and was not a success. The FULAGAR was later converted to steam and sold and her name changed (I think to Brereton). She finished her days on the Splough Rock off Carnsore Point whilst running for shelter at Rosslare and became a total loss.

I eventually installed myself in the forecastle, which was typical of the period, dark, damp, below decks, wooden bunks, deal table and forms, a coal fired bogey, in each forecastle, paraffin lamps and supply your own bed and

25. A 'KIL' class Q-ship when in naval service.

bedding and eating utensils. The Cook/Steward supplied and cooked the food and charged 12/6d per week for doing so, the food was quite good for the first couple of days after pay day, reverting at the latter end of the week to stews and lob-scouse for dinner and porridge for breakfast. I suppose he was working on a tight budget, and it was the accepted thing that the cook would get his food free out of the profits, a practice which all cooks denied.

The KILMARNOCK had an open bridge, with canvas dodger, a steering wheel on a brass pedestal, brass engine room telegraph and two copper speaking tubes, one to the Captain, the other to the Engine room. A box mounted on the front held the binoculars and a wire lanyard to the steam whistle. On their respective sides were the Port and Starboard side lights which used paraffin oil, and their screens. There was no seat, so when you went there to stand your watch, you stood it, literally and physically. The steering wheel on the bridge was connected to the steam steering engine, which was in a house abaft the funnel, by a series of brass rods and cog wheels. The steering engine was connected to the quadrant by rod and chain fitments. She was an exceptionally good steering ship, and as a change from the average coaster used steam steering at sea, which was considerably easier on the arms than pulling away at hand gear. There was a very good chart room underneath the bridge, with good all round vision. It was fitted with a large chart table with drawers beneath it, as well as a cushioned settee and small folding table. The pipe from the saloon stove below it ran through it and kept it reasonably warm.

We loaded a cargo of coal at Garston, and after loading overnight, sailed the following early morning for Cork, the weather being then boisterous. Proceeding down the river she was going at great speed and overtaking everything, but by the time she reached the Bar Light Vessel, the steam must have been going down because she had slowed very considerably, and by now firemen and engineers were in the stokehold having trouble keeping steam. By the time we had reached the Skerries Lighthouse, off Holyhead, she had slowed down to about five knots, and with the wind freshening from the South West to a whole gale she was labouring and making heavy weather of it. Somewhere South West of the South Stack, Holyhead, by which time she was shipping very heavy seas and was awash fore and aft, I had just been relieved after doing my 'trick' at the wheel when she shipped a heavy sea at the same time that I reached the bottom of the bridge ladder and I was washed off my feet and thought that I had been washed overboard. I must have been carried over the whole length of the midship deck and the length of the after hatch, when I felt myself hit something hard, grabbed at it, and found it to be the quadrant under the grating aft. I was shaken up quite a lot, but managed to make my way to the door at the after end of the amidship accommodation and get inside, where I found the remainder of the crew who were off watch, huddled in the galley with the stove burning brightly and obviously much appreciated. Judging from the shouting coming from the stokehold it appeared that the firemen were having difficulty maintaining steam, and most of the firemen were in the stokehold assisted by the engineers. The engine was only turning very slowly, and the weather appeared to be getting worse. She was shipping very heavy water and was sluggish, and not freeing herself properly of the heavy water that was coming aboard. Suddenly she took a heavy roll, listed, and took a long time to recover. Then the weather seemed to quieten, the ship uprighted herself and was steadier; we had turned back. The firemen seemed to be having some success with the steam and the engines had picked up a little speed, although the ship was still taking on board very heavy water. She was still very sluggish and it was obvious that all was not well. After a couple of hours we entered Holyhead Harbour and anchored in the shelter of the breakwater.

The fore deck was about six inches under water so it was certain that something was wrong. The pumps were started, and it was well into the following day before the water was pumped out of her. The Board of Trade surveyors came on board and surveyed the hatches which were securely battened down and in good order. They found that water had got into the hold through two goose neck ventilators under the bulwark rail which had not been plugged before leaving. The forward accommodation was a shambles, water had got into it and was about a foot deep, with all the loose gear, boots and shoes, wooden forms and ashes from the bogey, washing about everywhere. We all turned-to together and had to bail the forecastles out with buckets. However once we had the water out of them we were not very long in getting them dry with the aid of the bogeys, which gave off a good heat when they were going full blast. The mooring ropes and spare gear which had been stowed under the forecastle head had washed adrift and were in a tangle, and it was obvious that we had been through a bad time.

Eventually after remaining in Holyhead for about 3 or 4 days, during which time we were fully occupied in tidying up after the gale, the weather moderated and we were able to continue our voyage to Cork, where most of the crew left her, including the Mate and 2nd Engineer who were both deep water

South Stack.

S.S. "KILDAVIN"

Length ~ 170'2" Registered.
Breadth ~ 30'0" Moulded.

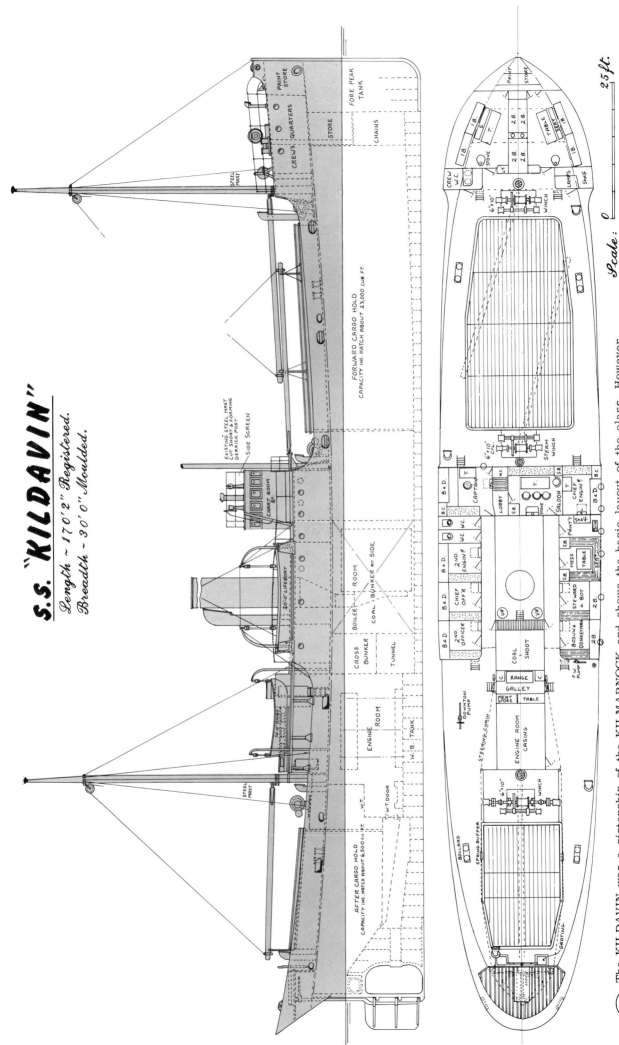

PAINT STORE

CREW'S QUARTERS

STEEL MAST

FORE PEAK TANK

STORE

CHAINS

FORWARD CARGO HOLD
CAPACITY INC. HATCH ABOUT 23,000 CUB. FT.

EXISTING STEEL MAST CUT SHORT & FORMING DERRICK POST

SIDE SCREEN

CHART ROOM &c.

20'0" LIFEBOAT

14'0" DINGHY

STEEL MAST

BOILER ROOM

CROSS BUNKER

COAL BUNKER AT SIDE

TUNNEL

ENGINE ROOM

W. B. TANK

W.T. DOOR

W.T.

AFTER CARGO HOLD
CAPACITY INC. HATCH ABOUT 6,500 CUB. FT.

BOLLARD

SPRING BUFFER

STEERING CHAIN

DOWNTON PUMP

CREW W.C.

STOVE

L.T.

LAMPS

SHELF

TABLE

SEAT

18

5

T

2 B

2 B

2 B

18

18

18

WINCH

6"x10" CYL.

STEAM WINCH

B.C.

T.

CAPTAIN

W.C.

LOBBY

S.B.

STOVE

SALOON

T.

CHIEF ENGINR

B & D

B.C.

B & D

W.C.

2ND ENGINR

W.C.

PANTY

SHELF

S.B.

MESS

TABLE

SEAT

SINK

B & D

CHIEF OFFR

S.B.

STEWARD & BOY

2 B.

B & D

2ND OFFICER

VK

VK

BOSUN & DONKEYMAN

2 B

F.W. PUMP

COAL SHOOT

RANGE

GALLEY

MEAT STORE

TABLE

C.

C.

ENGINE ROOM CASING

WINCH

6"x10"

GRATING

Scale: 0 — 25 ft.

27 The KILDAVIN was a sistership of the KILMARNOCK and shows the basic layout of the class. However when they were adapted for commercial trading, they were reconstructed to a number of different plans so the cabin and deck layouts differed in details.

men, and swore never again to put their foot aboard another coaster. I remained, because I reasoned that if she could survive what she had come through, she would survive anything. We took on crew replacements in Cork, and the Mate having left, the Bosun was promoted to Mate and I, being the only other deck rating who had remained, was promoted to Bosun/Acting 2nd Mate, in which position I gained much watch-keeping experience.

From Cork we went to Swansea in ballast. At Swansea we loaded a cargo of steam coal for the French Navy in Cherbourg, at the same time filling our own bunkers with Welsh steam coal, which we were assured was the proper coal for furnaces with Howden's force draught fans. We left Swansea, and before we were a couple of hours out, the steam started to drop back and the engines almost stopped. The Engineers blamed the bunkers, so we turned around and limped back to Swansea, where we were boarded by an army of Chemists, Surveyors and other V.I.Ps who took samples of the bunkers for analysis and also took measurements of the boiler, furnaces, etc.

After lying there a couple of days, it was decided to discharge the bunkers, and replace it with a different type of coal. All this took time because the bunker hatch, although quite large enough to receive bunkers, was too small to allow a decent sized cargo tub to be lowered into it and consequently had to be discharged with 5 cwt. baskets. This made it a slow job, but after a further 2 or 3 days, the old bunkers were out and replaced so we set off again. The new bunkers were a little better, but we were still having problems. Whilst we had steam for an hour or so, we would average about 10 knots, but as soon as the fires began to get dirty we would be down to about 5 knots.

However the weather was kindly to us and we duly arrived in Cherbourg where we berthed in the Naval dockyard, near the old Mauretania which was also lying there having repairs done to her. Perhaps our having to turn back influenced the French, because they came on board almost daily and took samples of the cargo away for analysis. They made no attempt to discharge us and we lay there for 5 or 6 weeks whilst they took samples and argued. In the meantime the discharging time has expired, and the ship came on demurrage (compensation for delaying the ship by exceeding the agreed time in the charter), and apparently on this occasion, this was paid according to the amount of cargo remaining in the ship when her time had expired. In our case we still had a full cargo and we were well over our time, so the demurrage must had been considerable. When I discussed this with Mr. Leeson, when I knew him better, some years later he confided to me that that particular voyage cleared the purchase price of the ship, but he must have lost a lot of money with her later, because she was always problematic with only having the one boiler. Various methods were used to try and overcome the steaming problem, first the uptake tubes were removed, this resulted in flames coming out of the top of the funnel! Then dispensing with the 'Howden' force draught fan and converting to natural draught, this was worse than ever, and so the experimenting continued.

In the meantime we were getting around fairly well under the circumstances, and ran several cargoes of bunker coal from the Bristol Channel ports to Falmouth where it was discharged into a bunkering elevator craft. This was a steam self-propelled craft of about 1,000 tons which had a conveyor type belt from the hold carrying coal to a gantry above her bows, which held a movable pipe with which it used to supply ships with coal bunkers. It was used extensively by passing coasters in particular and was very efficient and could handle 50 to 60 tons of coal an hour with ease. There were several of these bunkering stations along the English Channel ports and I am sure they did some good business. With the advent of the Motor ships and decline of the steamers, they became obsolete and finally disappeared. A pity because they provided employment for quite a number of men both directly and indirectly. We used our own winches and derricks to discharge our cargo into the elevator, whilst we were lying to an anchor in Carrick Roads, Falmouth. As we were lying some distance from the town, a 'liberty' boat which attended the bunkering craft would give crew members a lift ashore and return them, but I rarely went ashore from the anchorage.

One afternoon, the ship chandler came on board with provisions which the cook/steward had bought. The cook/steward still being ashore, I took delivery from the ship chandler and whilst I was doing so, the Captain who was passing, asked me to hand him the bill and he would check them off as I handled them. All went well until we came to a parcel of bacon which was very obviously short weight. The Captain asked me to get the scales and we weighed every thing and found lots of items short of weight. The ship chandler remonstrated and said he hadn't got time for this, but when the Captain threatened to bring the Police on the job, he broke down and blamed it on the cook/steward who he said had persuaded him to fiddle the bill. The cook/steward eventually arrived back on board, having apparently regaled himself at the local tavern with his ill-gotten gains. The Captain was waiting for him, and after listening to his explanation, fired him on the spot. This very soon sober-

Senhouse slip.

ed him up especially when the Captain told him to pay his own fare home out of the money he had stolen from us: I never did care much for that cook/ steward. He used to regale us with his experiences in what he referred to as the 'Cuckoo boats' which was a local nickname given to a line of little passenger steamers of the Liverpool and North Wales Steamship Co. which ran daily services from Liverpool to Llandudno, Beaumaris and the Menai Straits. They commenced operating in May (when the Cuckoo arrived) and laid up for the winter in October (when the Cuckoo left, hence the 'Cuckoo' boats). They had a paddle steamer called LA MARGUERITE and a couple of screw steamers. The cook/steward had served on the LA MARGUERITE as a steward and told how they made money on 'swanks'. Apparently a 'swank' consisted of all the dregs from Bass beer bottles poured into a bottle and recorked, and of course resold. It was the custom at that time when pouring a bottle of beer particularly Bass to leave about three-quarters of an inch in the bottom of the bottle on account of the sediment it contained which was also reputed to be a fairly strong laxative. With so much beer left in the bottle, it would not be very difficult to make a few swanks. I was always very wary drinking bottled beer after that, especially if it was mixed with draught beer or stout.

From Falmouth we sometimes went to Fowey and loaded china clay occasionally for France or Holland but mostly for Runcorn. This was a dirty trade, together with the coal which was full of greasy black dust which penetrated everywhere during both loading and discharging. Then the holds had to be brushed and washed out scrupulously clean before loading the china clay which was used for making pottery and cosmetics. The china clay was loaded by tipping it into the hold down a chute from a 10 or 12 ton wagon, a cloud of white dust covered the ship whilst this was in progress and a coating of dust about $\frac{1}{2}$ inch thick settled over the whole ship. If it started to rain during loading, then loading ceased and the hatch had to be covered. Many foreign coasters and also British foreign going ships carried 'cargo tents' for this purpose, these were both handy and quick. They were made of canvas in the shape of a bell tent, the derrick was plumbed over the centre of the hatch, and the peak of the tent hoisted up on the runner and the skirt of the tent draped around the coamings of the hatch and secured to the hatch cleats which normally held the wedges when the hatch was battened down, I never saw a British tramping coaster with a cargo tent, they would have saved many accidents of men falling down holds which was only too common. The china clay once it got water on it, became as slippery as ice, making it dangerous to even walk on deck let alone scramble over beams. We were always pleased to see these cargoes battened down and the ship washed down. Our trading was not confined to short runs, we made several trips to Dublin, Cork, Waterford and Limerick with coal cargoes and also cargoes of bulk grain and flour in sacks. We also traded from the North East coast where we loaded coal for the bunkering hulks of Gravesend and South coast ports and also to Continental ports.

We had continual changes of crew, especially firemen, who found the job too heavy for them. The ship was by then burning 22 tons of coal in 24 hours, which meant that each man had to shovel 7 tons of coal plus ashes a day. The firemen were on a three watch system of 4 hours on and 8 hours off, but after their 4 hour watch, they spent another hour heaving ashes up from the stokehold. This was done with a hand ash winch and dumping the ashes overboard, so that instead of an 8 hour day they were working a 10 hour day (without overtime). The heat in the stokehold was intense and the noise and vibrations from the Howden fan which was always running flat out, was enough to try the patience of a Saint. It was not surprising that the firemen became dissatisfied, their growls and grumbles no doubt influenced the sailors because we had a considerable turnover of sailors also.

By picking up replacements at different ports, we gathered quite an assortment, one of whom I think deserves a mention. This was the Newfoundland fisherman, a real 'blue nose' (every finger a marline spike, every hair on his head a rope yarn, and every drop of blood Stockholm tar). A first class seaman he was always respectful and quiet. He dressed in the Newfoundland type oilskins (which were reminiscent of the days of Nelson) in bad weather, in which he seemed to revel. He was a big man and not handsome by any means, and called himself 'Newfoundland Sam'. At day break each day we took in the paraffin navigation lamps. The masthead lamp had to be taken down from off the forecastle head. If the ship was shipping water over the bows, we sometimes had to ease down the main engines for a few minutes whilst the man was on the forecastle head. Sam would never hear of the engine being slowed down. When he had lowered the lamp down, he would go right to the stem and look down into the water for two or three minutes before taking the lamp below to the lamp room. Although the ship may have been putting water over the bow before he went there, she would not put another drop over until he came down. Whether he went to the bows to say his prayers or whether he was a 'Jonah' I do not know. Occasionally a well dressed young woman would come down to the ship in a car, and Sam went ashore for a few minutes and

spoke to her and then she was gone. Their meeting was never more than ten minutes so we wondered what she saw in Sam. It might have been his daughter, but whatever the connection we never found out. One day Sam announced that he was leaving (no reason) and he went along to the Captain and settled up and was off. A few days later a couple of detectives came on board making searching enquiries about Sam and his girl friend. What they had been up to I do not know, but the police said that they had been after them for a long time and were keen to get their hands on them.

I was very happy in KILMARNOCK as I was in charge of the bridge on watch at sea, with a fine chart room and free access to the charts. I was not interfered with by the Captain whose standing order was "Call me if you want me" and he rarely came on the bridge at sea. I made full use of my opportunities and gained a great deal of bridge experience. Unfortunately in May, about four months after I joined her, the owner decided that it was time he made some improvements to her boiler, so he laid her up in Clarence Dock Liverpool to do so, and paid off all the crew with the exception of the Captain and Chief Engineer. So it was back to looking for work again, fortunately within a fortnight I had been able to get myself a berth in another steam coaster called FLORENCE which belonged to John S. Monks & Co., Rumford Street, Liverpool.

The FLORENCE was a little ship of about 300 tons and traded mostly Ireland, Bristol Channel, Solway Firth, and River Mersey. She carried an occasional cargo of gravel loaded from a bucket dredger in the Workington channel in the Solway which was taken to the Bromborough dock in the River Mersey for use in the building of the dock there. Her Master was Captain Bill Lewis whose father was also Master and two of his brothers also sailed with his father. They were very much a coasting family. Bill and I were to become very firm friends in later years and worked a great deal together until his death, he was a fine man. The FLORENCE was a happy little ship, but the recession was setting in and after four months, she also laid up and paid off, so it was look for work again. Within a few days I received word from Captain H. W. Moore, the Master of the KILMARNOCK, that she was starting up again and my job was there if I wanted it, so I accepted and rejoined KILMARNOCK ten days after leaving the FLORENCE.

Mr. Leeson had made many modifications to the KILMARNOCK including the installation of somebody's induced draught patent which was apparently on a similar principle to that used in the steam locomotives. A small steam pipe from the top of the boiler was led through the smoke box, where the steam was supposed to be dried, to four semi-circular troughs underneath the fire bars of the furnaces. The fire bars were athwart ships with only a quarter of an inch space between them and the dried steam was supposed to blow through these spaces and induce the fires to burn. On paper the system probably looked fine, but practically it was a proper flop. However modifications and experiments had to be tried out. We never made any record passages but we 'got around' and with her speed so much reduced, she was very comfortable at sea, at least on the bridge.

We carried on like this until the December of 1924 when we were loading a cargo of flour and bran at Rank's Mill, Birkenhead for Limerick when I had the misfortune to fall down the after hold whilst putting on hatches for the night. It was about two o'clock at night, raining, and the beams and hatches were slippery. Fortunately there was a layer of bags of bran on the bottom of the hold which saved me a lot, but I struck my head on the beam and propellor shaft tunnel on the way down and sustained some bad cuts which sent me to hospital, where I was kept in. The ship sailed next morning without me and the Captain wrote he would keep my job for me until I was better.

The KILMARNOCK made her passage to Limerick, and was returning to Swansea where I was to rejoin her. Unfortunately she did not make Swansea. Somewhere near the Smalls Lighthouse, her furnace crowns collapsed and that was the end of the boiler. She was picked up by a steam trawler and towed into Milford Haven where, as was the custom, the crew were paid off with the exception of the Captain and Chief Engineer, so there the KILMARNOCK and I parted company, and it was back to earth again.

During the time she was at Milford Haven, the Board of Trade started making enquiries and the Chief Engineer decided to disappear. I met him many years later when he was Chief Engineer of a big factory. I asked him why he had run away and he confided that he was sailing on his Father's certificate (who was dead) and the Board of Trade surveyor had rumbled it.

I think the KILMARNOCK was sold after that. I had decided to get something a bit bigger under my feet for the winter and signed on as Able Seaman aboard the S/S WINIFREDIAN a cargo and passenger ship belonging to the Leyland Line of Liverpool. She was a big four-masted Western Ocean liner and at one period the largest single screw ship in the world. Quite a change of environment, but that is another story.

Engine Room
Telegraph.

6.

"Matje" & "Wythburn."

31. MATJE at Preston.
Photo: John Clarkson.

Owen G. Spargo

Towards the end of 1928 I was at home, having recently completed a voyage to the Far East and being newly married, I was not relishing the idea of having another long absence from home. Fortunately I received a telegram from Captain H. W. Moore under whom I had served in the KILMARNOCK and ADAM SMITH, offering the mate's berth in the MATJE and asking could I join her at Eastham, the exit from the Manchester Ship Canal, at 10 o'clock that night when she would be arriving there on passage from Manchester to Pwllheli in North Wales. I wired back accepting the job, hopefully thinking that now, being married, I would enjoy a little more home life. I packed my sea bag and made my way towards Eastham by tramcar, ferry and bus. When travelling by trams, it was the custom for a seaman to deposit his sea bag on the rear platform under the stairs, always with the conductor's permission and the recognised tip, sixpence that very often could be ill afforded.

It was a long walk from the bus stop on the main road to Eastham Locks and there were two ways of getting there, by going through Eastham village which was poorly lighted, or by going through Eastham woods which was much shorter, with a good defined path, but was without lights. Although dark, the night was fine and clear so I chose to go through the wood. Putting my bag on my shoulder I entered the woods and had only travelled a few hundred yards when I heard footsteps behind me. I stopped and the footsteps stopped. I asked "are you coming along?", but got no reply. I continued on my way and again the footsteps followed me. I stopped; the footsteps stopped. By now I was getting curious, so putting my sea bag quietly on the ground without stopping. I turned around and retraced my steps to confront whoever was following me and ran head on into a donkey. I do not know who got the biggest shock but he must have been an old and lonely animal for he was very friendly, and after I had stroked and spoken to him, he walked beside me to the end of the wood where I patted him and bid him "Good night".

After I had been at Eastham for about an hour the MATJE showed up. The only lights visible on her were the navigation lights and the dull lights from the portholes in her forward bulkhead, whilst the light from the galley lamp and the reflection from a 'duck' lamp burning smokily in the stokehold was the only illumination on the after deck. To use an electric torch to get around the decks in those days was almost unheard of. I went on board and reported myself to the Captain, who showed me to my room where I deposited my bag,

Stopper knot.

by which time the ship was lowered down in the locks to river level and the dock gateman was calling "come ahead". I went to the forecastle head which was my docking station. I hauled in the ropes, coiled them down and secured them. After ascertaining that all was secure, I reported to the bridge and very soon made myself at home as I was used to sailing with Captain Moore.

The MATJE was a trim little craft of 278 gross tons (Plate 72). She was built in 1890 and was thus 38 years old when I joined her. She was strongly constructed and in common with many ships of her era, had a bar keel and stem. Despite the fact that she had hand steering from the open bridge, by means of a large wheel, she was a good steering ship and easy on the wheel even in bad weather. She had a raised forecastle head on which stood a steam windlass and anchor crane. She originally had stocked anchors which had been replaced with stockless anchors. However, these still had to be stowed on the forecastle head because the hawse pipes were too small to accept them.

She had one long hatch between the fore and main masts with a derrick and steam winch at each mast. There had originally been a small hatch forward of the foremast, but this had been altered to a sliding scuttle leading to the crews accommodation which had been part of the hold. This had been partitioned off with a wooden bulkhead, which although reasonably dust proof, did not prevent the smell of the cargo penetrating. The only light and ventilation was that which was provided by the scuttle when it was open, otherwise lighting was provided by a paraffin lamp which hung from a nail in the bulkhead. The original crew accommodation had been under the forecastle head but for some reason had been condemned, probably due to lack of headroom.

The masts passed through the deck and fitted into sockets in the keelson. They were secured at the deck by wood wedges over which, and around the mast, was a canvas cover, called a 'mast coat'. These were hand made and required some skill. I had the pleasure of renewing and making them when I was in her, and was very proud of the job that I made of them. The hand steering gear with wheel, binnacle containing the compass and the engine room telegraph was all the equipment on the bridge. The compass was illuminated by a colza-oil-burning light which more often than not had to suffice with paraffin due to the lack of colza oil which at that time was 6d a gallon. The bridge had a canvas surround to waist level, which had been coated with paint until it was solid, and above this was a canvas dodger. Despite its starkness it was comfortable enough and only rarely did spray reach there in bad weather. It was approached by a ladder at the after end. Under the bridge was the bridge deck, which held the main mast just in front of the bridge, in front of which was the derrick and steam winch for the after end of the hold. Behind the mast was a very ornate skylight to the accommodation below. At the after end of this deck stood the drinking water tank holding 600 gallons. It was the only fresh water tank on board and a pipe led to a tap in the galley which was on the after deck in the fore end of the boiler casing. This tap was a continual source of annoyance as people would draw water from the tap, particularly shore people working on board in port and not turn the water off properly, consequently it would not take very long for the tank to empty itself. We had to fit it with a lock and key in the end and that, apart from a voyage I made in a pilgrim ship to Jeddah, was the only time I saw the drinking water locked up during my whole time at sea.

The accommodation below the bridge deck was quite roomy but was divided up into a lot of little rooms and cupboards and had obviously had many alterations over the years. This accommodation was entered from the after end on the starboard side, where an alleyway led to the Captain's and Mate's cabins which were in the fore part, behind which was a small but comfortable saloon. There was a table built around the mainmast which passed through from the deck above down into the hold beneath. This part of the mast was so well polished that you could see your face in it. At the after end of the saloon was a cushioned settee which served as a seat at the table for meals. Over the table hung a brass lamp with a white shade, whilst each room had a paraffin lamp in gimbals (lighting throughout the ship was by paraffin). On the port side was a small stove and little pantry. Abaft this accommodation was another saloon and cabin where the Chief Engineer lived. On the starboard side of this alleyway when entering was a W.C. (drawbucket flushed), a lamp room, two cupboards and at the fore end a store room where paints and ropes were kept. The accommodation was comfortable if old. The beds were the usual wooden bunk type and we all provided our own bedding and utensils.

Binnacle.

She had one boiler with two furnaces which were fired from the after end which was common with the engine room. She had a compound engine with engine driven pumps and a good turn of speed. She could do 9 knots when driven, but this increased her coal consumption, so she was run at 8 knots and could keep this up in all but very bad weather. She was a very good sea boat and I was out in some very bad weather in her, on some occasions hove-to and I rarely saw her put any heavy water on board.

The second engineer lived in accommodation below decks right aft which was entered from a scuttle on the deck and consisted of two very cramped rooms one at each side of a small mess room which contained a triangular table with seats around it. The woodwork was all done out in panelled mahogany, all showing signs of neglect. It looked more like the cabin on a schooner than on a steamer. It was a very dark place as the single porthole each side had their dead-lights permanently closed on account of leakage. Heating was provided by a small coal burning bogey stove and lighting was by a single paraffin lamp on the bulkhead; it was a dreary place.

The second engineer who occupied this accommodation was a character to himself, an Irishman from Arklow, he was a very quiet man and could neither read nor write. By writing letters for him to his wife and reading his wife's reply to him we soon became firm friends. I often wondered if he was an Irish tinker, he was so well versed in weather and folk-lore; he lived very close to nature. I could never understand how he knew so much about the tides. Sometimes I would ask him, to test him, "how is the tide now Joe?" He would reply, "well let me see, the moon was so and so last week, the tide is with us for the next four hours." He was never wrong. Also I would ask him "what time is it?" he would reply without looking at the clock and was rarely more than five minutes out. I do not think he ever had a watch.

The Chief Engineer was a very friendly and likeable man who came from Anglesey. He spoke very broken English and very rarely went ashore. A typical Welshman, he was always ready for a yarn and like the second engineer was well versed in folk-lore. He had at one time been 'chief engineer' of a steam-driven thrashing machine which toured the farms in Wales at harvest time. Some of his anecdotes of that period would have compared very favourably with George Borrow's stories of 'Wild Wales'. He sadly lost his life when the WYTHBURN was blown up and sunk by a mine in Barry Roads.

The general atmosphere on board was one of friendliness and good feeling with everyone pulling together and assisting each other whenever possible. The one A.B. was a Japanese who had been in the ship a long time. He was a very agreeable and dependable man and an excellent seaman. The remainder of the crew, a Fireman and an O.S. were often birds of passage because it was the owners' practice that when the ship was going to lay over a weekend in the Mersey, say from Friday night to Tuesday morning, to pay off these unfortunate individuals and put the remainder of the crew on half pay. By losing the Saturday's work they were unable to sign on the dole and would also get no dole pay for Monday, so it was only to be expected that they did not stay. Still times were bad and it was not difficult to get others to take their place.

We traded all around the United Kingdom and near Continent, carrying whatever cargo offered. We carried many cargoes of granite chippings from the Welsh quarries to, amongst other places, Pomona Dock, Manchester which was as far up the Ship Canal as we were able to go. We did not relish a journey to Manchester because it often meant that we would go up the canal during the hours of darkness and as we had to negotiate four locks doing so and sometimes have to tie up to allow traffic to pass, little or no sleep was to be had by any one on board during transit of the canal. On arrival at Manchester, a steam crane with grab would completely discharge the cargo during the day, when it was impossible to sleep with the noise of the grab, and by 5 or 6 o'clock in the evening we were on our way down the canal again, cleaning the hold on the way ready to start loading another cargo at 8 o'clock next morning at one of the Mersey ports and sail again the same night. Again if the ship was to lay in Manchester or the Mersey Ports over the weekend, the half pay/pay off rule applied, so that local men had no reason to look forward to a run to the Mersey.

After I had been in the ship for a month or two I was given the opportunity to bring my wife with me, and seeing that we were newly married and had no ties, I quickly availed myself of the offer. My wife quickly adapted herself to shipboard life, and she sailed with me for quite a long time. We had a very happy time together, especially in the small ports where we joined in local events and soon got well known. It suited the Master that I had my wife with me, for he knew that we would always be on board and so he could leave the ship without worry. Also with my wife doing the cooking we were getting proper food and regularly. She spent a long time on the bridge with me at sea, and very soon learned to steer and would steer the ship happily for hours on end or sit on a seat reading in the wing of the bridge. The Captain was an Amateur Radio enthusiast and was forever tinkering with sets that he made himself. We were always sure of a radio programme, provided that he could find a garage to keep the glass accumulator (battery) charged up.

One of our favourite ports was a very small one in Southern Ireland called Kilmacsimons Quay which was on the river above Kinsale above a bridge, the Western bridge at which was also another quay where a coal merchant did

Side-light.

business. Kilmacsimons quay consisted of a small quay that could take up to two ships each about 150 feet in length. It dried out at low water when the ships lay aground. There were about a dozen typical small Irish cottages with the half door to keep out the animals. Some of the cottages had earth floors and all used peat for fuel, which had a distinguishing and not unpleasant smell of its own, and of course a public house. Dennis the publican was also a coal merchant and shipped occasional cargoes in on his own account. He also acted as agent for ships that brought cargoes of coal or grain for the merchants in Bandon and the surrounding countryside. His pub was well patronised by the ships crews who were very often drinking and singing there until the small hours of the morning, Dennis sitting in a small window on the river side with a commanding view of the road in both directions to keep a look out for the police. During the many times that I went there I never saw a policeman, who would have had to come from Bandon several miles away in any case, and despite the long drinking sessions I never saw a case of drunkeness. Occasionally when they were musically inclined they would serenade us for half an hour or so after Dennis had called time. When we took a cargo of grain, all the village poultry would congregate at the ship's side to pick up the spillage. We could always buy fresh eggs and vegetables there cheaply and would get fresh milk, butter-milk and farm butter from the nearby farm.

The river was only navigable in daylight and discharging was slow work using our own derricks and winches and discharging the cargo into horse drawn carts which had a long distance to take it. It is surprising how much employment that small ship provided for so many people and yet showed a profit.

On one occasion we were bound for Coleraine, a small port on the River Bann in County Antrim, Northern Ireland. The River Bann has a notoriously bad bar at its entrance. Several ships have been lost on it over the years, the story going that ships once they hit it never got off. We had been anchored at Moville for a couple of days because there was too much sea on the bar to enter. When the weather moderated we proceeded towards the entrance and struck the bar in doing so and bumped our way along the stone retaining wall at the bank, but luckily we got over it and were able to make our way to the berth where, after discharging, we proceeded to Loch Sween and loaded beech logs for Garston. I had been to Loch Sween some years before in the GLEN HELEN. On this occasion we were there over a weekend and as Sunday work was unheard of in Scotland we had a free day. So on the Sunday, taking the ship's lifeboat which we were using to load the timber, together with a couple of the crew, my wife and I went exploring the upper reaches of the loch, landing on a couple of Islets in the centre of the loch on which there was a lot of bird life. The nearest habitation was several miles away. It was very quiet and remote. At night time, all that could be heard was the occasional call of an owl. The timber was felled and dragged down to the water from where we ferried it out with our lifeboat to the ship which was lying with anchors out ahead and stern ropes made fast to trees on shore, the logs were then lifted on board with our own derricks and winches.

After discharging at Garston we loaded a cargo of coal for Howth, a small port just North of the Bailey in Dublin Bay and close to Ireland's Eye, a small island off the Bailey. Here the cargo was discharged into horse drawn carts with our own derricks and winches. There was a considerable fleet of fishing vessels working from Howth and we were able to get a good feed of excellent fresh fish. From Howth we went to Carreg-y-llam and loaded a cargo of granite chippings for Glasson Dock, a small port with a dry-dock on the River Lune between Fleetwood and Lancaster. This was a good piece of strategy on the part of the owners, because the ship was going into dry-dock there for repairs. The dry-dock was owned by Nicholsons and they were able to start on repairs whilst we were discharging. Nicholsons was a small family firm with skilful craftsmen who took pride in their work. I think most of the workers lived in Glasson Dock or not very far away. The crew with the exception of the Captain, Chief Engineer and myself were paid-off on arrival, and the boiler blown-down for cleaning. After discharging the three of us pulled the ship across the dock by hand and into the dry-dock since we had no steam on the boiler. We dry-docked in the evening and on the following day were surveyed, after which the Captain and Chief Engineer went home on unpaid holiday until repairs were completed. My wife and I remained on board on half pay which was £1-15-0 per week, which after I had paid my National Insurance and paid the rent of my house ashore, left us with about £1-3-0 to feed the two of us for a week.

We were in Glasson Dock for about a month before repairs were completed, and although I only received half pay, it did not prevent the owner from sending along a couple of gallons of paint with instructions to get on with chipping and painting the hold. He would also phone Mr. Nicholson periodically and enquire of my progress. Nevertheless my wife and I were very happy. There was only one small general shop combined with a post office and two public houses, no butcher (a van came once a week) and only two buses a day to

Sheet bend.

Lancaster so that if you went in by the morning bus, you had to return by 5 o'clock at night. That did not worry us, we would walk to Lancaster market on a Saturday and buy sufficient meat and provisions for a week, after which we would go to the cinema for the matinee (two seats at 6d each, half a pound of chocolates 1/-, 20 cigarettes 4½d, and a box of Swan Vesta matches 1½d, total cost 2/6d) or in present money 12½ new pence. After coming out of the cinema we would walk back to Glasson Dock, a total distance there and back of 14 miles and arrive back fresh and contented. We never thought of using the bus, it was pleasant countryside and we enjoyed it.

The MATJE had one fault which kept recurring, that was the tail-end shaft used to wear down the stern tube quickly. Shortly after I joined her the tail-end shaft was drawn and the stern tube which was lined with lignum vitae wood was found to be badly worn. This was replaced with green-heart wood which still wore down before its anticipated time. Before I left her the tail-end shaft had a brass sleeve shrunk on to it and the stern tube fitted with a brass bush. We did not have many other mechanical troubles, but eventually the manilla rope rings on the circulating pump plunger would wear out and had to be renewed. Occasionally we would have a leaking boiler tube, which the engineers would deal with themselves. We had one collision during the time I was in her when a Liverpool grab hopper dredger the MILES K. BURTON which was over-taking us, collided with us in the Rock Channel in the Mersey. Apart from the bump, little or no damage was done. As they were both strong ships we continued on our voyages.

She was kept well occupied and when the trade fell slack on the West Coast, she was large enough to trade successfully on the East and South Coasts and near Continent, carrying whatever offered. There was also at that time a seasonal trade with salt herring and salt mackerel from the small ports and bays on the West coast of Ireland, where they were caught, cleaned and put into barrels for shipment, mostly to Continental ports. Some were shipped to the Mersey for onward shipment to Russia and the Mediterranean countries. We took several cargoes to the Continent. On another occasion we took a cargo of steel plates from Cardiff to Derwenthaugh on the River Tyne. We were glad to see these discharged because they were very low in the hold making us very stiff and we would have rolled heavily. Also had they shifted, they would have been too heavy for us to handle them. Fortunately we had fine weather all the way. Other cargoes we carried were china clay from Fowey, Par and the Clay Ports to Lancaster, Preston and Runcorn; also to Rotterdam and the French ports. Going to so many different ports and carrying such a variety of cargoes was very valuable experience for me which proved very useful in later life.

My wife remained with me for most of the first year and eventually Captain Moore was transferred to a larger ship, the KYLE PRINCE (ex. ITA) and was relieved by a man who was very soon referred to by the crew as the 'horizontal navigator.' He would come on board in his cups when the ship was ready to sail and could not get to his bed quick enough with a bottle of whisky and you would rarely see him until we had got the pilot on board at our destination. He left the chart on the table and left me to get on with it. I was not too worried except that he would not get up to keep his watch, leaving the sailor on the bridge by himself for the full four hours. I was more concerned in case the sailor should fall asleep or get into difficulties whilst he was on his own. Fortunately the Japanese seaman was very reliable. On several occasions he woke me up when he could not get sense out of the Master. In due course the ship laid up owing to a shortage of cargoes and everybody was paid off including myself.

During the depression of the 1930s many ships were laid up through shortage of cargoes, with the consequent paying off of their crews. I was often paid off for this reason, but by hard work and looking for work it was possible to scrape a modest living even though there were many hundreds of seamen unemployed. I had served for over two happy years as Mate of the s/s MATJE a 300 ton steam coaster built by William Thomas of Amlwch, North Wales as the PRINCE JA JA, although William Thomas was better known for the many schooners he built.

After spending 5 days on the dole I was offered and accepted a temporary job to relieve the mate of the s/s WYTHBURN who together with her Master, Captain W. Evans of Moelfre, had to attend an enquiry concerning some stem damage (photograph, 36) the ship had sustained when she had been run down whilst at anchor. Gathering a few clothes together in my sea bag I proceeded by train to Barry Dock in South Wales where I found the WYTHBURN berthed under the coal tip waiting to load coal. The relief Master, Captain W. Donnan of Portavogie was on board with Captain Evans, both of whom I knew. I reported myself and having deposited my bag into my cabin, quickly changed into my working attire and started work.

The WYTHBURN (Plate 2), was a long raised quarter deck type of steam coaster, built by Williamson of Workington and carried about 500 tons of cargo.

Clove hitch (ratlines)

36. The WYTHBURN (note the stem damage). Standing at the bow is Will Lewis of Moelfre, Mate and brother-in-law of the Master, Captain William Evans of Moelfre who is at the wheel on the bridge with the pilot to his left. The second man on the forecastle is standing below the tackle and messenger chain which drove the anchor windlass from the forward steam winch.

She had two hatches with a derrick and steam winch at each hatch. The anchor windlass on the forecastle head was driven by a chain messenger from the forward winch. She had an open bridge surrounded by a canvas dodger. Below the bridge was the wheelhouse which housed the steam steering engine, and below the wheelhouse was the Master and Mate's accommodation. On the open bridge stood the wheel and pedestal which was connected to the steam steering gear by a rod extension, the magnetic compass housed in a teak binnacle with a brass top and the engine room telegraph. The steam steering was only used for manoeuvring in port and narrow channels, elsewhere the hand steering gear was used to save on bunkers and fresh water for the boiler, when it was carried. She had a steam capstan aft, which was a very useful piece of equipment when she was loading coal, which saved a lot of pulling and hauling when the ship was moved during loading. She was a single bottomed ship and at that time very slow, rarely making more than 6 knots when loaded and unless the weather was favourable or fine, it was futile to try and make a passage with her in ballast. Nevertheless she would go ahead, if slowly, in bad weather when loaded. Because she was too slow to hurt herself and more or less hove herself to in bad weather, she was considered a good sea boat.

She carried a crew of nine which consisted of Master, Mate, one A.B., two Ordinary Seamen, two Firemen and two Engineers. The usual catering conditions prevailed, each crew member providing and cooking his own provisions in the one community frying pan and kettle provided in accordance with the recommendations of the National Maritime Board. Washing and bathing facilities consisted of the usual buckets, lighting by paraffin lamps and heating by slow combustion bogey stoves. The sailors and firemen lived in a forecastle forward, which was furnished with the usual two tiered wooden bunks, deal table and wooden forms, whilst the Captain and Mate lived in accommodation under the wheelhouse consisting of a cabin each separated by a small saloon, which was entered from the after deck. The two engineers lived in separate cabins which opened off the after end of the engine room. There was an athwartship galley in the engine room casing abaft the funnel, this had three boiling rings and one oven where the entire crew did their individual cooking. Wages were paid weekly, and on pay-day or the following day there was occasionally a demand on the stove for an exotic fry-up but more often than not, the only evidence of cooking was a pan of stew (scouse or lobscouse), or if we had a few Welshmen on board a pan of 'stwnch' this being potatoes boiled together with a vegetable (swede, turnip, carrots, peas or broad beans), generally swede turnip, the whole when cooked mashed and a lump of butter added with pepper to make a very tasty, cheap and filling dish. These dishes were often evident on the day preceding pay day when cash was short.

Although the WYTHBURN was no 'oil painting', she was a homely ship and had a happy crew. We loaded a cargo of coal for Westport on the West coast of Ireland and although it was the first week in January the weather was quiet and settled. We sailed from Barry Dock and after clearing the Breaksea Light vessel and Nash Point, set course for the Fastnet Rock Lighthouse a distance of about 270 miles, which I thought was imprudent at that time of year in a low powered ship. However the weather kept fine and we eventually reached the Fastnet and passed between the Rock and Cape Clear after which it was inside everything; the Lemon Rock, Calf Sound, the Bull, Cow and Calf Rocks, the Skelligs, through Blasket Sound, then across the mouth of the River Shannon and Galway Bay to Slyne Head and on round Clare Island into Clew Bay at the head of which lies Westport in County Mayo.

It was a very interesting voyage with the weather keeping fine. I am afraid it would have been a different story if the weather had broken. Westport was then a small port at the entrance of which are many small islands, it was well sheltered and dried out at low water when ships lay aground at the quay. It was typically Irish with very friendly people, many of whom went to sea or had relatives at sea, the remainder being mostly farmers or fishermen. I had been there before several times and had on one occasion been to the top of Croagh Patrick, a mountain nearby, from where Saint Patrick was reputed to have banished the snakes from Ireland, and a place of pilgrimage.

There was a couple of coasters there including the BRIARTHORN (Captain Ebenezer Griffiths) owned by W. J. Ireland of Liverpool, who ran a fairly regular trade there with grain and coal. The Limerick Steamship Co. also maintained a fairly regular service from the Mersey, often taking back cattle to the lairage at Birkenhead. We were a couple of days discharging our cargo using our own winches and derricks, the crew driving winches. After completing discharging, we cleaned out the holds and loaded a cargo of potatoes in sacks for Liverpool. During the time that we were there we bought a 'leg of lamb' from a butcher who was hawking it from a pony and cart. It was very cheap even at that time, but unfortunately when it was cooked, it was as tough as an old boot. The Captain swore that it was the leg of a goat that had been running wild around Croagh Patrick probably in Saint Patrick's time!

After loading the potatoes, the tide being suitable, we sailed at daylight for Liverpool in the continuing fine weather. When we were clear of the quay and I was on the forecastle head lashing the ropes and preparing to secure the anchors, the engine stopped and the ship took a sheer outside the channel. I was ordered to let go the port anchor and hold on to the chain. This I did but the ship still had way on her and took the ground outside the channel. There was a great deal of activity between the bridge and wheelhouse and the bridge and engine room. It appeared that the steering engine had jammed and seized up. The captain dashed down from the bridge to convert to hand steering and in doing so had got the gears jammed, and so the steering gear was out of commission. What had actually happened was, the steam steering normally exhausted to the atmosphere when the ship was manoeuvring and the engineer thinking that there would be no more manoeuvres had switched the steering engine exhaust to go through the condenser to save his boiler water and had not informed the bridge. The condenser could not cope with the extra load from the steering gear exhaust and a pressure built up. The Captain thinking that the steering gear was fouled or jammed stopped the main engine thus aggravating the position. It was clearly the fault of the engineer who eventually admitted it. By the time the steering problem was sorted out, the ship was firmly aground and as the tides were falling, the prospect looked rather glum, especially as it was high water when we ran aground and the following tide was predicted much lower.

We had grounded on stony but fairly level ground and were able to walk all round her at low water when we carried our spare stream anchor to the channel and connected all our wire hawsers to it. The following tide, when the ship started to rock in her berth, we hove on our anchors, but the ship did not float and we hove both anchors home without moving the ship. That tide the BRIARTHORN sailed and offered to pull us off the bank. His offer was declined with thanks. The following low water we again ran out the anchors, but this time we doubled them up and waited until the ship was almost afloat before heaving on them, after which the ship came off the ground without any difficulty and we quickly resumed our voyage. We then made good time to the Mersey, making full use of all the short cuts. When we arrived at Liverpool, the Captain was waiting to rejoin her, and after discharging, there being no further cargo for her, we moved her to a laying up berth where everybody with the exception of the Master was paid off.

I was very fortunate on this occasion, for the following day I secured a berth in one of J. & P. Hutchison's ships, the ARDENZA of Glasgow, a collier type of ship of about 900 tons, but on foreign articles and on a regular general cargo trade to Bay of Biscay ports and had a very good name for maintaining a regular schedule. Her Master was seventeen years in her and had only gone to shelter once during that period and that was only for four hours to replace his hatch tarpaulins which had been washed off during a gale. I had sailed with him before and I was one of the few who could get along with him. It was a change from wondering if and when you were going to be paid off and revert to the dole.

The WYTHBURN was blown up by a mine whilst heaving up her anchor in Barry Roads preparatory to entering Barry during the 1939/45 war. All the crew lost their lives with the exception of the Mate, Mr. Barney Richardson. Many of my friends were amongst those who lost their lives.

Breaksea
Light Vessel.

THE
BRITISH ISLANDS

COMPILED FROM A CHART OF 1913.
MAGNETIC VARIATION FOR 1926.

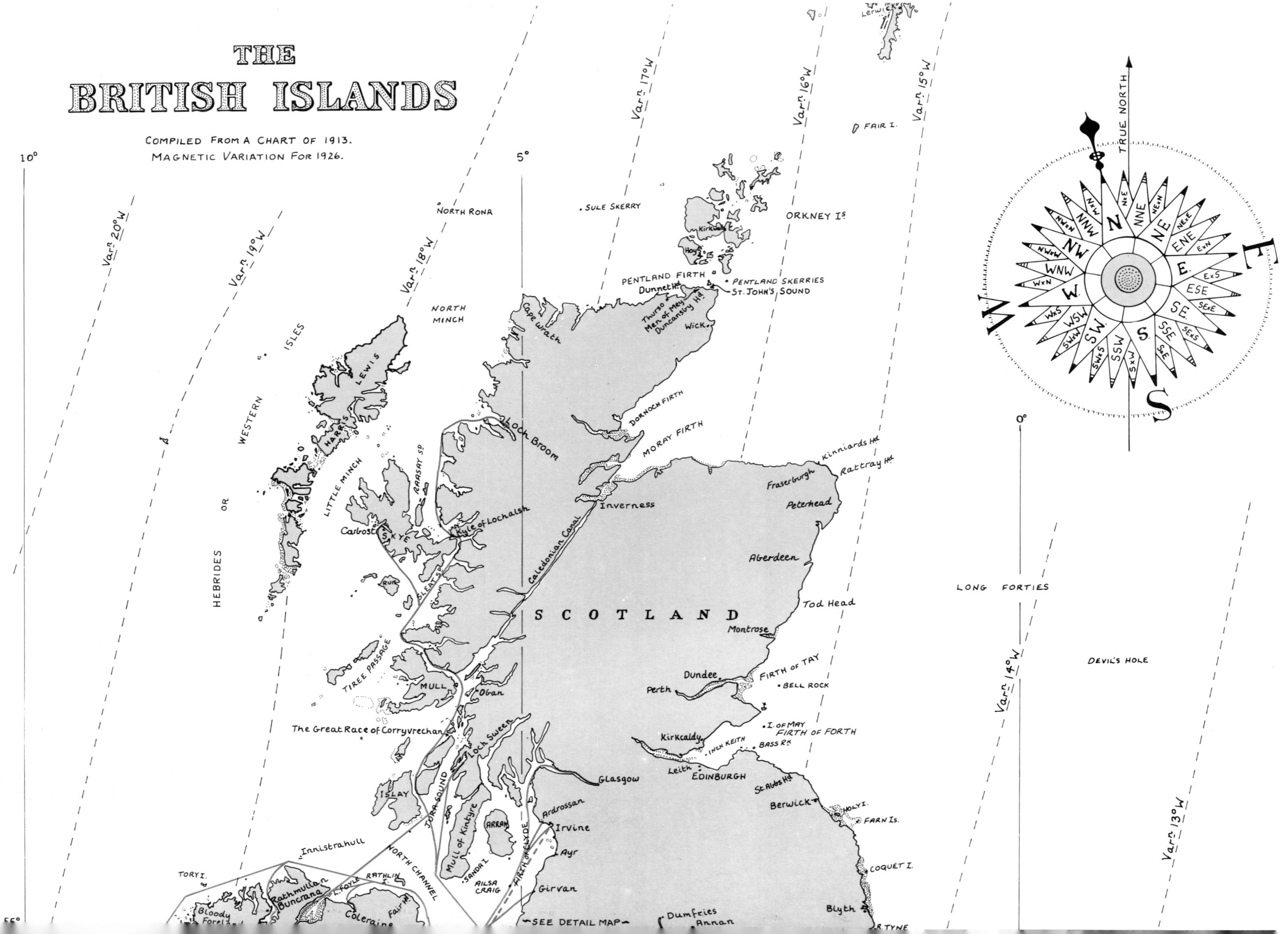

TRUE NORTH

E

ESE
E×S
SE×E
SE
SE×S
SSE
S×E
S

E
E×N
ENE
NE×E
NE
NE×N
NNE
N×E
N
N×W
NNW
NW×N
NW
NW×W
WNW
W×N
W

W×S
WSW
SW×W
SW
SW×S
SSW
S×W
S

DEVIL'S HOLE

Var.ⁿ 13°W

LONG FORTIES

0°

Var.ⁿ 14°W

Var.ⁿ 15°W

Var.ⁿ 16°W

Var.ⁿ 17°W

Var.ⁿ 18°W

Var.ⁿ 18°W

Var.ⁿ 19°W

Var.ⁿ 20°W

Lewis

FAIR I.

ORKNEY Iˢ

Kirkwall
Hoy Iˢ
PENTLAND SKERRIES
PENTLAND FIRTH • ST. JOHN'S SOUND

SULE SKERRY

NORTH RONA

NORTH
MINCH

LEWIS

HARRIS

WESTERN
OR
HEBRIDES

ISLES

LITTLE MINCH

Cape Wrath

Dunnet Hd
Thurso
Mel or Duncansby Hd
Wick

DORNOCH FIRTH

MORAY FIRTH

Inverness

Loch Broom

Loch of Lochalsh

RAASAY Iˢ
Kyle of
SKYE
SLEAT Sᵈ

MUCK
EIGG

TIREE PASSAGE

SCOTLAND

Kinnairds Hd
Fraserburgh
Rattray Hd
Peterhead

Aberdeen

Tod Head

Montrose

Dundee
FIRTH OF TAY
BELL ROCK

Perth
I. OF MAY
FIRTH OF FORTH
INCH KEITH
Kirkcaldy
BASS Rk
Leith EDINBURGH
St. Abbs Hd
Glasgow
Berwick I.
COQUET I.
MAY I. FARN Iˢ

Dumfries
Annan

Caledonian Canal

Oban

MULL

The Great Race of Corryvrechan

ISLAY

Ardrossen
Irvine
Ayr
FIRTH OF CLYDE
Girvan
SEE DETAIL MAP
ARRAN
Holy I. SANDA I.
AILSA CRAIG
Loch Sween
Mull of Kintyre
JURA SOUND

Inistrahull
NORTH CHANNEL
RATHLIN
Coleraine

TORY I.

Bloody Foreland

5°

10°

0°

Var.ⁿ 16°W

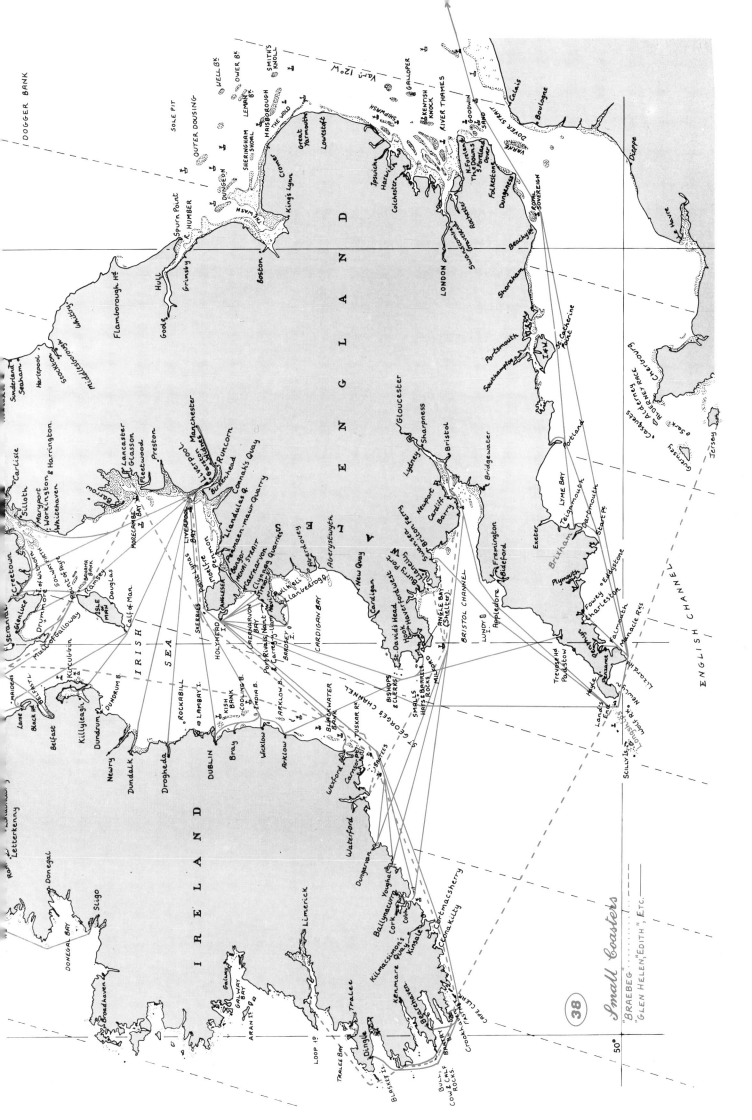

Small Coasters

"BRAEBEG" ———
"GLEN HELEN", "EDITH", ETC. ————

38

7. Outside the Limits in "Kyle Firth."

Owen G. Spargo

By 1930 I had served in many foreign going ships and seen a great deal of the world. I had just completed a deep sea voyage when I heard that the s/s KYLE FIRTH which had been bought by Monroe Brothers of Liverpool from T. G. Gillie & Co. of Glasgow, was going on a voyage 'outside the limits' which meant that she was going to a destination beyond the Home Trade limits, which were the River Elbe and Brest, and by so doing would have to comply with the B.O.T. manning scale and increase her complement and fulfil various other conditions. She now required amongst others a Second Mate which I applied for and got the job.

We took a cargo of coal from Swansea to Quimper, a very small port just South of Brest, from Quimper we went in ballast to Antwerp where we loaded a cargo of chemical fertiliser in bulk for Kirkcudbright and Palnackie, small ports in the Solway Firth. The KYLE FIRTH was a long raised quarter deck type of steam coaster and carried about 500 tons, although she was on Foreign Articles for that voyage, she had not deviated very far from coasting conditions. We still had to provide our own food, bedding and eating and cooking utensils, with the exception of the customary communal kettle and frying pan. As we did not carry a Cook, everybody including the officers had to cook for themselves.

The Master was an inoffensive elderly man, unfortunately more than a little addicted to the bottle. The Mate, also getting on in years, had served in deep water sailing ships and large liners. He was a real old 'shell back' and a very good seaman. He tried to run the ship on big ship lines, which never worked in coasting ships (he was to serve under me in several ships in later years). I got along with him very well but he also was fond of his drink. After leaving Swansea we had a very fine passage down the Bristol Channel and around the Longships lighthouse at Lands End, until we had almost reached Ushant, when we ran into very dense fog. Ushant is a place very much to be avoided in dense fog, on account of the strong currents and tides, also the convergence of ships at this turning point. Nowadays with radar it is not quite so fearsome, but despite the advantage of radar, collisions do still occur.

When I came on watch at 4 o'clock in the morning, I found the ship stopped in very dense fog, with a calm smooth sea, and everywhere deathly silence that you could almost feel. The fog remained until noon when it cleared suddenly and we found ourselves surrounded by rocks, the nearest of which would be about a couple of hundred feet away. We had no idea where we were, but the Captain managed to "con" her out clear of the rocks, and eventually we were able to verify our position and proceed to Quimper, where on arrival, we were informed that we were too deep draughted to get alongside the berth. We spent a couple of days transferring cargo from aft to forward to lighten the draught, and by other methods, such as filling the fore peak tank, transferring the anchor cable from the chain locker to forward of the windlass, topping the derricks vertical and using all the methods we could think of, we were able to put the ship on an even keel and get within working distance of the quay, where after a few tons had been discharged, we were able to get into berth. Quimper at that time was a small town with very friendly people, and almost as much Breton was spoken as French and several of the older people told me they were Bretons not French. We enjoyed a couple of days there discharging, after which we went in ballast to Antwerp.

Double bend.

We had an uneventful and fine passage to Antwerp, during which the crew had to wash out the hold after the Swansea coal, ready to load the chemical fertiliser. Shortly after we arrived in berth at Antwerp the Captain went ashore 'to the Brokers', and that was the last we saw of him until he arrived with the Pilot when we were ready to sail. Most of the crew wanted provisions and went ashore to get them, leaving one or two to assist in the loading. When after a couple of hours the crew had not returned, the Mate went ashore to 'look for the crew'. By the time he returned with his merry men, all the worse for drink, the ship had completed loading and I had battened down the main hatch and was in the process of battening down the fore hatch. The Mate immediately objected to my battening down 'his hatch' so I left him to get on with it. About half and hour later a taxi drew up alongside the ship, with the Captain, the Agent and the Pilot. The Captain was just about capable of making his way to the bridge. We cast off and proceeded on our way to Kirkcudbright. The weather was rapidly deteriorating, and by the time we were in the North Sea we were bucking into a South Westerly gale.

I relieved the Mate at 4 am. and found him suffering from a bad head from the previous day. He gave me the course and disappeared with a grunt and I took over the watch. We were now passing through the Straits of Dover, the wind had drawn more to the Westward and there was quite a nasty sea running. The ship was putting the occasional sea on board. By the time dawn approached I saw that the tarpaulins were coming off the fore hatch. I sent the A.B., who was on watch with me, to call the Captain to come and take the bridge whilst we secured the hatch and slowed the ship down. The Captain came up immediately, arousing the Mate as he passed his room. The Captain took the wheel from me whilst I went on deck with the A.B. to secure the hatch. The Mate meantime had got up and was standing on the lower bridge in his underpants (long johns) issuing orders. I told him to come down and finish his work. He was affronted, but fair play to him, out of bravado he joined us and pulled his weight with plenty of blasphemy.

Whilst we were securing the hatch, the ship took two or three seas on board and we were working up to our waists in sea water for about an hour until we had finished, by which time the Mate had well sobered up and disappeared to his cabin to finish his watch below. I relieved the Captain who went to his cabin and returned with an enamel mug half full of rum which he handed to me without a word. I shared it with the A.B., drank my share and returned the mug with thanks. I think he must have finished the remainder of that bottle himself. I did not see him again until we arrived in Portland in the early hours of the following day, where we went alongside the bunkering hulk, which was anchored in the harbour and took on board about 30 tons of coal bunkers. From Portland to Kirkcudbright we had an uneventful passage, but during our stay at Kirkcudbright the crew went on the beer again. We discharged our quota of the Kirkcudbright cargo and with the help of a couple of the crew who were half sober, I covered the hatches and made the ship ready for her passage to Palnackie.

Palnackie was a small port on a river to the eastward of Kirkcudbright. It is entered on the East side of Hestan Island and has the village of Kippford on the East bank, a little way inside the entrance. Thence the narrow and winding channel, including an almost horseshoe bend, at the head of which was a rock locally known as the Porter stone, was navigable as far as Dalbeattie. Palnackie itself was situated on the left bank a few miles below Dalbeattie. It was difficult of access as to the depth of water, the winding channel, and also the entrance was exposed to the South Westerly winds. It was what we referred to as a 'Spring Tide Port'. Despite this there was a thriving trade there in grain, animal feeding stuffs, coal and general cargo from the Mersey and fertilisers from the Continent. There were several small ships owned and trading there locally, one of which was the SOLWAY LASS, a very smart looking motor ketch. Cargoes were also available at Creetown granite quarry in Wigtown Bay which was not far away. It was not uncommon to see two and sometimes three ships discharging at Palnackie with another couple discharging at Dalbeattie. Discharging was carried out from dawn until dusk, using the ship's winches and derricks, the crew driving the winches. This entailing a twelve hour stand driving a winch, together with an extra hour opening and closing the hatch before and after loading, was a customary day's work for an A.B. in this trade with no overtime paid.

It was to this small port that the KYLE FIRTH was to take the remainder of her cargo. We sailed from Kirkcudbright at about eleven o'clock on a very dark but calm and clear night, which was not customary because Kirkcudbright was really a daylight port. The channel was unlit but as the Spring tides were almost over, and there was a danger of the ship being neaped at Palnackie, I suppose this was an incentive to take a chance. The crew by this time had plenty of opportunity to get well and truly 'lubricated'. The Mate and crew duly arrived on board followed by the Captain and Pilot supporting each other The Captain promptly went below to his cabin, leaving it to the Pilot to take

A well tarred barrel...

the ship away. The Mate went on the bridge with the Pilot as soon as we left the quay, and the crew disappeared to 'sleep it off'. After we had been steaming for about an hour, the Mate called to me to 'stand by to anchor'. The crew by now were well in the 'land of Nod', so I went to the windlass on the forecastle head and had hardly reached there when I was ordered to let go the anchor. This I did, and by the amount of cable that ran out, I knew that we were in shallow water. I called to the Mate and said "We are in shallow water, do you want a sounding?" I was told to mind my own b----y business and slack away the cable. "In that case," I said, "you had better go astern as the cable is up and down." He must have put the engine full speed astern because the cable just rattled out. After I had rung the bell five times indicating that five shackles (75 fathoms) had passed out, he told me to hold on. After applying the brake to the accompaniment of a shower of sparks, I was able to secure it with the cable stretched in a long line ahead. The Mate then told me "you don't need anchor watches or an anchor light here, nothing will come near us and she won't drag"; how true that was.

I got up at 6 o'clock the following morning, and I could not see the sea! We were high and dry on a sand bank, obviously we had not gone far enough out before anchoring. I managed to get the news through to the Captain and Mate and there was "panic stations"! However there was nothing we could do but wait. Eventually at about two hours before high water we were afloat, and then it was up anchor as quick as possible and all speed for Palnackie. We arrived at Kippford where we boarded the Pilot at High water, which was really too late to proceed up river, but because the tides were falling, and the following day's tide would not be high enough for us to berth at Palnackie, the Pilot was persuaded against his better judgement to take a chance, and we entered the river. When negotiating the bend in the river, the ship grounded and a wire rope was run to one of the channel buoys (a very well tarred barrel) to heave her off. The buoy's mooring chain broke and we hove the buoy up to our after fairlead where it hung, and we carried it with us to Palnackie. After we had overcome that obstacle, we managed to get moving again, but we struck the Porter stone when negotiating that part of the bend and lost one of the blades of our propellor. We eventually arrived at Palnackie but about two ships' lengths from the berth, she took the ground in the middle of the river and remained fast. Efforts made on the night's tide to move her were unsuccessful, and with the tide falling and the following day's tide smaller still, she was 'neaped' and would have to remain where she was for about a fortnight.

A few days later I was instructed to join the smaller coaster FERRUM, which belonged to the same company, as Mate. I left the KYLE FIRTH reposing comfortably in mid-stream, well aground with a wire rope to the bank at each end, and the black barrel still hanging from her stern, and the swans swimming peacefully around her.

This KYLE FIRTH was lost several years later on 13th May, 1940 when she sank off the Skerries near Holyhead, after her cargo of granite shifted whilst on passage from Carreg-y-llam to the Mersey. There was no loss of life.

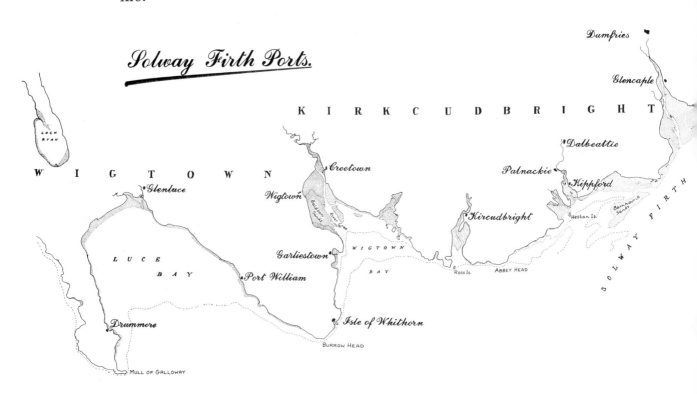

Solway Firth Ports.

8.

43. The single hatch coaster FERRUM.

"Ferrum".

Owen G. Spargo

My instructions were to join the FERRUM at Otterspool, which was at that time a stretch of foreshore between Garston and Dingle on the River Mersey, now a beautiful landscaped park. Being a native of that part of the world, I had no difficulty in finding the FERRUM, which was laying afloat with her head down river and moored amidships against a single vertical pile which had been driven into the beach, with an anchor out ahead and a wire out to a ground mooring astern. Work was in progress building a wall on the foreshore parallel with the river. A large concrete mixing plant had been erected on the beach, also a "Scotch" steam derrick and grab which was used for discharging the ships and general work in the construction.

The FERRUM was loaded with a cargo of granite chippings which she had brought from Porth y Nant, a quarry between Nevin and Trevor, in Caernarvon Bay. She had apparently not commenced discharging and was about 40 or 50 feet out in the river without means of access. As I stood on the foreshore, the derrick driver appeared and told me to put my sea bag into his grab and get in with it. He then swung me out with the derrick and landed me on the FERRUM's deck. The cargo surveyor and dischargers came on board later by the same means.

I reported to Captain W. Hughes, her Master, whom I found at his breakfast in the very clean little saloon, the woodwork of which was gleaming, and with a white tablecloth spread on the table, an uncommon sight on small steam coasters. He gave me a cup of tea and after we had talked awhile I remarked "I suppose I had better get my uniform on". He looked at me, and no doubt knowing that I had just come from deep sea ships thought perhaps that I meant it. However, when I emerged clad in well worn dungaree trousers and a jersey, well, we understood each other immediately! He told me that the cargo surveyor was coming on board shortly to 'measure' the cargo and would want me to assist him. He said "Let him assess the quantity, and as long as it exceeds 250 tons accept his figure, but if it is less, dispute it." The surveyor duly arrived and I assisted him by holding the end of the tape whilst he stretched it over the heap of granite chippings. After he had taken a few measurements and written a few figures, he informed me that we had 306 tons on board, so who was I to dispute it? I replied "Is that so". The ship could only carry about 240 tons, so who was fiddling who I do not know, but when I told the Captain, he replied "Champion, that is about what he generally gives us". Whether anybody got anything out of it I do not know, I certainly did not, neither do I think did the Captain.

After discharging the stone, we went to one of the Liverpool docks, where we loaded a cargo of maize in bulk, overside from one of the big ships for Garlieston, a small port in Wigtown Bay in the Solway Firth. We also took on board several wooden barrels of treacle (molasses) as deck cargo, the treacle being for use in the process of making cattle-feed. When we had completed loading, I battened down the hatch and was about to put lashings around the barrels on the deck. The Captain told me not to bother and to bring along a sledge hammer which was kept forward. I brought the hammer and handed it to him. He placed it on the lower bridge, and said, "This is kept here with these cargoes, this is your 'barrel lashing'. If any of those barrels break adrift and start rolling around the deck, just knock their heads in with this." They were put on board at shipper's risk and he was not going to have them floating around doing damage to his tarpaulins, or have one of us hurt trying

Half hitch.

to save them. He also told me that the molasses had the same effect on the sea as oil and as he described it "gave good smoothings". Fortunately, we did not have to resort to the hammer, but I did not disbelieve him.

The FERRUM was a good example of a 'big' little ship (45). Apparently when she was built, attempts had been made to reduce her registered tonnage (to reduce dock dues, light dues, harbour charges and other expenses) by giving her an extra large engine room and various other dodges, this would give one the impression that she carried more than she actually did. She was a very nice model, and a very good sea boat loaded, but being single bottomed she was the same as any other single bottomed coaster when in ballast, all right when the weather was good. We traded mostly to small shallow-water ports which were only accessible on Spring tides, such as Dalbeattie, Palnackie, Glencaple, Drummore, all in the Solway Firth and Rathmullan, Ramelton, Letterkenny, and Buncrana in Lough Swilly. We also traded a great deal to the Welsh quarries in Caernarvon Bay and Cardigan Bay, also to the small ports in the South West of Ireland.

I got along very well with her Master, Captain W. Hughes who came from Cemaes on the North coast of Anglesey (inside the Skerries rocks). When we were on passage and passing Cemaes he would go very close inshore and there would be lots of whistle blowing and waving to his wife and relatives and friends ashore. Occasionally he would anchor in Cemaes Bay for an hour or two and visit his home. He invariably used the passage inside the Skerries unless of course it was a lee shore or in very dense fog (and it had to be very dense) but, daylight or dark, it was always inside the Skerries and when coming from the Caernarvon Bay quarries we could often make a much quicker passage by doing so. Plenty of coasting men would go inside the Skerries during daylight, but very few would do so in the dark. Captain Hughes would tackle it at any time, and as we got to know each other better, he would hand the bridge over to me regardless of where we were, so I became very well acquainted with that dangerous part of the coast line. Occasionally Captain Hughes would bring his wife and family for a trip, then FERRUM was very much a family ship, and we enjoyed Mrs. Hughes home cooking.

The accommodation was generally good for a small ship of that period, the ratings, consisting of one A.B., one Ordinary Seaman and one Fireman slept in a forecastle below decks forward where they also ate their meals. It was fitted with the usual bare wood furniture of two-tiered bunks, forms and table, coal burning bogey stove and paraffin oil lamp illumination, and two small portholes at either side (which could not be opened when the ship was loaded). Washing and bathing facilities were by the customary galvanised bucket method. Above the crew's accommodation at either side on the main deck was a W.C. with the usual draw bucket flushing system, and opposite it a similar small room which was used to store the paraffin navigation lamps when they were not in use.

Under the open bridge was a chart room with a chart table with drawers underneath on the foreside and a single bunk on the port side where the Captain would sleep when he had his family on board. At the back of the chartroom, a stairway led down to a small saloon with a room on the port side for the Mate and another room on the starboard side for the Master, which he used when he was on his own. There was also a W.C. at the foot of the stairs, these two rooms were fitted with folding wash basins which had receptacles under them to catch the used water and had to be emptied after use, unless these receptacles were emptied out often and scalded, they could very soon create a horrible smell. The saloon was done out in pitch pine which had been scraped and varnished and was very attractive. It held a cushioned settee between two sideboard cupboards on the forward side, a table in the centre with a chair at either end. The floors were covered with linoleum. In the recess underneath the stairs at the after end was a small coal stove with two boiling rings and an oven which was well "black leaded" and polished until you could almost see your face in it. Over the table was suspended a hanging paraffin lamp with a white shade. All the accommodation had portholes, but these could only be opened in very fine weather. Lighting throughout the ship was by paraffin lamps. The two engineers lived in separate rooms at the after end of the engine room at deck level. Their rooms were small but very cosy and they were both very content in them. The FERRUM's stokehold and engine room were separate so she carried a fireman in addition to her engineers. They kept her engine room immaculate with all the brass and copper gleaming. She carried a crew of seven, quite a large crew for a ship of that tonnage at that time. Trading mostly to small shallow water ports which were only accessible during the daylight hours, where owing to lack of illumination it was not possible to work cargo during the night also with only one derrick for discharging, she was as far as the crew were concerned a 'comfortable little job'. The customary 'feed yourself, provide your own bed and bedding, cooking utensils, etc.' still prevailed. She was a happy little ship and on account of her light draught and handiness for shallow water ports, was kept

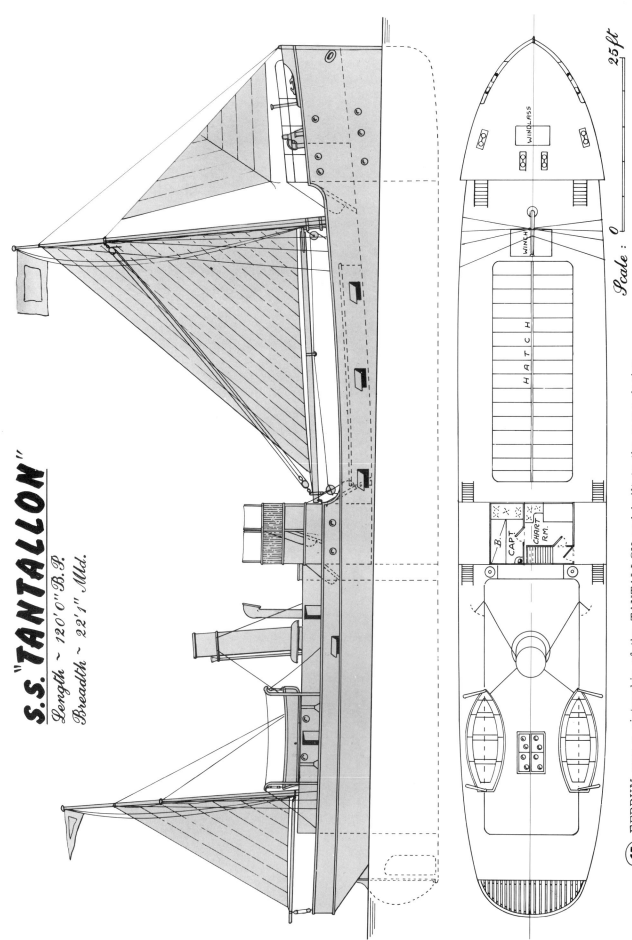

S.S. "TANTALLON"

Length ~ 120'0" B.P.
Breadth ~ 22'1" Mld.

WINDLASS

WINCH

HATCH

B.

CAPT

CHART
RM.

Scale : 0 _____ 25 ft

45 FERRUM was a sistership of the TANTALLON and built to the same design.

more or less in constant if not (by owner's standards) profitable employment.

After a while Captain W. Hughes was promoted to a larger ship in the Company. A North of Ireland man relieved him. He was a friendly man, but very nervous and excitable. Shortly after he joined, he called me one day to come on watch and told me "the dinner is on the table". I looked at the table, and there reposing in the middle of it, on top of the white tablecloth, were two cast iron saucepans, one containing potatoes which had been boiled in their jackets (with their peel left on) and the other a piece of bacon which had been boiled together with cabbage. It was a very tasty and filling meal which could have been presented in a bit more appetising way. Still it kept body and soul together and many would have been glad of it then. So started the trend down to reality and the comforts of the Captain Hughes' era soon disappeared. While we had this Irish Captain in command, we went to one of the Caernarvon Bay quarries to load a cargo of granite chippings for the Mersey. That he was not very well acquainted with the Quarries was apparent, and he was timid in approaching them, so was late getting alongside the jetty and consequently we were late on tide leaving and so lost the benefit of the strong tides around the South Stack and Skerries.

Under these circumstances it was the practice of Captain Hughes to keep well inshore, and very close around the South and North Stacks and into Holyhead Bay and the bays inside the Skerries to avoid the strong tides. I went on watch about half an hour after leaving the jetty, it was then dusk, clear and fine weather. The Captain immediately retired to his bed, leaving no instructions of any kind, so I carried on the same as I had been doing with Captain Hughes. By the time that I was due to be relieved at midnight, we were halfway through the Skerries Sound and just passing a reef called 'Harry Furlong' which was marked with a black beacon with a white band. The white band was quite distinguishable in the reflection of the Skerries lighthouse light and although it was very dark, it was very clear. I had taken the ship through this sound in the dark many times under much worse conditions. At midnight the Captain arrived on the bridge in his long underpants and nearly exploded when he saw the Skerries light on our port side, he said "My God, you have lost my ship" and started to give all kinds of orders, which if I had carried them out certainly would have lost his ship. After he had calmed down I told him that I was accustomed to being where I was and that his ship was quite safe, to which he replied, "Well, you have got her in here, you can bloody well get her out" and left the bridge. I carried on and passed between the Middle Mouse Island and the land as was customary. Had Captain Hughes been there, I would then have carried on close to the land passing North of the East Mouse Island until I reached Point Lynas, but under the circumstances I had no option but to haul away from the land until the light on Point Lynas (which showed that we were clear of the land) became visible and set her on a course for the Liverpool Bar Light vessel. I then went down and told the Captain, "There you are, Lynas is open and she is on a course E$\frac{1}{2}$S for the Bar." He had obviously had a shock, and told me, "As long as you are with me in this ship, never go inside there again even in daylight". I replied "All right, if that is the way you want it".

We made several voyages to the Solway Firth ports with maize and loaded granite chippings from Creetown to the Mersey and Manchester ship canal. Eventually we were ordered to Arklow to load a cargo of gravel aggregate for Birkenhead.

Arklow was then, and probably still is, a port to be treated with caution. Situated on a river which rises in the Wicklow mountains it has at times strong freshets, which wash down the gravel and when the weather is bad outside, cause a bar to form across the entrance. There are two piers forming the entrance. A concrete groin had been built on to the North pier, extending into the channel to break the sea with Easterly winds and the loading jetty was a short distance inside the entrance on the South pier. A small narrow gauge railway ran from the beach to the jetty, on which ran tipping trucks. The trucks were filled by men with shovels from the beach, and then pushed manually to the ship, where they were emptied by tipping into the ship. The bar was very unpredictable and varied very much with the weather. There could be 12 feet on it and in a few days it would dry so much that you could walk across it. A small dredger did its best to keep it clear, but was not very successful.

The range of the tides in that part of the world is also a bit of an enigma, the rise and fall in Arklow harbour is about 10 or 12 feet whilst only a few miles off shore on the Arklow bank, the rise and fall is only 3 feet 6 inches. There was at that time a family of father and several sons called Hall who did the Pilotage and boat work. They were very capable and even the local men would employ them, because they kept a constant watch on the bar and knew exactly what changes were taking place. They were all very efficient at 'handling' a ship. So between the shallow water on the bar and the unpredictable strength and direction of the freshets coming from the river, and the concrete groin on the North pier which the locals nicknamed the 'graveyard', most ships' captains when entering Arklow would take advantage of the pilot's local knowledge and let him get on with his job and not interfere. Not so our hero who had different ideas, he decided that the pilot was going too fast with the ship and stopped the engine. The ship sheered towards the groin, he panicked and put the engines full speed astern which made her sheer worse, the freshet caught her on the port bow and she hit the "Graveyard" stem on. Fortunately, we were light ship, so that the hawse pipes being above the groin were not affected, but from the keel upwards for about six feet the stem and plates were knocked back flat to a depth of about 18 inches. When we had untangled and extricated ourselves, we proceeded to the dock which is on the South side of the harbour a little above the gravel jetty. By pumping out the fore peak tank and filling the after peak tank and putting water in the engine room bilges up to the engine room plates, we were able to tip the ship and lift the damaged part clear of the water.

The Superintendent Engineer, a Scottish gentleman by the name of Campbell and renowned for his prowess with cement boxes, arrived from Liverpool next morning, followed by a donkey and cart loaded with several bags of cement. After unloading the cement we went with the donkey and cart and brought several loads of sand and gravel from the beach. The Superintendent and ship's engineers meantime built wooden "shuttering" in the fore peak tank, in the way of the damage to contain a cement box. When this was completed, it was all hands mix and carry concrete until there was a solid cement box in the fore peak behind the damage. The Captain was then transferred to the ADMIRAL, another company ship, where he gained notoriety over the "Fishy story of a fish's tail".

After 24 hours the cement was pronounced 'set' and a new Master having joined us, we proceeded to the gravel jetty where we loaded our cargo of gravel for Birkenhead. The damaged bow was submerged when we were loaded and not a drop of water got through. After discharging, the fore peak tank was filled for ballasting and no sign of leakage was found, consequently repairs were held 'in abeyance' and she continued trading in that condition for several months, certainly for a long time after I had left her. The damage was not obvious when she was loaded because it was below the water line, but when she was in ballast it made her look 'very sorry for herself.'

The new Master was also from Cemaes, but had a very different temperament from Captain Hughes. Where Captain Hughes was always cheery, this man had a permanent 'chip on his shoulder' and thought the whole world was against him. He was forever chasing the engineers for more speed and more steam, which was not necessary because we had a very conscientious and hard working staff in the engine room. On one occasion we were bound to Ramelton in Lough Swilly. At about midnight, when passing through Innistrahull Sound, in a gale from the Westward with the ship pitching into a very heavy head sea, the Chief Engineer came on to the bridge and told the Captain that the main steam pipe had fractured and advised him to nurse the ship as much as possible and get her into port as soon as he could. When the Engineer left the bridge the Captain told me "go down and see what you think about it, that old bugger wants me to turn back."

I went down and saw that the pipe had fractured at the neck of the flange nearest the boiler. Whilst it was a crack and not a hole, a great deal of steam and water was coming through it. I covered it with sacks and managed to put a bandage of sacks around it which I secured with seizing wire and lashed the pipe with seizing wire which I tightened with a 'Spanish windlass'. Whether this helped or not I do not know, but we got in with it. When I returned to the bridge, the Captain asked my opinion. I told him what I had done, and that I thought it was serious. I was told I was only aiding and abetting the Engineer. We reached Lough Swilly and anchored close to the jetty at Rathmullan where we would board the Pilot at daylight. After we had been anchored for about half an hour, the Chief Engineer came along and informed us that the pipe had now fractured right around and would have to go ashore for repairs. We had been exceptionally lucky, if the pipe had gone whilst we were outside we would not have stood a chance.

We were close enough to Rathmullan pier to pass ropes ashore and were able to warp the ship alongside the jetty and start discharging there and transport the cargo by road to Ramelton, but as this was done by horse and cart, it was a very slow job. The main steam pipe was dismantled and taken ashore for repairs, it could not be repaired locally and had to be taken some distance, possibly to Letterkenny, which all took time. Eventually repairs to the steam pipe were completed, and after discharging our cargo we went up river to Ramelton where we loaded a cargo of potatoes in sacks for Preston. Potatoes were considered a good cargo, because the holds were completely full, and the ship would not be 'down to her marks', also there was no danger of the cargo shifting and she was in good trim.

Admiral.

48. FERRUM was built in 1900 by J. McArthur & Co., of Paisley. Her registered dimensions were 120.0' x 22.1' x 8.8' and she had a gross tonnage of 235. She was one of several almost identical coasters built by McArthur's for various Glasgow owners around the turn of the century. Another of this series of coasters was the TANTALLON, also completed in 1900, Fortunately a plan of this vessel has survived and is reproduced (45). FERRUM had a long life and a number of owners before she joined the Monroe fleet during 1924. This John Clarkson photograph was taken during her time with Monroes. She left their fleet in 1936 when sold to other Liverpool owners and was finally sold for scrap by the Galleon Shipping Co., of Newcastle in 1953 after 53 years coasting around Britain.

So the weather being fairly unsettled we sailed, the wind then being Southerly fresh to strong, as the wind was 'over the land' (coming from the direction of the land). We were making a good passage in sheltered waters and safely negotiated Innistrahull Sound. By the time we were abeam of Inishowen Head at the entrance to Lough Foyle (Londonderry) the wind had gone to the Westward and was blowing a full gale. This was still in our favour being a fair wind and along we went merrily, with an ever increasing sea behind us, and headed for Rathlin Sound. Before we reached Rathlin Sound it was taking two of us at the wheel to steer her and she was normally a very easily steered ship. When passing through Rathlin Sound where even in fine weather there are always eddies and overfalls due to the very strong tides, the sea was just a mad boiling mass. Fortunately, the tide and wind was in our favour. Had the tide been against us I shudder to think what would have happened. After passing through Rathlin Sound we rounded Tor Point closely. Here we altered course more to the Southward, thus bringing the wind off the land again and we were once more in sheltered waters, although we were having some difficulty in keeping the ship up to the wind, but by keeping very close to the land which is 'steep to' in that part of the world and keeping inside the Maidens Rock and Hunter Rock off Larne, we made good time. Before we had reached the Copelands (Mew Island) at the entrance to Belfast Lough, the wind had shifted to the North West and increased. We now had to alter course to the South East to clear the Mull of Galloway in Scotland and around the Point of Ayre at the North end of the Isle of Man.

There is a very bad tidal race off the Mull of Galloway. Fortunately, we were able to avoid that and headed for the Point of Ayre though it was now taking two of us to steer her again, but she was flying along. At the East side of the Point of Ayre is a gravel bank with at that time about 12 feet of water on it which had broken water on it in bad weather. It was marked by a lighted buoy called the Whitestone Bank and the channel lies between the bank and the Point of Ayre and is less than a mile wide with very strong tides. When going around the Point of Ayre we had to alter course to South which brought the wind and sea about four points abaft the beam. Though we still had the wind and sea in our favour, there was really too much sea for us but we still had to carry on as we would not have been able to turn around. When going around the Point of Ayre she took some exceptionally heavy rolls and the sea just broke solid across her. I was thankful that she was loaded with potatoes and not grain or any cargo that could shift. Before we reached Ramsey we had the shelter of the Manx land and we hauled into Ramsey Bay where we found close on a hundred ships to an anchor sheltering from the storm, which was not an uncommon sight at that time, for we did not even have broadcast receivers then, the Masters relying on their weather lore and the barometer as weather criterion. Storm signals were hoisted at various lighthouses, headlands, coastguards stations, etc. They were a cone, point uppermost hoisted on a flagpole by day and a triangle of three green lights apex uppermost by night, when a gale was expected from the Northern half of the compass and similar shapes and lights with the point or apex at the bottom when the gale was expected from the Southern half. The coaster men were inclined to accept these with reserve, because very often the gale passed miles away and they were still kept flying. Their idea was that if you ran for shelter every time you saw a gale warning, you would never make a passage, so by and large not a great deal of notice was taken of them.

It was not an uncommon sight to see a large collection of ships sheltering in Ramsey Bay, ships bound for the Solway and Cumberland ports also Millom, Barrow, Fleetwood, Preston and the Mersey and Welsh Quarries when the wind was blowing directly into them. In fact most ports on the West coast were better avoided during Westerly and North Westerly gales, and most of the 'old timers' would keep clear of them until the weather moderated. Many ships have come to grief by trying to negotiate the Mersey bar with the wind from the North West including the Isle of Man passenger ship ELLAN VANNIN about which a song is written, also the s/s BRADDA and in more recent years the Liverpool pilot boat, to mention just a few. In all cases there was a large loss of life. So into Ramsey Bay we went and anchored amongst the other ships that were sheltering. When daylight came, we were able to recognise some of them. There were several of our Companys' ships bound to the North of Ireland ports and the Mersey, several Kelly and Craig ships loaded, bound for Belfast, many steam trawlers and also several tramp steamers of about 10,000 tons.

By now our bunkers were beginning to get low and we were in a position where we might just scrape into Preston with sufficient coal, but would not have enough to return to Ramsey Bay if we could not get into Preston. I had been in a similar position in another ship in the past, in which case we had run into the Mersey which is more accessible than the River Ribble, and bunkered at a bunkering stage near Cammell Laird's shipyard called "Monks Ferry" (now demolished), after which we anchored in the Mersey until the weather was suitable to enter the River Ribble. The Chief Engineer suggested to the Captain that we go into Ramsey, where the harbour dues amounted to less than 10/- (50p) and neither Pilot nor boatman was required and take on a few tons of bunkers. He was only rebuffed and told that he was trying to get him (the Captain) the sack.

After a couple of days the weather moderated a little and four or five of the ships that were bound to leeward, hove up their anchors and resumed their journeys. We did the same, the wind was still North West so that we still had a fair wind. All went well until we were about halfway between the Isle of Man and the Nelson buoy which marks the entrance to the River Ribble, when the wind shifted to the West North West and freshened considerably. This is about the worst wind you can have for the Ribble. Two of the ships turned back for Ramsey and those that had been making for Preston altered course for the Mersey. Our Captain's comment on this was that they were 'scared'. He went below at the end of his watch, instructing me to call him when we were near the Nelson buoy. By the time we reached the Nelson buoy it was about an hour after low water, and blowing a whole gale from the W.N.W. with a nasty sea. I called him when we were about a mile from the Nelson buoy and also told him the state of the weather. He instructed me to "heave her to and ease her down," I turned her around and put her head to sea and slowed the engine down, she then rode the sea comfortably.

Ferrum swept by
breaking seas.

After an hour or so, my watch being over, the Captain relieved me. He asked my opinion of a Pilot getting out to us, when I replied there was little hope, he then told me that he was not acquainted with the Ribble and did not have a large scale chart and had I been there before? When I replied that I had, he then said "Well, you can take her in". I told him that I was sorry but I was not that well enough acquainted, especially in this kind of weather and went below, leaving him to think it over. Before my watch below was over, he came down and called me, saying "it is an hour to high water, and no sign of the Pilot. I am going to run her in. Will you help me?" I replied "I suppose I had better do so, considering you are determined to go on." So we turned the ship around and ran before the sea towards the River Ribble. The River has revetment training walls on each side which are marked by perches, some of which carried lights and a narrow approach channel marked by lighted buoys. In rough seas these buoys often struck the bottom, putting the light apparatus out of action and making them unreliable in bad weather. On the port-hand side of the approach channel is a sand bank called Salters Bank which in those days, dried out at low water. It was marked with a black can buoy with a red flashing light.

Proceeding at a slow speed, we had a heavy breaking, following sea, she was running comfortably, although her fore deck was constantly awash. Occasionally a sea would break right across the hatch and carry on over the forecastle head. I took the wheel along with the Captain, the sailor standing by to help when necessary. There was a good moon which disappeared occasionally behind the scudding clouds, but generally the visibility was good. After we had run for about half an hour we picked up the Salters Bank buoy, the light of which was extinguished, broad on the starboard bow. It should have been on the port bow. We tried to put the helm over, but too late. She struck the Salters Bank with a thud which almost threw me off the wheel. She then shipped a heavy sea right over the stern which swept over the whole length of the ship. She would not now answer the helm but after bouncing on the bank for about half an hour, she slid off it and was afloat again in much quieter and smoother water, only to strike the bottom again, but this time there was a hard grinding sound and there was no mistaking that it was rock that we had hit this time, so we had presumably struck the revetment wall at the side of the channel. We bounced over this into much quieter water, where the Pilot boat came alongside and we took the Pilot on board.

The Pilot boat had been unable to go to sea on account of the weather. We were the first ship to arrive in Preston for several days and the first and only one on that tide. We passed the ships that had lain with us in Ramsey Bay, coming in the following day as we were going out. Ned Olsen, the Preston Pilot who took us in, was very forthright in his opinion of ship masters who brought their ships in under these conditions, and said we had been extremely lucky in getting over the Salters Bank. He also gave some advice, which I pass on and bears to be reflected on. It was as follows 'If ever it should be your misfortune to ground on Salters Bank in bad weather do not try to get out of the ship by launching the lifeboats or raft or any other method, but make yourselves comfortable in your cabins and batten yourselves down and make a cup of tea and wait until the tide goes out and at low water put a ladder over the side and walk ashore.' In view of tragedies in that area in later years, it bears thinking about.

On arrival at Preston we were able to look at our damage on deck, which considering what we had gone through was only trivial. We sounded the hold bilges, and found over a foot of water. The pumps were started and very soon the bilges were dry, the pumps were then stopped and having prepared the hatch for unloading we went to bed. When I got up a couple of hours later to start work, I again sounded the hold bilges, and found eighteen inches, so I went to the Engineer to ask him to pump these bilges out. When he went into the engine room to start the pump, he found the engine room bilges also flooded, so obviously we had bottom damage.

The pumps were able to contain the leaks, and after discharging our cargo and taking on bunkers, we proceeded light ship to Birkenhead, where after putting the ship into dry dock, the crew with the exception of the Captain and the Chief Engineer were paid off. I was transferred to another of the Company's ships, the STAGHOUND, which they had bought from John Hay of Glasgow. She was a very much larger ship, and a very good sea boat. I had sailed with her Master, Captain William Evans of Moelfre in several other ships and we got on well together, so I was very happy there. We made a round trip from Birkenhead to Cork, Cork to London, London to Antwerp, Antwerp to Stranraer, Stranraer to Carreg-y-llam and Carreg-y-llam to Liverpool, where after discharging, there being no cargoes available, the crew were paid off with the exception of the Captain and Chief Engineer who remained on half pay, which incidentally was at that time, less than the full pay of an A.B.

'Rock Dodging' in "Deneside".

Owen G. Spargo

By June 1931 the shipping slump was at its peak and one had to look very hard to obtain work. Many foreign going and coasting ships were laid up in the various back waters, where they would pay very little or only token harbour dues. I had served several short spells in different Monroe ships which would only run for a week or two and then lay up. My last ship had been the STAGHOUND, she laid up, and I had been on the dole for almost four months during which time I had applied everywhere, and had tramped the whole length of Liverpool docks daily looking for work. I was walking past North Canning Dock, Liverpool one day, when a small coaster called the DENESIDE was approaching the quay. As there was nobody on the quay to take his mooring ropes, I stopped and put his ropes on the bollards ashore. When she was tied up the Captain thanked me. We got talking and when I told him that I was looking for work, he said "I can give you an A.B.'s job". I gladly accepted, and went home to gather my effects to join her and start work the following day.

She was a handy little ship of about 300 tons and carried a crew of eight which consisted of Master, Mate, two Able Seamen, Chief and Second Engineers and two Firemen. She was a very good sea boat when loaded, and did about eight knots, but as she was single bottomed and only carried fore peak and after peak tanks for ballast, she was very poor 'light ship' and used to slam very heavily, and would blow right around in a moderate sea, but given the wind anywhere abaft the beam, when light, she would roll very heavily but run like a witch. She had arrived with a cargo of sandstone paving stones which she had brought from Liscannor, a small port on the west coast of Ireland just North of Loop Head at the mouth of the River Shannon. All of these stone slabs were quarried in a similar manner to the slates of North Wales. Similar stones were quarried in the Clyde area and exported to Liverpool and are still very evident on many of the city pavements.

The DENESIDE then belonged to the Mersey Ports Stevedoring Co., whose offices were in Oriel Chambers, Water Street, Liverpool, a popular building for small coasting ship firms, and it held the offices of several. The principal of the Mersey Ports Stevedoring Co., was and ex-sailing ship Master called Captain MacClure who had also been Master in the 'Branch Line' ships of Sunderland, which were noted for their large number of derricks. He ran a thriving stevedoring business in partnership with a man called MacKnight. They also bought and sold coasters as the mood took them, probably for a hobby as much as anything. Captain MacClure was a very fair man, a good employer and a very competent seaman. A typical deep water man, he could not understand his ships taking shelter. If you had been hove-to for a couple of days, he did not seem to mind, but he must have thought we were skulking when we were anchored windbound. He also introduced into the Mersey two wooden steam herring drifters which he converted into derrick barges, and did a roaring trade with them. I was to get to know him well in later years and to take command of one of his ships the PERDITA until he sold her to the Italians. The Captain of the DENESIDE was a Captain W. Smyth, later to be decorated with the M.B.E. He was a North of Ireland man from the Island Magee, Larne and his father was lost at sea, when a coaster he was in foundered. He never either smoked or drank, but was not a bigot either. The Mate was Andrew McNeilly Wright, later Captain A.M. Wright, and affectionately known to his friends as 'Big Andy'. He was a very high principled upright man, and as straight as a die, but more of him later.

The DENESIDE had a fairly regular run from the Mersey to Kilrush, which is a small port on the River Shannon near Scattery Island. We were restricted

Shackles &c.

to the highest tides at Kilrush by the depth of water, so we only took a cargo there once a fortnight. Over the neap tides we would take an occasional Kilrush cargo and discharge it at Cappa Quay or Carrigaholt which are both small harbours just inside the mouth of the Shannon on the North bank. The Kilrush cargoes consisted mostly of bulk maize and occasionally coal, together with about ten tons of general cargo in the hold, and about 20 or 30 barrels of lubricating oil on deck, as deck cargo. The deck cargo was carried 'at shipper's risk'. There was a curious thing about the deck cargo, we always had at least one barrel leaking. This was very noticeable in bad weather when the sea would break about a couple of hundred feet away from the ship, which would be in calm water. It was a very good illustration of the benefits of oil in bad weather, whether the leaking barrels were a coincidence or not I do not know, but it was certainly a boon and would last for the voyage, by which time one or more barrels would be empty. From the Shannon we would go to wherever cargoes offered and often took flagstones from Liscannor to the Mersey and Bristol. The flagstones were stowed on their edges and, as they were low in the hold, made the ship very stiff and she would do some heavy rolling which was uncomfortable. We also loaded cargoes of granite chippings at Crookhaven which is between Mizzen Head and Cape Clear, but our great stand-by was the clay ports where we loaded many cargoes of china clay at Charlestown, Par and Fowey for Runcorn and Lancaster or Glasson Dock.

The accommodation was similar to most coasters of her tonnage, the crew were accommodated in forecastles at deck level forward, with the customary two tiered bunks and deal table, forms and bogeys, paraffin lighting, no washing facilities other than a galvanised bucket which was provided, and kettle and frying pan for cooking purposes. The amidship accommodation consisted of a small chart room under the bridge, and beneath that a small saloon with a cabin at either side for the Master and Mate. The two engineers lived aft in small rooms opening off the engine room. The ship was kept in as clean and good condition as could be expected in the trade in which she was employed, and with the competition which was prevalent was driven to her utmost.

Captain W. Smyth, her Master, was a very experienced coasting master. He did not hold a certificate of competency, and was inclined to be a little cynical of those who did. He had the reputation of being a 'rock dodger' and he fully deserved the name. He never went around anything that he could cut inside of. I went through Sounds with him that I had never even heard of before, and many I have never been through since:- Ramsey Sound, Jack Sound, Broad Sound, inside Crow Rock, all off Milford Haven. Inside Longships, Portland Race, Owers Banks and all the channels around the Channel Islands. On the Irish coast we went inside Tuskar, Barrels, Saltees Islands, Coningbeg Rock, Cape Clear Sound, Fastnet, Skelligs, Lemon Rock, Blasket Islands, inside Bull Cow and Calf Rocks, through Dursey Sound, and all the sounds around the Irish coast, many of these sounds he went through in pitch darkness. Radar was unheard of then and he relied only on his eye-sight and the sea breaking on the rocks as his guide. The chart was always on the chart room table, but I never ever saw him draw a course on it or lay down a bearing and he never streamed a log. He would hold the chart in front of him when sailing along a coast and look at it like a motorist would look at a road map. Nevertheless, that he was competent there was no doubt, he was Master from a very early age, starting with a little ship called HOLYHEAD.

He commanded several over 1,000 tons for very many years. He did become unstuck on at least one occasion when he lost a ship on the North Bishops Rocks off the Pembroke coast. I do not think that there was any loss of life, and it might have happened in fog, but it certainly did not stop him 'rock dodging' until he retired. No doubt taking short cuts saved quite a lot of time and, in the winter, avoided a great deal of bad weather. I think of all the men I sailed under, Captain Smyth was definitely the champion 'rock dodger'. Andy Wright, the Mate, who had spent a lot of his sea time with Captain Smyth copied him to a large extent when he eventually got command. After I had been in the DENESIDE a month or two, the Mate went on leave and I was asked to take his place, until he returned, which I did. When the Mate returned the Captain had to go ashore to the 'Nautical Academy' to prepare to obtain a Mersey pilotage certificate and in his absence the Mate took command and I remained as Mate which lasted for another month or more and we all got on very well together. In my new position, I came more in contact with the owner than I would have done as an A.B. and I got to know Captain MacClure very well.

I soon made friends in Kilrush with going there often. They were friendly kind people and I once had the experience of shaking hands with the great Mr. Eamon DeValera himself who was canvassing his constituency before an election, Kilrush being in County Clare which was Mr. DeValera's constituency. We spoke for a few minutes and he seemed a very nice man. On one occasion we had arrived at Scattery Island Roadstead in the River Shannon which was the Pilot station. We were bound to Kilrush, and came to an anchor

Holyhead.

to await the tide. The Pilots at that time used a curragh, which is a canvas boat, for boarding, as also did the Islanders to do their shopping on the mainland. The Pilot had boarded us and about half an hour later fog shut down upon us, very dense, with a light Southerly breeze, when out of the fog came a curragh with two of the Scattery Island women in it who had lost their way in the fog. They had no compass and I smiled when I heard the Pilot instructing them how to reach Kilrush. "Keep the wind in your left ear, until your oar touches the bottom," he told them. Considering that the curragh only drew a few inches of water, I would imagine they would be pretty close in by then! It must have worked because a few hours later when the fog cleared and we tied up in Kilrush, we saw the curragh tied up ahead of us and the two ladies shopping.

Going through some of the sounds, especially at night, could be very exhilarating, in fact very exciting, because in many of them there were hidden dangers to be avoided; the Kettle Bottom and Sharks Fin Rocks inside the Longships, the Baillies Race inside the Tuskar, the Horse Rock in Ramsey Sound, the Pinnacle Rock inside the Blaskets, the Victoria Bank inside the Skerries, or as the Welshman called it Bar Gro to mention a few. Rock dodging also had its chilling moments, on one occasion whilst I was Mate with Captain Wright, I was relieving him at midnight on a calm, moonlight and slightly hazy night whilst on passage from Kilrush to Crookhaven. I could see the land on either side. Andy said "she is doing well with the tide, there is the Blasket on your starboard beam". I remarked, "That looks too low for the Blasket". He was a little annoyed when I disagreed, but a few minutes later, the land showed up right ahead and all around us. Then it was a case of 'about turn' as quickly as possible and get out. He had mistaken a deep inlet in the coast to the South West of Brandon Bay (I think it is called Smerwick Harbour, but it is not a harbour) for the Northern end of the Blasket Sound and had entered it, a narrow escape, but all's well that ends well. Shortly afterwards Captain Smyth returned, the proud possessor of a Mersey Pilotage Certificate, which meant that the ship was now exempt from Pilotage dues in the Mersey pilotage district whilst Captain Smyth remained in command. Andy reverted to Mate and I reverted to A.B.

The owners were quick to avail themselves of the advantages of the pilotage certificate and we traded more frequently to the Mersey. One thing I always admired in Captain MacClure was that he paid his pilotage. As I was to find out some years later, when I took command of one of his ships, the PERDITA. It was a pity some of the other coasting shipowners did not follow his example. Regretfully almost all the other coasting ship owners, greedily exploited these amenities, taking advantage of the unemployment problem to do so. It was not until many years later that a ruling was given by the Maritime Board, that officers possessing Pilotage exemption certificates, should be paid an extra percentage of their wages in recognition of their additional qualifications. I think it was about six or seven per cent or a similar ridiculous figure. Many coasting Masters held pilotage certificates for several ports. I knew of several men who held 8 or 10 different pilotage certificates and I myself held three on one occasion. A ship owner once told me that a Pilotage certificate was of more benefit to him than an extra Master's certificate from which he did not gain any monetary advantage. How true he spoke!

All went well for several months and we ran quite frequently to the Mersey until one occasion when we had brought a cargo of granite chippings to Birkenhead, where we arrived in the evening. After preparing the ship for discharging, I went home for the night. When I returned the following morning, I found that the ship had been on fire during the night and was gutted from the bunker to the stern. Fortunately the bridge and amidship accommodation and forecastles were not affected. The Engineers who both lived locally were at home, but lost all their effects. The after deck plates were buckled like a switch back railway as also were several ship side plates. So it was lay up and pay off the crew again, and back to Canning Place to get into the dole queue.

The Captain, Mate and Engineers remained in the ship, on full pay. Captain MacClure never resorted to half pay, he once told me, that if he could not afford to pay a man his full wages he would not employ him. On the other hand he would not stand for any work dodging and was very quick to comment in no uncertain terms when he came across any. Some time later Captain MacClure bought another little ship the SHELLEY in which Captain Smyth was appointed Master and 'Big Andy' was promoted to permanent Master of the DENESIDE, where he remained until a short time after the DENESIDE was sold to Howdens of Larne. Later he was Master with Kellys of Belfast, and eventually returned to Captain MacClure's employ when Captain MacClure bought a ship called KILRAE from Kellys, and Andy took command of her. I was asked to rejoin the DENESIDE when she was repaired, but by then I had got myself another job and was not available. Sadly all of these men are now dead, I remained very firm friends with them until the last.

Bowline on the bight.

10. *"Edith"*

Owen G. Spargo

The shipping slump of the 1930s was in full swing, when, after walking the length and breadth of Liverpool Docks unsuccessfully seeking work, I received a message from Monroe Brothers of Liverpool asking could I join their s/s EDITH to replace the Mate who had been taken ill. I got in touch by telephone with Monroe Brothers who informed me that EDITH was lying in West Birkenhead loaded with a cargo of coal for Killyleagh and would I get myself over there as soon as possible. Killyleagh is a small port in Strangford Lough, Co. Down, Northern Ireland, and about an 18 hours run for EDITH in fine weather.

I hurriedly packed my sea bag, a large white canvas kit bag, which I had made earlier in my career and of which I was quite proud, because these were quietly observed by other seamen, who assessed your abilities by the workmanship displayed in them. This held among other things my bedding, my clothing and my sea boots. The latter were of leather, hand sewn and wooden pegged with no metal nails used in their manufacture, and made to measure in Rotterdam. They cost about £2 and were an ambition for all seamen at that time. Also I included an oil skin coat and sou'wester, both very necessary items on EDITH which had an open bridge. Apart from the meagre shelter afforded by the canvas dodger, which came up to about eye level at the front of the bridge, I would be exposed to the elements for the whole period I was on watch, at least 12 hours out of every twenty four. My bag also contained sufficient provisions for the voyage, consisting mainly of tea, sugar, condensed milk, bread, butter and potatoes also cooking and eating utensils, none of which were at that time provided by the shipowner.

These items packed into my sea bag, I then put it on my shoulder, and by way of tramcar and ferry boat proceeded to Birkenhead. The combined fares amounted to 7 pence, cheap enough you may think, but after a month on the dole, receiving the large amount of twenty three shillings and eight pence a week to maintain a house and family, every copper counted. No joining expenses were offered or asked for, and no fares were paid, even when you were paid off many miles from home. With hundreds of ships laid up all over the world one had to be grateful for any job.

I found EDITH, a small steam coaster of about 240 tons and 100 foot in length, moored near the coal tip, battened down and ready for sea, putting my bag on board I made my way to the Captain's cabin, where I found him in company with the sailor. The pair of them were on their hands and knees poised over a large 'blue-back' general chart of Ireland, using the nautical almanac as a paper weight on one corner, and a shoe similarly on the opposite corner. The Captain was an old man and held a magnifying glass in his hand very intently perusing the chart.

I introduced myself, and he told me casually that I lived in the forecastle with the remainder of the crew and he hoped I had brought enough food with me for a long trip. When I told him that I had sufficient, he asked me, "do you know where we are going?" I answered "Yes", to which he replied, "Have you been there before?" again I affirmed I had. Immediately his attitude changed. "How far is it from Killybegs?" he asked. "About the breadth of Ireland", I replied, and then he had to ask me "Where is Killyleagh?" When I told him then he remembered, and I was accepted.

I made my way to the forecastle, which was about three feet below the level of the main deck and had one door. Inside it was divided by a fore and aft bulkhead made of wood, and at the after end stood a large coal fired cooking stove and a large wood coal bunker, which held about half a ton of coal and was kept full by the spillage of coal from the hatch when loading a coal cargo and the hold sweepings after discharging. The wood bulkhead down the centre divided the forecastle, forming a small room on the starboard which held a two tiered wooden bunk, a small table, two small lockers and a couple of wood forms. The floor was the bare wood and devoid of any covering. To give a bit of comfort, the occupants had spread a couple of sacks normally used for securing grain cargoes, which were strong and of fine texture.

Lighting was from a cheap paraffin lamp which hung from a nail over the table on the bulkhead. This had obviously been smoking, because the glass was black. The two engineers occupied the starboard side which also had two small portholes with their deadlights down and screwed up and appeared to have been leaking. The port side of the forecastle had two double tiered bunks at the ship's side and a small table on the centre bulkhead which was on hinges and could be lowered when not in use. There was a small wooden form at the table and wooden forms alongside the bunks. There were dirty dishes lying on the table. The stove was out and its ashpan full to the top with ashes. The paint which had originally been white was black with the smoke from the stove and the fumes from the lamps. The whole place was covered with a heavy film of coal dust which had got in during the loading. The place bore an air of neglect and squalor. The two forward bunks were for the sailor and myself whilst the two unoccupied bunks were used for storage of the anchor lamps, anchor shapes, life jackets, and other items required by the Board of Trade. The flags of the International code of signals were contained in two sacks, there being no flag locker. These were jammed between the lamps to secure them.

After changing into working clothes I made my way aft, where I found the remainder of the crew, Captain included, busy sealing the cabin, engine room and bunker doors and lids. I asked, "Should I put the hose on her and wash her down?" "No", replied the Captain, "just get the draw bucket and throw a couple of buckets around the bridge. She will wash herself down when she gets outside."

So being all ready for sea, we cast off, after giving the Berthing Master the customary allowance of 2/- for letting go our moorings. No pilots or boatmen were employed. We made our way towards Alfred Lock which is the access to the River Mersey, and after entering the locks, the gates were closed behind us and we were duly lowered down to the river level and when the outside gates opened we were instructed by a voice from the quay above us to "come ahead Captain, blow your whistle if you have got one" and after letting go our ropes, we duly came ahead and entered the river and started on our voyage.

After securing everything about the deck, I reported to the bridge, and watches were set. The Captain and sailor keeping the first four hours together, whilst I would keep the alternate four hours by myself with instructions of, if I needed him to call the Captain by banging on the deck, which of course was over his head. I only once had to resort to this, and he was not amused. That was when the visibility had decreased to less than half a mile and I was pulling my soul-case trying to steer the brute and keep a lookout at the same time. The Engineers, kept alternative four hour watches when they kept steam on the boiler, attended to the boiler feed water, oiled and attended to the main engine, bilges, etc. and loaded, pulled up and dumped the ashes they had made when cleaning the fires.

I remained about the bridge and deck doing odd jobs until we reached the Bar Light Vessel, when it being my watch off, I went below, where I cleaned out my predecessor's bunk and dumped his mattress overboard and made a bit of a clearance. After making myself a cup of tea I gladly lay down on the bare bunk boards to sleep, and only too soon was I called to go on watch.

So after muffling myself up, I went on deck and after watching for a slight lull, the decks now being awash, I made my way to the bridge. The mode of travel going on watch was an experience in itself. A lifeline was rigged from the foremast to the bridge over the top of the hatch and one climbed over the front of the bridge. The Engineers then carried on over the back of the bridge to where a ladder was lashed on top of the main engine cylinders up to the

engine room skylight above, through which they made their entrances and exits.

Having negotiated this 'obstacle course', I eventually arrived on the bridge to take over my first watch, where I found the Captain sitting on top of his cabin scuttle, fully attired in oilskins and sou'wester calmly observing the sea and the sailor wrestling with the wheel. I relieved the sailor at the wheel who repeated the course to me (she was about a point off) and handed the wheel to me with the final opinion of "and she is steering like a bastard". He repeated the course to the Captain and then disappeared over the front of the bridge in a flash to make the most of his four hours off.

The Captain remained seated for about half an hour when after checking the course with me and telling me to bang on the deck if I wanted him, he disappeared to his cabin. The two side lights (port and starboard), fixed in portable screens where they were kept permanently, were on the bridge wings and burnt paraffin. A binnacle with its brass top well polished had two lamps designed to burn colza oil for illuminating the compass, but which were now burning paraffin. At the side of the binnacle stood the engine room telegraph, with its brass well polished. On the port side was the scuttle to the Captain's cabin and, at the after end of the bridge, the steam steering gear, a common enough piece of machinery in many steam coasters at the time, which by means of a clutch could quickly be converted into manual (hand steering) gear. It was only used for manoeuvring in docks or in narrow waterways, being converted to manual (Armstrong patent) at sea to conserve bunkers, and very often the ships steered a better course in hand gear, than they did in steam gear which was inclined to be too quick when steering a compass course, also the helmsman could get the 'feel' of the ship better when he could 'feel' the weight against the rudder. And of course that other important piece of equipment, the steam whistle, the lanyard of which stretched from the whistle on the front of the funnel to a dodger stanchion at the front of the bridge at about six inches over one's head, and down which rain drops used to travel when it was raining to drop either right down one's neck or down one's sleeve, either to irritate you or to rouse you if you tried to nod.

The EDITH (61), was one of four similar ships bought by Monroes from Monks of Liverpool who had traded them on short trips of about twelve hours, mainly on the North Wales, the Lancashire coast and near Irish ports.

However, Monroe Bros. had different ideas when they acquired them, and traded with them extensively to the very small Irish ports, where freights were good and where there were many coal and grain cargoes to be found, ranging as far afield as Bantry around the South and West and Sligo around the North and West. They also traded extensively to the granite quarries in Caernarvon bay, Cardigan and Liverpool bays and the small ports in the Solway. There were also some trips to the Hebrides, Firth of Clyde and Bristol Channel ports, and occasionally English Channel and near continental ports. I suppose, because they were not on any regular run, one could describe them as small coastal tramps. Perhaps taking into consideration the conditions in which the crew lived, coastal vagrants might describe them better.

The EDITH had a raised forecastle head, flush main deck with bulwarks, one hold, one hatch and two side pocket bunkers. The bunkers were filled from two round holes in the maindeck and when full were covered with heavy steel lids similar to the lids used on the coal cellars in old houses ashore. A half-turn given to them when in place secured them and they were then made water tight by filling the gap around the edge with tallow, very necessary as they were always awash at sea when the ship was loaded. They each held about fifteen tons, almost every ounce of which had to be shovelled in and trimmed, this duty being performed by the Mate, two Engineers and Sailor for which they received a bonus of five shillings to share between them. The princely sum of one shilling and three pence each, which small as it was, would however at that time purchase 35 Woodbines and a box of matches or two pints of very good beer, 10 Woodbines and a box of matches. She had one steam cargo winch and two masts with a wooden derrick on the foremast. The anchor windlass on the forecastle head was driven by an endless chain (called a messenger) and connected to the cargo winch and worked similar to an endless belt on any other machine, except that tension was provided by passing the upper bight of the messenger through a snatch block suspended on a tackle from the hound's band on the foremast, the tackle then being tightened as necessary to give the required tension. It was a noisy operation heaving up the anchor, but never the less quite effective, providing the messenger held out. A number of spare split links were carried to be used as an emergency repair when a link broke which was not uncommon.

At the after end of the hatch, on the main deck was the Captain's cabin; at either side of which was an alleyway to allow passage along the deck. In the port alleyway at the ship's side was a small galley with stove and coal bunker. The steel door of this galley opened into the alleyway as also did the Captain's cabin door which was opposite. A handy arrangement you may think, but unfortunately, these alleyways were always awash at sea except in flat calm weather, so both doors had to be securely battened down at sea and so were of no benefit. A similar construction on the starboard side formed the W.C. which had a draw bucket flushing system, but this place was also inaccessible in bad weather and the 'bucket and chuck it' method had to be resorted to when nature demanded or if more comfort was desired with less privacy, by a 'squat' on the stokehold plates and cremating the result in the furnace. Fortunately the Captain's cabin also had a vertical ladder inside which led to a small scuttle giving access to the bridge which was over his cabin. The bridge was on the same level as the top of the engine room casing which continued from the back of the bridge and carried the funnel and two cowl ventilators behind which was the boat deck, this had a lifeboat at each side carried in radial davits. Between the lifeboats was a small skylight giving light and ventilation to the engine room and abaft the skylight, the mizzen mast. She was ketch rigged and had originally carried a mizzen boom and tri-sail which had probably worn out and not been replaced.

The engine room held the boiler in addition to the main engine so the two furnaces were on the after end of the Scotch boiler. They were fired from a position just forward of the engine. The engine was a compound with condenser incorporated and boiler feed pump, air pump, circulating pump, and bilge pump, all working off the main engine. She also had an independent general service pump which would do practically everything from pumping ballast and bilges to feeding the boiler and supplying water to wash down decks. The engine room had doors at each side at deck level which were divided in two the top half being capable of being opened whilst the lower half remained closed. The lower half was fitted with a strong steel bar which could be fitted across the doorway, the door being attached to it with a bolt and nut. The lower half of the door after being draped around the edges with tallow soaked sacking was secured with this bar which acted as a draw bar and drew the door tight, and although this may have looked very 'Heath-Robinson', it was quite effectual in keeping out the sea water which continuously reached this level when at sea. It also allowed the engineers to open the top half and dump their ashes through it on to the deck where they seldom remained more than a few minutes before being washed over the side through the scuppers. The Captain used a similar method to keep his cabin watertight and to secure his door at sea.

EDITH was a very hard ship to steer when loaded, as were her sister ships which I sailed in later either as Mate or Master, possibly due to the fact that they were inclined to load by the head. That is they were inclined to draw more water forward than aft, and probably to counteract this, a wooden bulkhead had been constructed in the fore part of the hold, which resulted in them not being able to load to their marks when full with a coal or grain cargo. They were about four inches light when the hold was full. This little reserve buoyancy made a big difference to them in a seaway. They were still very wet, and with a cargo of granite or similar heavy cargo they were terrors.

A few months prior to my joining EDITH she had rolled her funnel over the side whilst carrying a cargo of granite from Carreg-y-Llam, a quarry in Caernarvon Bay, to Liverpool and the Captain had brought her to Liverpool with a 'jury' funnel constructed from corrugated sheets and odds and ends.

After a four hour wrestling bout with the steering, especially on a bad or wet night I was glad to get to my bed and could have slept on a bed of nails, let alone the wooden bunk boards. These little boats were aptly nicknamed 'Monroe's Training Ships'. They invariably put a newcomer on trial in one of them, to see what he was made of, and more than one highly qualified foreign going ship's officer met his match in one of them. They rarely remained more than a few weeks until they found a more congenial job. After a while I got the brute tamed a little with the wheel.

Captain Thomas Davies, The Master, was an ex-deep water sailing ship Master who came from Cardigan and held a Master's square rig foreign going certificate. He was a real old 'Cape Horner', a splendid seaman, but a little out of place in such a small ship. He was not conversant with some of the short cuts and dodges used by the regular coasting Masters that I had sailed with, and believed in 'keeping plenty of water under her'. This could mean

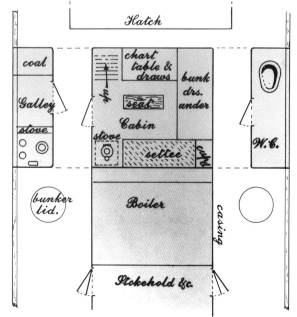

57. Cabin Layout of the EDITH.

that we were often in the track of the big ships which frequently meant that we got the full force of the bad weather whilst the coasters would be going along under the lee of the land in smooth water.

A typical deep water sailing ship man, he was a very quiet gentlemanly man, who never admitted to his age, but he was probably well in his sixties if not seventies. He rarely spoke and used to sit for hours on end on the scuttle of his cabin just looking at the sea, and occasionally dozing. He must have been a very meagre eater, for I rarely saw him cooking, and one or other of us would bring him a can of tea when we came on watch. He would never take the wheel if he could avoid it.

At first I resented his remaining on the bridge when I was on watch, thinking that perhaps he did not trust me, but he never interfered, and when I got to know him better he came out of his shell. We became firm friends, and he became quite talkative. He told me the reason that he did not remain in his cabin was that the after end of his cabin came directly against the forward end of the boiler and it was so hot that at times he could not bear his hand against it. He slept on the settee, his bunk being the receptacle for all his oddments, too numerous to mention.

He had very fixed ideas on how a sailor should dress (we rarely referred to them as seamen in those days). His ideas were: sailors should always wear a jersey and blue double breasted serge suit, which indeed most of them did. Their jerseys being mostly hand knitted by their women folk, and it was quite easy to tell which part of the country a man came from by the pattern of his jersey. He contended that a sailor should only wear a collar and tie on very special occasions, such as going to chapel, or a funeral or wedding, and on one occasion when I bought myself a pair of grey flannel trousers to wear with a blue serge suit, the trousers of which had worn out, and an open necked shirt, it being summer time, he told me that I looked disgraceful.

He was not very keen on running for shelter, preferring if he was caught out in bad weather to heave to and fight it out, but if on the other hand he was sheltering, and the other ships ventured to have 'a look at it', he would remain in until the weather really settled and so once he decided to shelter he wanted a lot of dislodging. In those days we did not have any weather forecasts as we have today, the only indication we had of bad weather coming, apart from our own predictions, was the storm signals which were exhibited on various headlands, and which were observed with doubts, because very often the storm did not materialise or had already started. Yet at the end of the year his turnover must have been as good as the rest, otherwise he would not have been tolerated. I also think the owners had a soft spot for him, on account of his age, and also the fact that he was a widower and made the ship his home and very rarely left it. This let him get away with a lot.

The two Engineers were typical coasting 'shovel' engineers. They were not tradesmen or qualified engineers and had probably graduated from fireman or donkeyman in larger ships. One of them was proud of the fact that he had been in charge of a threshing machine driven by steam which went around the farms threshing the grain at harvest time. They were very hard working men, and worked alternate four hour watches, during which time they were kept very busy, because besides having to look after the main engine, they had in addition to attend to the water level of the boiler and bilges and also stoke the fires and keep steam on the boiler, and as the ship burned about six tons of coal a day, this meant that they had to shovel three tons of coal each and every day in addition to cleaning the fires which was a very hot and dirty job. Yet despite this, they managed to keep themselves very clean with the plentiful supply of warm condensed water available to them from the drains of the main engine.

The drinking water was carried in a 200 gallon tank in the fore part of the hold and was obtained with the use of a hand pump, which was about worn out and very temperamental and frustrating when trying to get water in bad weather. Their method of cooking at sea, also deserves a mention. They would bring a tea can of cold water on watch with them, also an enamel or tin plate. They would then take a shovelful of hot coals from the furnace and put it on the stokehold plates (floor) and place the can of water on it to boil. They would then put a couple of rashers of bacon and crack an egg with it on their dinner plate. The plate was then placed on the firing shovel which was held under the furnace to grill whilst the can boiled to make their tea. Another method they had, was to put raw potatoes unpeeled in the ash pit under the furnace and in due course they had baked potatoes in their jackets. This method was also common practice with the drivers of steam rollers and steam lorries of which there were plenty on the road at that time.

The engine room in bad weather, was as close an impression of Dantes Inferno as one could imagine, with both doors sealed and both ventilators turned away from the wind to prevent water coming down them. The only outlet for the heat was through the small skylight. The smell of hot lubricating

'SLICE' 'RAKE'

Firing irons.

oil, the washing about of the bilge water, the smell of salt water on red hot ashes, and of escaping steam from the main engine glands mingling with the oil on the cross head guides and emulsifying all, had characteristic smells of their own, which if anything was a cure for sea sickness, that certainly was.

Upon coming on watch, the engineer would first drain and then close the boiler water gauge glass to ascertain that he had sufficient water in the boiler, then check if the main engine was running cool by feeling the bearings with his hands. Then after checking that the bilges were reasonably dry and that there was a good head of steam on the boiler he would take over the watch. These men although they were rough diamonds in many ways, were very meticulous in the way they handed over the watch. The understanding seemed to be that if the engine ran hot in the first half hour of the watch, then it was due to the negligence of the man who had just gone off, and I saw many an argument over this point.

His next job was to clean the fire, to do this he would stoke up one of the two furnaces and then 'wing' the other. That is, he would move the hot burning coals to one side, exposing the clinker on the fire bars. He would then remove this clinker with a steel rake, and then by winging the hot coal to the cleaned side he would remove the remaining clinker, afterwards spreading the remaining coals and stoking up the fire. He would then 'draw' the pits, meaning that he would pull out the fine ash from the ash pits which were under the furnaces. When he had these on the stokehold plates he would then wet them with sea water from a valve fitted in the ship's side for this purpose called the ash cock. The fumes and smell from this was enough to make anybody cough. If you would like a demonstration try letting a panful of sea water or strong salt water boil over on your stove! He would then put the ashes into ash buckets, in this case discarded ten gallon drums with the top removed and two handles made by cutting holes in their sides. They held about one hundred weight of ashes when full. These he would pull up to deck level by means of a rope rove through a block shackled to the engine room deckhead, and then empty them on to the deck by way of the top half of the engine room door, often getting a good wetting in the process, not a hard job you might think, but when you consider he had to do this by himself and it meant going up and down the engine room ladder once for every bucket and he would have seven or eight buckets full every watch, and the ladder was about ten or twelve feet, it was equivalent to climbing a ladder of about eighty feet and that done at the double in a rolling ship would compare favourably with many commando courses.

If the quality of the bunkers was bad and they were very often, because owners only bought the cheapest coal they could get for bunkers, then the engineers would often have to clean two fires a watch to keep a full head of steam, giving them double the work, and if the steam pressure dropped, then the engine slowed down and the speed dropped, and the Captain would very soon detect this and demand an explanation in no uncertain terms, as also would the owners from the Captain if he was making slow passages. As there was no shortage of men, any laxity from any crew member regardless of rank would not be tolerated and often resulted in instant dismissal, and many of these little ships were at sea in gales or wind when they should have been sheltering, either because the Captain was trying to show his ego with the chance of getting promotion or was scared of getting fired to make room for somebody better qualified or more ambitious, knowing there were hundreds of men available and ready to step into his job.

On our arrival at Killyleagh we opened the hatches, topped the derrick and removed the beams, and shore labourers commenced to discharge our cargo into horse drawn carts, using our cargo winch and iron self tipping tubs we carried which held half a ton each, the engineers maintaining steam for this purpose. In some small ports the deck hands had also to drive the winch. Not a very pleasamt prospect if you had kept a watch at sea during the night and arrived in port at say seven in the morning to find you had to drive a winch for about ten or twelve hours, and then go to sea again at night and keep sea watches during the night, and very often have to clean the hold out ready for the next cargo before doing so, with no overtime paid, and the prospect of being paid off without notice if there were no cargoes available. Crews were automatically on twenty four hours notice before arriving at the Mersey.

However, in this case we did not have to drive our own winches, so taking my bed tick, which I always carried I made my way to a nearby farm, where for a few coppers I had it filled with clean sweet straw. This I then brought on board and placed in the fiddley over the boiler to air and also kill any residents which it might contain, and whilst it was airing I thoroughly cleaned out my bunk and forecastle, and then put my new 'donkey's breakfast' in my bunk and made up my bed, and after my wrestling bout with the steering gear on the passage over, and spending my watches below on the hard bare bunk boards, with a good feed of scouse under my belt and after a good hot bath

in a bucket in the stokehold, I turned into my new bed and never slept in a more comfortable one.

I awoke fully refreshed at six o'clock in the morning when the dock labourers returned to resume discharging, they having worked until dusk the previous day. The method of discharging although simple was quite efficient and although on occasions we could discharge our cargo in a working day, we would often be restricted to one tide a day by the fact that many of the very small ports we went to were unlit and had no navigational lights so that we could only navigate during the daylight hours.

When discharging was completed, we brushed the hold and loaded a cargo of potatoes in bags for Liverpool. The potatoes were brought alongside the ship in horse-drawn carts, and wooden chutes were rigged into the ships hold, and the sacks of potatoes were slid down the chutes, with this cargo we had to stand over the hatch and tally (count) the bags, which we did by getting a docket off each cart driver and checking the number of bags as it was being unloaded, and on this count the Captain signed the bill of lading. I never ever saw a ship's tally which corresponded with the bill of lading - contents, quality, weight and number of bags unknown (or so many bags in dispute). I do not suppose it made a great deal of difference. One good custom they had in these small Irish ports was that the shipper invariably put a bag or two on board for the use of the crew as a gratuity. Whether this was to discourage us from stealing them or an act of charity towards us, I do not know, but either way it was very much appreciated by us and helped our budget a lot.

We took the potato cargo on this occasion to West Brocklebank Dock in Liverpool, arriving at six o'clock in the morning where the Liverpool dockers were not long in relieving us of our little cargo, and at six o'clock the same night we were on our way to Garston where we arrived and were under the coal tip loading coal for Courtmacsherry, West Cork the same night. After being on our feet all night attending ropes and moving the ship back and forth to facilitate loading we were loaded, battened down and on our way to Court-macsherry by seven o'clock in the morning of the following day, and so the grind went on, only this being a longer passage we did get a bit longer in our beds to recuperate after our unpaid night's work at Garston.

We duly arrived at Courtmacsherry which was a very small Irish port, and were received with typical Irish hospitality by the friendly villagers, many of whom had either been at sea themselves or had connections with the sea.

After discharging at Courtmacsherry we went in ballast to Crookhaven, which was another very small port between the Fastnet and Mizzen Head and I would mention in passing that this part of the world is exposed to the full force of the Atlantic, we loaded a cargo of granite chippings at a quarry there for Swansea, and so the time passed. We always had the excitement of wondering where we were going to next, and we got a very good selection, which was interesting and was to prove very valuable experience to me in my future.

Sadly a great many of the small ports we went to are now finished such as the granite quarries in Caernarvon Bay of Clynnog, Trevor, Port Rivals, Porth-y-Nant, Carreg-y-llam, and the Cardigan Bay ports of Pwellheli, Portmadoc, Llanbedrog and Abersoch, also the quarries in Liverpool bay such as Penmon, and Penmaenmawr. Also gone are the small ports in the River Dee of Point of Ayr, and the small ports of Widnes and Warrington in the River Mersey and as far as Pomona in the Manchester ship canal. Similarly the small ports in the Solway Firth such as Isle of Whithorn, Port William, Kippford, Palnackie, Dalbeattie, Kirkcudbright, Garlieston, Harrington, Whitehaven, also to many small ports in the Hebrides and North West of Ireland, such as Loch Sween, Loch Broom, Lough Swilly ports of Buncrana, Letterkenny, Ramelton, Rathmullan, Portsalla, and others.

I suppose the variety of ports we visited offset the conditions we worked under, because we rarely went to the same place twice, and I daresay we averaged at least two cargoes a week, possibly five cargoes in a fortnight, and running to small and often exposed ports, where freights were high. They must have shown a good profit at the end of the year, and although conditions on board were crude to put it mildly, after a while when I had settled down, and with a fairly regular, if not permanent wage, because the threat of laying the ship up and either paying off, or half pay was always hanging over your head, I was quite happy, and never felt afraid in these small ships probably because I knew that they could not shift their cargo, for with the majority of cargoes they were full up all over and not loaded down to their marks. They had that much reserve buoyancy that although they were very wet and shipped plenty of water, it did not remain on board for long. I think the water splashing up from the beltings also had a lot to do with them being so wet.

On one occasion we made a voyage to Antwerp, and at that time there was competition between the Dutch and Belgian Pilots for the pilotage to Antwerp, where the ship has to pass through the Dutch international waters on her way

Potatoes
in sacks....

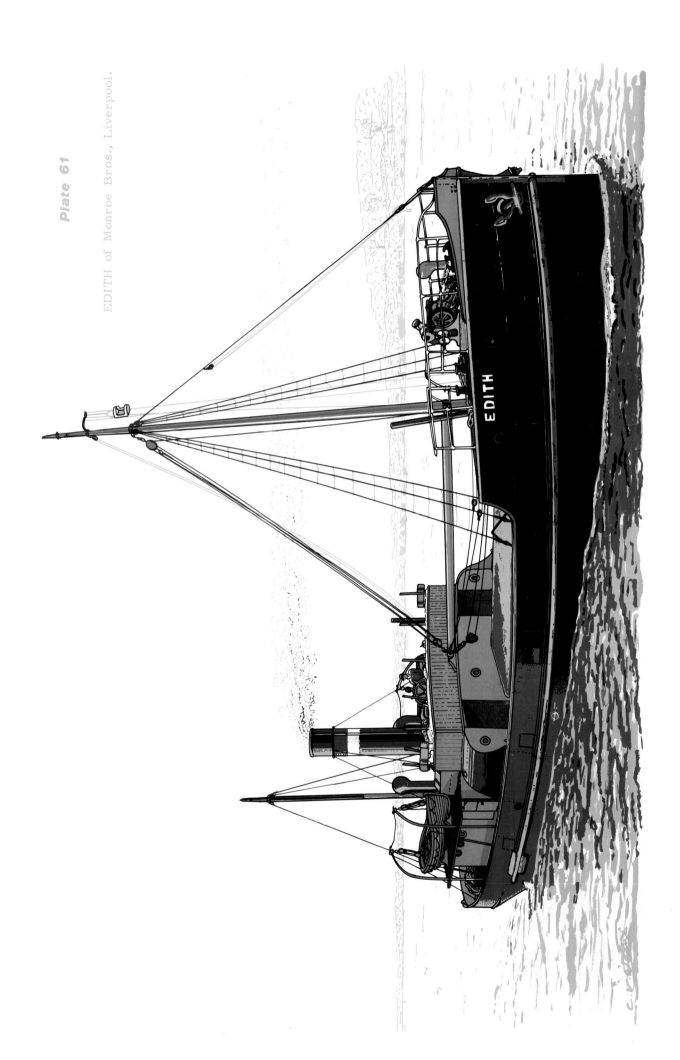

Plate 61

EDITH of Monroe Bros., Liverpool.

to Antwerp. We picked up a Belgian pilot who was 'not amused' at the prize he had picked up, or the conditions he had to contend with. However, by the time we had reached Antwerp he had resigned himself to his fate, and when he left the ship he turned around a couple of times to have a last look at her. I would not be sure whether it was a look of relief or a look of gratitude or even incredulity at having reached Antwerp in one piece.

On another occasion when bound to Queens Dock, Glasgow, the pilot asked for the International Code flag 'B' to be hoisted on the fore stay, which was the signal that we wished to enter Queens Dock. Simple as this request was, it was a major operation on board EDITH because it meant emptying two sacks of flags on to the forecastle floor and rummaging through them until we found the flag, which in this case we did not; it was missing. It was found several weeks afterwards under the Captain's settee. An amusing incident resulted when the bridge operator got awkward when told "we did not have a B flag". He accused the Captain of swearing at him. I never heard the Captain swear all the time I was with him. It was only when the pilot told him that, "we havna got any bloody B flag" that the message got through and we were allowed to enter with a few sarcastic comments, about being a menace on the high seas.

I very rarely went ashore and then only to post my wife's money home, or to buy food, for one thing my wages would not allow any extravagances. My wages were £3.10.0 per week consisting of 7 days and whilst no agreed number of hours was specified, as there were only two watches, it could not possibly be less than 12 hours per day or 84 hours per week minimum. Overtime was unknown and a naughty word, not to be mentioned. After I had paid my National Health contribution of 10 pence and 5 pence for a registered envelope to send my allowance of £2.0.0 to my wife to keep a home over our heads, I was left with the princely sum of £1.8.9. to feed and clothe myself for a week and to build a reserve to pay my fare home in the event of no cargoes being available which often happened. At such times occasionally the owner would get big hearted and offer us half pay (but not half work), but this was totally unacceptable in my case and I frequently took a job on another ship as A.B. where I was paid more money.

If the ship was to lay in a Mersey port from say Friday night to Monday morning, the custom was to pay everybody off except the Captain and Chief Engineer who remained on at half pay, and then resume work on full pay on the Monday morning, very often starting work at six o'clock on the Monday morning and working all day discharging, and then working all night loading. Thus when you were paid off on a Friday night you not only lost Saturday's pay because you could not sign on the dole, the dole office being closed on a Saturday and also because you were paid on a seven day week basis. You also lost Sunday's pay which in the case of the mate, whose wages worked out to 10/- per day, a loss of £1 thus reducing his wages to £2.10.0 per week which was about 12/6 a week less than Able Seamen were being paid elsewhere, but work was scarce and employers were never over generous and were indifferent because they knew that they could, as the saying goes, get men two a penny.

I had now started to study for a certificate and when we got a quiet night in port, I had the forecastle more often than not to myself. The others either being ashore or sleeping. I would get out my books and start studying. The Captain who also very rarely went ashore would, at about 8 o'clock wander along forward ostensibly to assist me with my studies, but which invariably resulted in a series of yarns from which I learned the art of sending spars up and down, club hauling, box hauling, running out anchors and kedging, during the course of which he would be tearing a strip off the newspaper which we kept spread on the table as a table cloth to light his pipe from the stove gradually using it up until a strip about a foot long remained. After a few puffs he would take his pipe out of his mouth to continue his yarn and out would go his pipe again for relighting. By about 10 pm. the table cloth being almost fully consumed, I would make a cup of tea for each of us. After which he would always thank me and bid me good night, always in English and although he was a Welsh speaker, I never heard him speak in his native tongue. I also presented him with the remains of the table cloth which used to amuse him.

I was sorry to leave him, when I was transferred to one of the Company's larger ships, the EDITH unfortunately having failed to get alongside the quay on a falling tide at Glencaple and lay there neaped for about 10 days only about 10 feet from the quay. He wrote me a splendid reference in beautiful copperplate handwriting, which I still have. We had become very good friends and tears were in his eyes as he wrote it. He was a grand old man, and although I remained in the company for several years afterwards, I rarely came across him. So ended my acquaintance with EDITH. It was hard, at times very hard, but I had made a good friend, and also gained a vast amount of experience which was to stand me in good stead throughout my life, and also some time later when I took command of one of 'Monroe's Training Ships'.

Sheepshank.

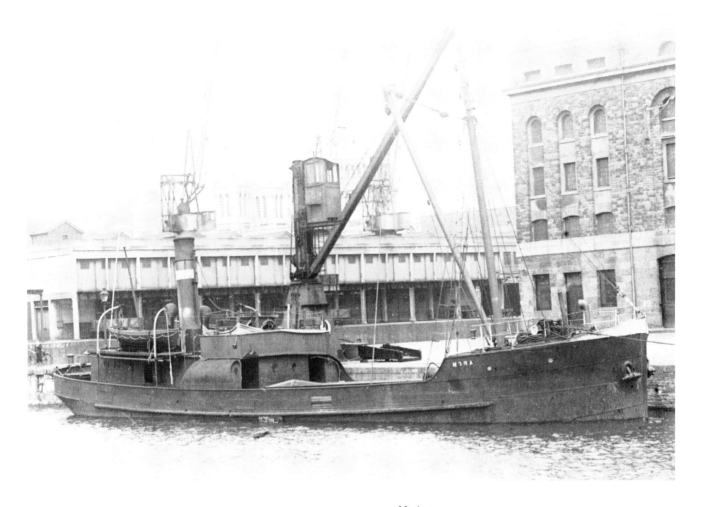

11. *First Command ~ "Nora."*

63. s. s. NORA.
E. N. Taylor

Owen G. Spargo

For a good many years it was possible, in fact I believe it still is, for a seaman to command a ship of any tonnage without a certificate of competency provided he was sponsored and could satisfy the underwriters of his ability to handle and navigate the ship. He could then trade with her from any port in the United Kingdom to any port within Home Trade limits, that is, between Brest and the River Elbe, but could not carry more than 12 passengers.

At one period there were many uncertificated Masters and Mates but these men did however hold Pilotage exemption certificates for various ports where Pilotage was compulsory, enabling them to navigate the ships of the Company in those waters without employing a Pilot. Many Masters held two or three certificates, some in the regular traders holding as many as twelve. In ports where Pilotage was not compulsory a Pilot was employed and then only for a first visit, during which the Master was expected to familiarise himself with the area sufficiently to do the Pilotage himself on future occasions.

Pilotage certificates were gained by examination before a local committee, which generally consisted of several local Pilots, representatives of the local shipowners, a Board of Trade representative and the Superintendent of Pilots. The examination which was mostly oral, was not a 'walk over' by any means and could sometimes last over two hours. An awful lot of questions can be asked in that time, some very searching, and failures were not unknown by any means. Proof of local knowledge and trading experience to the port, having made a certain number of voyages to the port during the year and a good record, were required. After the candidate had satisfied the examination committee of his ability and knowledge, a certificate was granted. It was retained by the holder making a specified number of voyages during the year and the Owner making a small token payment annually into the Pilotage Fund. The certificate could be granted to the Master or Mate, but whichever held it had to take charge of the ship in Pilotage waters, often a very unsatisfactory arrangement when the Mate was the Pilot. These Pilotage certificates were very desirable and very much sought after by coasting shipowners for the financial benifits gained by them. The amount saved in Pilotage by these certificates paid the holders wages many times over, because the Master or Mate holding

these qualifications was expected to render these services as part of his duties, indeed in most cases possession of a Pilotage certificate was a condition of employment.

A candidate for a Pilotage certificate could not present himself for examination, he had to be sponsored by the Shipowner whose ships he was going to pilot and had to be a serving Master or Mate in that Company, and provided that he passed the examination a certificate would be granted to him for ships of that Company or group of Companies. A certificate of competency was not required in the early years, but if the candidate produced one, then he was exempted from examination in Rule of the Road as defined in the general regulations also the Rule of the Road as interpreted in the Mersey Docks and Harbour Board bye-laws, especially bye-law 10 which dealt with ships entering or leaving the main channel from a side channel and which could very easily be confusing and had been the cause of several collisions mostly by ships entering the Main Channel from the Rock Channel. The Pilots and B.O.T. representative, generally examined him on this subject and it was a much more searching examination than by the B.O.T. examiner who was the sole assessor for a certificate of competency.

In the early 1930s, the Liverpool Pilotage Authority made a bye-law which made it compulsory for a candidate for a Pilotage certificate to hold a certificate of competency either as Master or Mate before he would be accepted for examination. This was a blow to many of the old time Masters, because if for some reason his certificate had lapsed and he had lost it, unless he obtained a B.O.T. certificate he had lost it for good, and for many of them living in the Merseyside area it required some thought. By this time I had been sailing for a few years as an uncertificated Mate in several small coasters and gained much experience but I could see that unless I obtained a certificate I would not go far so I applied myself to my studies and eventually attended the Nautical Academy.

Prior to the first world war, a number of nautical schools opened up in Liverpool, some of which were started by ex-shipmasters assisted by ex-ships officers who had either fallen on hard times or married and 'swallowed the anchor'. Of these establishments I suppose by far the most popular to the coasting fraternity on the West coast of England was Darby's Nautical Academy in Queens Road, Everton, Liverpool. It attracted men from England, Ireland, Wales and in particular the Isle of Man and was very successful in preparing them for the Board of Trade examinations for certificates of competency and also for Liverpool Pilotage examinations, in fact it was the only school that prepared candidates for Pilotage certificates at which it was very successful.

Both Mr. Darby and his son Peter who assisted him, were affectionately known to their pupils as Old Peter and Young Peter. After Old Peter died, Young Peter successfully ran the school until his death, shortly after the second World War. All of the men who passed through their school had affection for them and will verify that they have a great deal to thank the Darbys for. The Academy was a large Victorian terraced house with a cellar in which the Darby family lived and I presume occupied the upper floors. The ground floor consisting of two large rooms served the purpose of the Academy, the front room for the candidates for Masters and Pilotage certificates, whilst the back room was for the use of candidates for Mates certificates.

Although he was able to prepare candidates for foreign going certificates, he apparently did not choose to do so, and invariably sent them to one of the other schools. In reverse, candidates who had attended other schools and failed in their seamanship examination would revert to Darby's as also would candidates for a 'sail' endorsement on their steamship certificate. Mr. Darby ran a very friendly and homely school and was not exhorbitant with his fees. He charged £2-10-0 for Mates' examination, £3-10-0 for Masters, and £4-0-0 for coaching for a Pilotage certificate. These fees lasted until you had gained your certificate, even if you failed at the first or subsequent attempts. The candidate provided himself with an exercise book, pen and ink and pencil, everything else was provided by the school, although the candidates invariably bought themselves books and drawing instruments which they generally gave to the school after they had passed their examinations, thereby increasing its stock and also helping future pupils, most of whom had scraped and saved to attend school and would be very grateful for them.

Mr. Darby would duly arrive in shirt sleeves (rolled up), minus a tie with his waist coat invariably open and seating himself at the head of the table, lessons would commence at 9 a.m. with all the students gathered around the long table for seamanship lessons. On the table were placed several models of sailing ships and steamships, also coloured balls on stands to represent the lights carried by different types of ships, also models of the different buoys and seamarks that one would be likely to encounter, an arrow to indicate wind direction and another arrow to indicate tide direction. Everybody had to attend these lectures regardless of rank, and each student had to answer a question in turn, which if answered incorrectly was then discussed. It was a friendly atmosphere, everybody getting personal tuition. Every possible situation that was likely to arise being thoroughly discussed both in sail and steam combined, in fine weather, bad weather and fog, by night and by day.

The seamanship quiz being over by about 10.30, the students would then disperse to their various tables, aspiring Masters to the front room, Mates and newcomers in the back room where Peter would set them navigational problems, explaining each one individually before settling them down and leaving them. Because there was no set term, students joined at different times, each was in a different stage of advancement and able to help others when Peter was otherwise engaged. No educational standard was asked for or expected, Mr. Darby's attitude being that he was there to teach, which he did very thoroughly. I have known students who had to start by learning their multiplication tables. At mid-day Mrs. Darby would produce a tray with a pot of tea, cups and saucers, each student paying one penny. One of the students would slip out for fish and chips for those that required them, others brought sandwiches depending on their means. On the day before 'dole day' it was generally sandwiches for everybody, most students' funds beginning to feel the draught.

No time was wasted at dinner and by 12.30 it was over, then one of the students would get hold of a pair of semaphore flags or the Morse lamp and we would practice signalling between us until about 1 p.m., when lessons would be resumed until about 3.30 p.m. In the first week in the month, the students who had not passed their St. John's Ambulance examination (which had to be passed, and a certificate produced, before a candidate would be accepted by the B.O.T.), would then proceed to the Mersey Mission to Seamen which was in Hanover Street, Liverpool for instruction in St. John's Ambulance by a Doctor Murray Kearns who by giving five lectures on five successive afternoons was able to prepare his students for examination. On Monday of the following week the candidate would then be examined to see just how much of Doctor Murray Kearn's teaching he had absorbed, there were occasional failures, but very rarely. I have since passed St. John's Ambulance examinations of the same category under shore conditions, where I have attended the same lectures over a period of three months, when the examination was no harder, which I think speaks well for the Doctor who was able to instruct us so well and whose teaching I personally was to find extremely useful in later years.

During the weeks that the first aid classes were closed, the candidates would attend the Royal Naval Signal School in Canning Place at 4 p.m. each afternoon (after school) for an hours instruction in the practice of signalling by International Code of Signals with the use of flags, also semaphore with hand flags, and Morse code by lamp and hand flag. The Signal Instructor was an ex-Yeoman of Signals, R.N., and very thorough, as the number of successful candidates bore out. Meanwhile at 4 pm, Mr. Darby having finished with his B.O.T. pupils for the day, the candidates for Mersey Pilotage Certificates would present themselves at the Academy, where Mr. Darby coached them in the intricacies of the Mersey Pilotage, which covers a very large area extending from St. Bees Head in Cumberland to the Isle of Man along the East coast of the Isle of Man to the Chickens Rock on the South coast of the Isle of Man, across to the North coast of Anglesey, and up the River Mersey as far as Eastham and Garston, all particulars of which had to be known by heart because it was an oral examination. He had no opposition in this subject, and the failures of candidates who had attended Darby's were extremely rare.

He always made sure that each pupil had plenty of homework to keep them occupied outside school hours which he would go over with each pupil individually to make sure they understood what they were doing. He was very patient and gave excellent service for his small fee. Twice a week lessons had to be interrupted for an hour or more to enable the students to sign on the 'dole', their only means of subsistence during the period they were studying, which amounted to 17/- for a single man and 23/- for a married man per week, so unless you had rich parents to subsidise you, or had saved a good nest egg, you had no time to dawdle or to be lax in your studies. Also the fact of having gained a certificate did not guarantee you a position by any means. You had to find a berth first, and that meant getting around and looking very hard for one and very often meant going back as an A.B. in which case your time would not count towards the next certificate.

After a very good coaching by Mr. Darby I presented myself at the Board of Trade office in Canning Place and after a thorough examination obtained my certificate of competency and after completing the necessary sea time I eventually returned and obtained my Master's certificate. The depression was still very much in evidence and it was a case of get work where you could when you could. I made several deep water voyages and also worked in steam dredgers, but these were only contract jobs which finished as soon as the work was completed, still they kept 'the wolf from the door' and I was very fort-

unate in being able to obtain work as there were plenty of men with Masters certificates sailing as Able Seamen. I eventually secured a berth as Mate of the s/s DAISY with Captain John Souter (Senior) a Scot from Stonehaven. The DAISY was a short raised-quarter-deck steam coaster which carried about 300 tons and had belonged to J. Monks of Liverpool before Monroe Bros. She was a very good sea boat and I had sailed in her as an A.B. some years before so I was well acquainted with her. I do not remember her ever being held up by bad weather during the time I served in her. I got along very well with Captain Souter and on his recommendation I was promoted as Mate to a larger ship of the same company. She was the ISLAND QUEEN which they had bought from the Channel Islands Steamship Co, but shortly after I joined her she was renamed KYLE QUEEN.

She had an engine amidships with a long raised quarter deck and carried about 900 tons in two holds with two hatches. She had a comfortable bridge with wheelhouse and a roomy bridge deck beneath it, off which were situated the Master and Mates' cabins. From an athwartship alleyway, abaft the Master's cabin, a very imposing stairway led to a nicely furnished saloon off which were four cabins, one of which was used by the Second Mate. At the after end of the saloon and leading off was a mess room with a cabin at either side where the two engineers lived, there was also a good pantry and bathroom. The accommodation amidships was very good but she did not carry a cook, everyone including the Master and Officers providing and cooking their own food. The crew consisted of two firemen, one Able Seaman and two Ordinary Seamen who lived in a common forecastle. Lighting throughout was by paraffin despite the flashy accommodation. One thing that amused me, was the several paraffin bulkhead lamps which were fitted around her engine room casing on deck, were very quickly removed and stowed away to save paraffin. She had been on the general cargo trade from London to the Channel Islands and carried a few passengers, a trade for which she was well suited, but now she was away from her fancy friends and it was intended that she should work for her living with a very much reduced crew than she had previously carried.

She was entirely unsuited for the coastal tramping trade due to the excessive amount of cargo trimming necessary and the propellor tunnel in the after hold prevented effective grab discharge. She was also single bottomed and not very good light ship. While she had been carrying general cargo she had rarely if ever been loaded down to her marks and had a good record for passage making. When she was down to her marks with a cargo of coal from Ayr to Liverpool or a cargo of pig-iron from Barrow to Bowling on the Clyde, she did not take kindly to it and could be as wet as any coaster. She was built by Swan, Hunters on the Tyne and a neighbour of mine had worked there and drawn up her plans and so was very interested in her. She was sold to the Khedivial Mail Shipping Co. of Alexandria, Egypt after a short time and ended up trading round the Mediterranean and Red Sea areas for which trade she was probably more suitable. By coincidence a school chum of mine, who I had not seen for many years, a Captain Frank Parker, was Master of her when she was under the Egyptian flag and thought the world of her.

Whilst I was in the KYLE QUEEN I was asked by the Owner if I was prepared to sit for a Mersey Pilotage certificate. When I replied that I was, he then told me that he would put my name forward and that he would promote me to Master of the NORA (sistership to EDITH and JANE, one of his training ships), in order that I could present my credentials to the Pilotage Committee as a 'serving Master in command', which he thought would be more impressive and would bear more weight.

So I took command of the s/s NORA and joined her in the Albert Dock, Liverpool where she had been lying for some weeks being prepared to undergo survey. The preparations were being carried out by crews of other of the Company's ships, which were laid up due to lack of cargoes. These men were working for half pay which averaged about 30/- a week and their free lodging on board the ship. Many of them were glad to do so, because it was slightly better than the 'dole' when they would have had to pay for their lodgings. They worked a full hard working day of never less than eight hours. Occasionally they would be taken across to Birkenhead to load and trim a cargo of bulk grain which was loaded into another of the Company's ships which were hired as store ships when there was no cargoes available and were laid up with just the Captain and sometimes the Chief Engineer on board (on half pay) to look after them. The regular crew of the NORA were pleased to see me joining her and getting her under way because it meant a return to full pay.

The boiler was filled and steam raised and whilst preparations for leaving were being carried out, I took the ship's register to the Custom House where it was endorsed on the back with an entry which stated that on this day I was appointed Master. I was then instructed to proceed to Port Glasgow, where I was to berth at Lamont's yard and hand the ship over to them for repairs and to return to Liverpool myself and attend the Nautical Academy to be coach-

ed for the Mersey Pilotage certificate and was expected to obtain it by the time the repairs were completed, in about three or four weeks time. Also, I was not to cast off from the berth before five minutes past midnight when the crew would come on full pay, a saving of about two pounds.

So at five minutes past midnight, the tide being suitable, we cast off and proceeded towards Canning Dock entrance to enter the river. The Liverpool docks at that time were very poorly illuminated, mostly by gas lights, and Albert Dock being surrounded by high warehouses was considered to be one of the darkest docks in the system. NORA was a strange ship to me, but I had served in two of her sisters which were almost identical, so I was not entirely lost. Because she was under the tonnage for compulsory pilotage, I did not employ a pilot, neither did we employ a boatman. Although I did not experience too much difficulty getting away, nevertheless I was pleased to clear Canning Dock entrance. On entering the River Mersey, I found that she would barely stem the tide which was still flowing, however as the tide eased she began to crawl ahead. By the time we had reached the Crosby channel we had a strong ebb tide behind us and my worry now was to avoid the buoys upon which she seemed to set with much affection. I also found when checking the compass course that I would be steering towards the Isle of Man on the way down channel, that she had an error of over a point. However the weather was fine and clear and she plodded along comfortably at about six knots. In common with her sisterships she steered like a brewer's dray, but she was not quite as bad as she would be when loaded.

In due course we sighted the Isle of Man where after proceeding through Ramsey Bay and around the Point of Ayre we headed for the Mull of Galloway and along the Scottish coast. During daylight I went on deck to get a better look at my first command; she was certainly due for survey. My old friend Joe from Arklow who had been Second Engineer of the MATJE when I was in her, was now Chief Engineer of the NORA. He took me to see his engine room. I asked him how was the engine running? He replied, "Like a stone crusher." and by the sound of it the description was very suitable. I went into the engine room, which like the others, was combined with the stokehold. It was very hot and very dirty to say the least. Her compound engine was loose on its bedplate and was secured with wire rope stays at each side to the ship's side. These were set tight with bottle-screws, despite which that the engine was loose was very obvious. I asked him "How long has it been like this?" He replied, "As far as I know, always." He was apparently familiar with it and was not too much concerned. The Master's cabin was exactly the same as the EDITH (57), except that the door to the deck had been blanked off with a steel plate, the only means of access now being from a scuttle on the bridge. Like the rest of the ship it was dirty, not having been lived in for some time and smelled damp and mouldy. With the portholes open, by the time we reached Port Glasgow it was just beginning to dry out with the heat from the boiler. The steam steering gear on the bridge had long ceased to function and the hand steering gear was permanently engaged. She was almost the same as the others, except that she had an athwartship saddle-back bunker between the back of the bridge and the funnel, leading to the pocket bunkers on each side. With this she carried a few tons more bunkers than the others, it also dispensed with the lids to the bunkers on the main deck which the others had, which was a relief to me. I was never really happy about those lids, especially after the JENNIE, another ship of the same class, had backed off Monk's Ferry coaling station without closing them and had filled with water through one of them and sank within minutes under Woodside ferry stage, fortunately without loss of life, which was rare in that kind of accident when ships got foul of the ferry stage moorings. The JENNIE was refloated, sold, was repaired and improved upon. She was renamed ASSISTANCE and traded successfully for several years afterwards.

To come back to my story, I arrived at Lamont's Yard, Port Glasgow, where I handed the NORA over to the repairers and returned to Liverpool where I attended the Nautical Academy where I joined a class with two other Masters who were also preparing for examination. Mr. Darby was giving his usual very useful and thorough teaching, and after about three weeks we went to the Pilotage office on Canning Pier head for examination where two of us were successful, the third being turned down for misinterpretation of the bye-laws, but he was successful at his next try. After I informed the Owner of my success, he was pleased and told me he would not be leaving me in the NORA for very long and would be promoting me to a larger ship, which was pretty obvious, because the NORA being exempt from compulsory pilotage on account of her size, my certificate was not working for him although it qualified me for the necessary compulsory trips every time I piloted the ship in or out of the Mersey, to retain the certificate.

I was fairly fortunate in the NORA (63), and got around without too much difficulty trading mostly to the small Irish ports and also the Caernarvon

Jennie.

Bay quarries to the Mersey and Manchester. The first cargo of stone that I took from Carreg-y-llam to Manchester was for the slate wharf in Pomona Dock which was as far as it was possible for a ship of that size to go in the canal and about 35 miles from Eastham, during which time we also had to negotiate five locks and several swing bridges. I entered the canal at Eastham just as it was getting dark. I had no pilot and with the ship steering wild I had to steer the ship myself all the way, the Sailor or the Mate being on the bridge to help me when she took one of her wild sheers. It took me 10 hours on this occasion to transit the Canal and after keeping my watch at sea and doing the pilotage in the River Mersey and again in the Canal, I had been on my feet about 30 hours and steered her for about half of it. I was exhausted when we arrived at the wharf and lay down on the settee to sleep. I was too tired to get undressed and get into bed. We commenced discharging at seven o'clock and at 5 o'clock in the evening discharging was finished, and it was proceed down the canal again that night to be in Birkenhead to start loading coal the following morning at 8 o'clock and sail from there the same night and do the Mersey pilotage again outwards. She was not too bad to steer when she was light ship and I made a quicker passage down the Canal. After a while I began to learn a few tricks when loading her to make her a bit more manageable and although I was quite happy in her I was not sorry when I was told that I was to go to a bigger ship. My successor was not quite so lucky with her, and piled her up on the Wigtownshire coast in November 1938, fortunately without loss of life. She was declared a constructive total loss.

68. The LETTY. Photo; John Clarkson.

12.

69. The KYLE PRINCE.

"Letty" & "Kyle Prince."

Owen G. Spargo

My new ship was to be the LETTY, she was a much larger ship and carried another hundred tons more cargo. She had the two cargo hatches and the bunker hatch forward of the bridge, so that from the bridge to the stern she could be kept reasonably clean. She also had a comfortable wheelhouse which contained the steam steering gear (which worked) although we used hand steering when at sea as was customary. She steered very much better than the 'training ships'. She had a derrick and steam winch at each hatch and a steam windlass on the forecastle head, also a steam capstan aft. The crew lived in the forecastle which was at deck level and was fitted out in the usual manner. It was dry and fairly comfortable, except in bad weather when the crew were unable to get along to it and either slept in the galley which was aft or on the fiddley gratings. The Mate and I lived in cabins underneath the bridge which were at after deck level and entered from the after deck, the Mate's cabin on the port side and mine on the starboard. My cabin had a small saloon and a separate bedroom. It was quite good accommodation with good lighting from portholes on the fore bulkhead and also on the ship's side. Unfortunately it was paraffin lamp illuminated as was the whole ship at night time. The amidship accommodation was panelled throughout in mahogany and must have cost quite a lot to build and it looked quite cosy when cleaned and polished up. The engineers lived in separate cabins opening off a mess room at the after end of the engine room from which it was entered. It was small but quite dry and comfortable. The engine room and stokehold were separated by a Scotch boiler with two furnaces, on account of which she carried one fireman, who was on watch with the Chief Engineer, the Second Engineer doing the stoking needed in his watch. She had a large triple expansion engine with steam reversing and was very handy when manoeuvring. She had a good turn of speed and could do a steady 10 knots without much difficulty, but unfortunately to maintain this she was very heavy on bunkers so I ran her at the more economical speed of 8 knots, only using the reserve speed when necessary. She had a main trysail which I bent on and set whenever the weather suited and it gave her an extra knot in a moderate breeze. I had one Chief Engineer with me who was very keen on it and would trim the sheet without being asked whenever it was necessary. As the sail was as old as the ship which had been built in 1908, and getting the worse for wear, I did not bend it on in bad weather for fear of losing it, but it was certainly a good help in not too strong winds. She had been on time charter for a number of years carrying market garden produce from Maasluis in Holland to Cherry Garden tier in the Pool of London, for this charter she had to maintain ten knots and also arrive on time for the markets. She kept up her time-table and was reputed to have made some very good passages, and being light loaded with produce very probably she did.

When this charter expired, long before I joined her, she returned to the West coast where she had to work for her living on the stone, coal and bulk grain tramping trades. She was quite a nice model of a ship and when painted up looked very smart. I was very pleased to get the command of her, but the Master that I relieved seemed just as pleased to be getting out of her, he was

Reef knot.

also going to a larger vessel. I asked him what he thought of her. He replied he was not keen on her, she was a dangerous bitch that shifted her cargoes, and did all kinds of bad things and predicted that I would soon find out. She was apparently one of three ships at one time owned by T. G. Best, Liverpool. The other ships were HAROLD and FRED. It seemed that the HAROLD had been lost in the vicinity of the South Stack, Holyhead, whether by stranding or foundering I do not know. There was at that time a green conical buoy between the North and South Stacks which would indicate the presence of a wreck; some of the older men maintained that it marked the HAROLD, but there was also a submarine fog bell (S. F. B. on the chart) in that vicinity and it was possible that was what it marked. These submarine fog signals were common at that time, many of the headland lighthouses and lightships were fitted with them and some of the larger ships had hydrophones so that they could obtain a 'fix' from them. I do not think they were a great success, probably being ousted by the radio direction finding system. As far as the coasting men were concerned they might never have existed.

I soon got used to the LETTY (68), and was careful to pay attention to the trimming especially when loading grain and coal cargoes. I found that when loading grain it was not possible to fill the main hatch and put the balance in the fore hold as was the custom with other ships because she would trim too much by the stern, so the procedure was to load on the fore end of the main hold and after end of the fore hold. This left a slope on both ends of the cargo to be secured, whereas if it had been possible to fill the main hold completely and put the balance in the fore hold, then there would have been only one end to secure, thus halving the chances of the cargo shifting. The grain cargoes were secured by placing sacks of grain on the slope at the ends of the cargo, each sack overlapping the other by half of its length and starting from the bottom and forming it up like stairs. Providing the wings were properly trimmed and filled and the ship not allowed to roll too heavily I rarely had any dangerous shifts of grain cargoes. It was one of the systems recommended by the Board of Trade and the cheapest.

I did on one occasion get caught out in a particularly bad storm and so I endeavoured to heave the ship to. I found that she did not heave to very well and would not on that occasion lay any closer than five points to the wind. When I tried to put her on the opposite tack, she would not head the sea to go about and I had to wear her round, not a very safe manoeuvre but it had to be done in order to put her on a course that would take her clear of the land. She would only lay five points to the wind on either tack. I could not run before the wind because there was too much sea and also I had a lee shore astern. I was very pleased when that storm was over. On another occasion we were running before a moderate sea, quite comfortably, with an occasional sea lapping over the forward bulwarks, when a freak big wave came at us from astern and she 'pooped' the sea right over the stern. It carried on along the whole length of the ship, over the boat deck and bridge until we were up to our knees in water in the wheelhouse. It entirely covered the foredeck hatches and winches and derricks and went over the forecastle head. Fortunately all the doors were closed, otherwise we could not possibly have survived it, as it was the engine slowed itself down due to the excessive weight of water. For a few moments the position looked very desparate as she heeled and staggered and eventually lifted and cleared herself. I slowed her down and after ascertaining that all was secure on deck, watched for a lull, turned her around and made for shelter. It was a frightening event which I had only experienced once before and that was in a big ship in the South Atlantic. My next experience was to be in light ship condition when she would not face up to a strong head wind and 'blew away' with me and I had to run for shelter. So although she was a nice model and had a good turn of speed and comfortable accommodation, she demanded respect, but despite her tricks, I was in her for a considerable time and grew very fond of her.

Unfortunately she was lost with all hands after leaving Liverpool on the 21st of August 1940 in a severe gale on a voyage to Buncrana. She took several of my friends down with her and was one of a number of coasters lost with all hands in that gale. I was pilot on board a similar coaster, the HARLEY, hove to in the vicinity in the same gale and had been unable to disembark at the Bar pilot boat. Fortunately the HARLEY was only part loaded otherwise I would not be writing this now.

From the LETTY I was moved to a larger ship called the KYLE PRINCE of about 480 tons deadweight capacity. She had been built by the Dublin Dockyard Co., and had been owned by M. Murphy as the ITA. She was quite a smart strong little ship (69) with a long raised quarter deck and two hatches with the bridge between them and had double bottom water ballast tanks. Her open bridge had the steam steering gear in a deck-house below it. Steam steering was in use all the time she was underway as there was no provision for hand steering, either on the bridge or in the deck-house below. She had many what were then patent gadgets such as pumps, an alarm bell which sounded when the engine was put the wrong way during reversing, a patent ash hoist (which did not work) and pumps which appeared identical but which were in fact opposites of each other. We did not find this out until we tried to cannibalise one to repair the other and found that they could not be substituted. She had a triple expansion engine with steam reversing gear and could be as handy as a tug when things were going well, but she had a patent H.P. valve which they called a 'Match-box valve' which nobody seemed to be able to set correctly and this had a nasty habit of jamming when reversing and the engine would not go astern. When this happened at close quarters she generally came off second best and had several new stems to her credit due to hitting quay walls and other things. She also had a reputation for shifting her cargoes due to very heavy rolling and was called by the seafaring fraternity in Dublin who had sailed in her, 'the rolling bitch'. A lifeline which was stretched athwartships across her bridge and fore and aft slats of wood on the bridge deck seemed to support this. By her movements I would think that she was very stiff; there was no stability data aboard. She could certainly roll and I could only compare her to a 'Kelly' lamp which was so weighted at the bottom that it quickly uprighted itself when tilted. She also had a reputation for being very wet in bad weather. But despite all these bad habits which were attributed to her, she was quite a smart looking ship and it had to be very bad weather to stop her, even if she did go through a head sea as often as she went over it.

I joined her in the West Float, Birkenhead where I found our Superintendent busily putting the finishing touches to a cement box which he was building on the starboard hawse-pipe, my predecessor having tried its strength against the quay when entering the Alfred Locks, for which he blamed the main engine sticking. His story however, was not accepted and he was accused of having too much way on the ship and suspended, hence my appearance. I made my way to the Superintendent who was working from a stage suspended over the bow. He was smoothing the cement with his hands into the shape of the moulding at the edge of the hawse-pipe and making a very neat job of it. I asked him would I be able to use the anchor? He replied, "Yes, but only in an emergency" also that he would not be finished with it for a couple of hours. So I left him to it and returned a few hours later to find him standing on the quay admiring his handiwork. The cement hawse-pipe was an exact replica of its partner even to the rivet heads which he had fashioned round the moulded edge, he had even painted it black and it was hardly possible to distinguish any repairs to it.

I left the berth to proceed to sea, having to pass through a lifting bridge on route, I had warned the Bridge Master I was coming so that he could be ready for me. I approached the bridge very slowly and endeavouring to use the main engine as little as possible to avoid having to put the engine astern, but the bridge was slow in opening and eventually I had to ring 'slow astern'. Nothing happened except the rattle of the reversing engine and hissing steam. By now the ship was getting closer to the bridge and the Engineer in his efforts to get the engine to go astern was giving her the occasional 'kick ahead'. I then rang for 'full speed astern' and getting no response, I told the Mate to let go the port anchor and after letting go a few fathoms of chain, to check her with it. The anchor taking hold brought the ship to a stop about a foot away from the bridge. I got the Mate to put a rope ashore to hold her and put the engine room telegraph to 'stop' and let the engineer sort out his problems. In the meantime the Bridge Master was nearly exploding on the quayside and shouting that the ship was a menace on the high seas (and probably me) and was not fit to cross the dock. I told him, "The next time I blow my whistle for the bridge to be opened try moving yourself a bit faster or I might be taking your bridge with me." I had a good many similar engine failures, but was fortunate in being in a position where I was able to avoid damage.

I carried many cargoes of grain, coal and also granite chippings from the Caernarvon Bay quarries without mishap or them shifting, the only cargo that moved in my time was a cargo of fire bricks which I took from Llanelly to Glasgow. These were stowed flat in stacks and were neat and tidy when stowed and were the last cargo you would expect to move. We had a little bad weather on passage but not enough to make us uncomfortable or hold us up. I did not think for a moment that it would affect the cargo. However when we opened the hatches on arrival in Glasgow, the whole cargo was in a shambles, it looked as if it had been lifted from underneath and shuffled. Apart from this occasion, I was never troubled with shifting cargoes but I always took great care with the trimming and securing of the cargo and personally inspected it before signing the stowage certificate and often had to make them go over their work again if it was not to my satisfaction. After all it was a letter of indemnity that I was signing and more or less accepting responsibility myself.

My predecessor relieved me in the KYLE PRINCE having 'done penance' in one of the smaller ships and was unfortunate in losing her when she sank in Caernarvon Bay when her cargo of granite chippings shifted. There was no loss of life. I was transferred to the larger TEST.

Swivel.

Plate 72   MATJE of Monroe Bros., arriving at Bristol Docks.

13.

73. SPRAY purchased with
the TEST.

The 'Armchair' - S/s "Test."

Owen G. Spargo

"She is an 'armchair' Captain!" So quoth the owner of the S/S TEST when
he appointed me as her Master in 1936. She had been acquired by Monroe
Brothers of Liverpool from Ellis & MacHardy of Aberdeen in 1934 together
with their s/s SPRAY (later renamed DUNVEGAN) for a reputed 'song'. Both
ships had been employed for years trading between Blyth and other North East
coast coal ports to Aberdeen, with occasional voyages from Aberdeen and
nearby ports with barrels of salt herrings to Hamburg and other Continental
ports. Both ships had the reputation of rarely being held up by bad weather,
and taking into consideration the fact that they would be full up with all cargoes
and also light on their marks they would be in very good trim and able to
take on anything in the way of weather that they were likely to encounter. That
they had made some very good passages there was no doubt, but that they also
had taken some very hard beatings in doing so was evident as I was later to
find out.

The TEST was a typical three masted, long raised quarter deck type
coaster of the period, except that she did not have a mizzen mast when I
joined her; it probably having been removed over the years. She had a raised
forecastle head, forward well deck between forecastle head and bridge and
raised after deck from bridge to stern. One very distinguishing feature was
her 'whale back' stern. She had two hatches to one hold, which was divided
by a wood bulkhead. She had a steam windlass, two steam winches, and steam
steering gear. Below the bridge was the wheelhouse with steam steering gear
and below the wheelhouse the Saloon and Master and Mates accommodation,
all situated between the two hatches. Access to the accommodation was by a
stairway at the after end of the wheelhouse on the starboard side. There was
no other means of access or exit, although both rooms had wash basins, water
for these had to be carried by bucket from aft. They drained into a receptacle
which had to be taken up on deck to be emptied. There was no toilet amidships, the officers toilet being in the after end of the engine room casing, so
that in bad weather the old 'bucket and chuck it' was not uncommon to escape
a wetting going aft.

The bunker, boiler and engine room in that order were aft of the main
hatch. She carried water ballast in double bottom MacIntyre tanks, the margin
plates of which developed a nasty habit of fracturing along the bend at the top
where they had been bent to join the tank top. There was a large fore peak
tank and small after peak tank. She had one Scotch Boiler with two furnaces
at its forward end. The furnaces were constructed of smooth riveted plates
and not corrugated as they were in later vessels and so did not have the
strength or rigidity of the corrugated furnaces. Abaft the stokehold, the engine
room was separated from the stokehold by a makeshift wood and tin plate
bulkhead. The main engine was big and gave an impression of power which
indeed it had, the cylinder tops being higher than the level of the after deck.
It was a triple-expansion engine with hand wheel reversing and had combined
circulating, air, feed, and bilge pumps all worked by a rocker shaft connected
to the cross heads. She had also an independent Whitworth type feed pump and
an independent general service and ballast pump completed the engine room
lay out. Lighting was by paraffin lamps as indeed was the remainder of the
ship. In the top of the engine room was a warping winch engine, the shafts of
which passed through the engine room casing at either side and connected to

large heavy cast iron warping drums. The shafts of these had been bent so many times over the years and faired by heating that the metal had become soft and eventually one shaft broke and had to be renewed. They were fine while they lasted, but whether the drum ends were too heavy or the shaft too weak I do not know but it was not long before they were bent again and turning eccentrically and with their ends painted white with red centres would make you wonder if you were seeing things when they were revolving.

The two engineers lived in separate rooms which opened off the after end of the engine room at deck level, whilst below deck, aft and over the after peak tank was a small messroom with two tiny cabins, the whole of which was occupied by the Bosun who received 2/6d. a week more than the A.B.s for which he had to trim all the lamps in the ship but excluding the engine room and perform the duties which were normally done in other ships by the Bosun, Lamptrimmer and Second Mate combined. He certainly worked for his 2/6d. a week and private accommodation. The Sailors and Firemen lived forward in a forecastle which was below decks and had at some time formed part of the fore hold from which it was separated by a wood bulkhead, which although fairly dust proof was certainly not gas proof, and when strong smelling cargoes were being carried, such as chemical fertilisers with an ammonia content or even cement or pitch, the smell reaching the forecastle could be very unpleasant to say the least, but despite these discomforts the crews remained, times were so bad, that they would suffer anything rather than be unemployed.

I joined the TEST at Berwick-on-Tweed, where I found her fully loaded with coal for Belfast, although she was no oil painting I immediately took a liking to her, and I found her to be an exceptionally good sea boat, easy to handle, and very easy on herself in a seaway, but she had been driven to her utmost and after forty four years was beginning to show it in many ways.

I once read a book on ship construction, in which to describe the stresses on the various parts of the ship, the author described an imaginary conversation between various parts of the ship commencing with a rivet in the keel and progressing to the different parts as they groaned and complained in a sea-way. The TEST did just that! My first experience of this was when I lay in my bunk I heard the ships' plates, beam-knees and wood work in the cabin creak and groan, more like one would expect to hear in a wooden ship. Later when I took my watch in the wheelhouse, I noticed the front of the wheelhouse swaying from side to side as the ship rolled and saw that two stays had been fitted to counteract this. These were held in place by nuts and bolts, and periodically with the working of the ship these nuts and bolts would work loose and had to be tightened. However, she was a very strongly constructed ship, with reverse frames and broad longitudinal stringers, bar keel and very many other constructional aids to strength and doubtless had been a very fine strong ship in her day and to me still was, but she had a good many soft spots which I was to find out during the several years I served in her, yet although at times she wobbled like a jelly, I believe the official term for it is wracking, I grew very fond of her.

We had an uneventful voyage to Belfast, going North about, through the Pentland Firth where I made the mistake of not putting the steering gear into steam steering before entering St. John's Sound; we had been steering with hand gear since clearing Berwick. St. John's Sound is the channel nearest to the Scottish mainland, between the mainland and St. John's Island, a very narrow channel with very strong currents and eddies and at its Western end a reef of rocks marked with a perch and having a strong tide race close to it called 'The Men of Mey'. Not too difficult a channel to negotiate in a good steering ship providing you chose the right state of tide, before the tide started to run too strong, but not a place to be treated lightly, where because of the strong currents and eddies and overfalls the helmsman needs to be very much on the alert not to allow the ship to sheer and where inattention could very quickly lead to disaster. On this occasion the TEST was still in hand-steering and although she was a very good steering ship normally, as soon as she felt the strong currents she became like something possessed and started to sheer very wildly. Had she been in steam-steering it would not have been very difficult to correct her sheers, but she was in hand gear which was much slower and harder to apply, and required a lot of strength. On this occasion I had got into a position where I did not have the room or time to change to steam-steering, so I just had to carry on with the hand-steering gear and with the wild sheers she was taking in the strong currents and eddies, I was very much relieved when she was clear of St. John's Sound and I had left the Men of Mey astern. I had experienced quite a thrill and had a few anxious moments and had also learnt the lesson not to tackle the Pentland Firth in hand-steering again.

The steam-steering engine was in the wheelhouse under the bridge and was connected to the quadrant by the rod and chain method. That is, there were two lengths of chain secured to the drum of the steering engine and then led around sheaves, one on each side of the lower bridge deck, to the after deck,

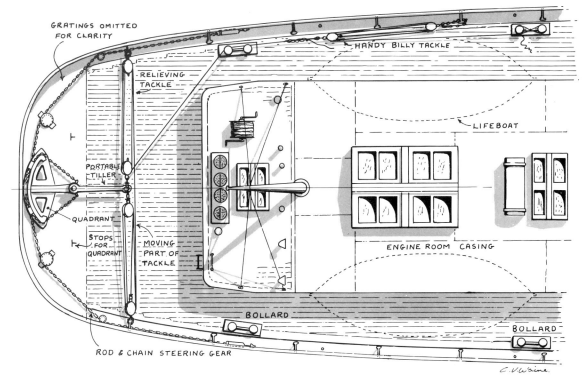

GRATINGS OMITTED FOR CLARITY

RELIEVING TACKLE

HANDY BILLY TACKLE

LIFEBOAT

PORTABLE TILLER

QUADRANT

STOPS FOR QUADRANT

MOVING PART OF TACKLE

ENGINE ROOM CASING

BOLLARD

BOLLARD

ROD & CHAIN STEERING GEAR

C.V.Waine.

75. The above method of rigging a relieving tackle was used on most coasters. The larger East Coast colliers were eventually fitted with a friction brake making use of a stout vertical axle on top of which was a pulley wheel. The other end of the axle was secured to the rudder quadrant. Around the pulley wheel was a turn of wire the ends of which were made fast to either side of the deck, and could be adjusted by means of a tightening screw. The 'Dunston' rudder brake came into use later and involved more mechanics and was very good and effective.

where they connected up to steel rods at the end of which they connected up with another length of chain in the middle of which was a steel spring, which was to ease the tension on the chain, and also acted as a safety measure. The chain then continued along the deck through various leads and sheaves to the quadrant, to which it was attached with a bottle-screw which was put there for the purpose of adjusting the chain when it became slack, which it very often did after a bad passage. To have to shorten the chain by as much as four links was not unusual when the bottle screws had taken up as much as they could. The steering chains came under the Board of Trade regulations, and were put ashore every so often for testing and annealing. The steam-steering gear could be converted into hand-steering by assuring that the quadrant and helm indicator were both amidships then shutting off the steam, and then very quickly disengaging the clutch to the steam gear and engaging the clutch to the hand gear, not a very difficult operation, but occasionally it would jam in transit when, especially if the weather was bad, it could be a bit of a problem for a few minutes.

The hand-steering was always used when in open water, for the reason that she steered better and she saved on bunkers and boiler feed water, but during heavy weather there was a heavy kick with backlash and constant jolting on the wheel, which could very easily throw an unwary helmsman over the top of the wheel. In these conditions it would sometimes take two men to hold her. This kicking and jolting caused wear and tear on the rudder pintles and also stretching of the steering chains. To reduce this wear and jolting we rigged an arrangement called a 'Relieving Tackle' not a modern arrangement by any means as it probably originated in the times of the very old sailing ships, but never the less a very simple and effective remedy. It consisted of two double luff tackles with a continuous rope rove through them. One tackle was connected on each side of a small portable tiller which fitted on the rudder post when required, the other ends of the tackle were made fast, often to bollards at each side. The falls were then set tight with a handy billy tackle, these luff tackles then worked with the movements of the rudder and acted as a very effective damper (75). This tiller was also for use as an emergency steering gear in the event of a steering chain or similar breakage, in which event two separate tackles had to be used preferably in conjunction with the steam winch or capstan as it was not possible to use the tiller, as such, on its own. The effect of rigging the relieving tackles was immediate. It effectively stopped the kicking and backlash, and although it had the effect of making the wheel harder to turn, it was much easier to steer, and with the tackles rigged we were quite comfortable in the wheelhouse even in bad weather.

From Belfast we went to Partington in the Manchester Ship Canal in ballast, and encountered strong head winds all the way which slowed her down a great deal, sometimes to as little as two knots, still she was easy on herself and making some headway. Bunkers were cheap, trade was slack, and the owners got very annoyed when their ships had to take shelter and lay windbound, so I kept her at it, tacking her like a sailing ship to assist her, and occasionally having to wear her when she would not go about on the opposite tack. After a long passage we eventually arrived at Partington where I went to the telephone to inform the manager of our arrival. Radio telephony was then very much in its infancy, and mostly confined to steam trawlers. We could pick up their conversations on our private receiving sets and used to listen to their conversations as a form of entertainment until the G.P.O. stepped in and requested them to use lighter adjectives. I often reminisce over the telephone conversation I had with the Manager. We arrived at about half past eleven at night, when he was probably just settling down. It went on these lines:-

Manager: "Oh, so you've arrived. Where have you been to an anchor?"
Self: "I haven't been to an anchor."
Manager: "Have you punched through all this?"
Self: "Yes."
Manager: "How much bunkers have you left?"
Self: "Two tons,"
Manager: "Good night."

I am sure he must have slept soundly after that news. On another occasion when bound to Sligo with a cargo of coal. I arrived off Sligo in a Westerly gale and the weather being unfit to cross the Sligo bar, I was left with the alternatives of remaining hove to and face the rigours of the Atlantic, or seek shelter. I decided to seek shelter and run to Broadhaven, a tiny inlet nearby, tricky to enter in a Westerly gale but giving excellent shelter once inside, and very sparsely inhabited then. I had only been anchored a couple of hours, when a man came off from the shore in a curragh (a canvas boat peculiar to the West of Ireland) with a telegram from the owners which read "presume another night in bed", so although we had no radio they got to know our whereabouts very quickly. After having experienced a hectic few hours approaching and negotiating the very narrow entrance to Broadhaven I was in no mood to make comment, so I sent the reply back via the boatman in one word "correct". I never heard any further on this, although I fully expected to on my return!

At Partington we loaded a cargo, of coal for Cork, and as we approached Holyhead the wind freshened from the S.W. and, as was customary in coasting ships, instead of setting a course for the Tuskar Light House off the S.E. coast of Wexford which meant we would be punching into a head sea, I set course for the Codling Light Vessel which is off Wicklow thereby putting the wind and sea a couple of points on the port bow and allowing the ship to make better progress. When getting near the Codling Light Vessel and by then getting the lee of the Irish land I would then set a more Southerly course to clear the Arklow and Blackwater banks. The new course would put the wind and sea now a couple of points on the starboard bow and with the lee of the land, allow us to make good progress. If the weather became very severe we would go closer to Wicklow and then inside the Arklow banks in smoother water under the lee of the land until we reached Rosslare, where if the weather had deteriorated we were handy to slip into Rosslare Bay which was a very good and favourable windbound anchorage for coasters, schooners and steam trawlers. I have seen over fifty ships anchored at Rosslare on numerous occasions. As a S.W. gale in this vicinity invariably veers to the West and then North West before it dies away and thereby comes off the land along the South coast of Ireland, we could then make a good smooth water passage by doing a bit of 'rock dodging' going between the Tuskar Rock and Carnsore Point and inside the Barrels and Coningbeg Light Vessels and then set course under the shelter of the land to the Westward.

On this occasion by the time we had reached Rosslare the wind had veered to the Westward and gone West by North which was barely giving shelter along the South coast of Ireland and had moderated to about force 5 with a moderate Westerly sea, so I shaped down inside the Tuskar and Barrels and Coningbeg lights and then set course towards Roches Point clearing the Pollock Rock. By now we were punching a moderate head sea but she was going along very comfortably and being now clear of any immediate dangers I went below and lay on the settee. After a little while she started to put some heavy water over the bows and I thought, "some arm chair!"

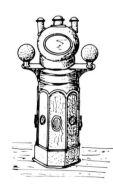

She continued to make heavy weather of it, so I decided to go up and see if the weather was deteriorating. When I reached the wheelhouse I found the weather to be improving but the helmsman having difficulty in steering, so I slowed the ship down and sent the Mate to sound the tanks and bilges, he returned after doing so and stated that everywhere was dry. In case he was getting false readings, I also instructed the engineer to try the pumps everywhere, and he came back with the same answer, so I hauled the ship in closer to the land to get as much shelter as possible, and was glad to reach Cobh harbour, where the Pilot greeted me with "she is very deep for'ard Skipper."

By now we were in smooth water and I was able to get down to investigate for myself and found that the original crew's quarters which was right in the bows under the forecastle head and below decks, over the fore peak tank, was full of water to a depth of about 4 feet and must have held 20 tons or more, so it was no wonder she was wet. There was no means of pumping this compartment, so early next morning I got all hands to it with buckets to bail it out until we could reach the manhole door cover to the fore peak which was in this compartment. Once this was reached it was fairly easy to ease this and allow the remainder of the water to drain into the fore peak tank. It was then quickly removed by the engine room pump. There was no lighting in this compartment other than from the electric torch I was carrying, which was probably why it had been condemned as accommodation. When I was able to enter the compartment and look around I switched off my torch and saw daylight coming through a small hole in a plate near the hawse pipe. I knew it could not be damage because I had never been near enough to anything to do any. I asked for a knife to further investigate and of course nobody had a knife, so I sent one of them to obtain one and also to bring a hammer and drift from the engine room, thinking to enlarge the hole and seal it with a bolt and grommet. Whilst I was waiting for the tools I put my hand into my waistcoat pocket and found the stub of a lead pencil so I poked this into the hole and without any difficulty pushed the pencil right through the plate. By the time the tools arrived I had found several holes and did not need the hammer to force the drift through to enlarge them, I enlarged them with the aid of a marline spike and then fitted bolts and rubber insertion pads, on top of which making full use of the reverse frames, I built a cement box in the frame spaces around the leaks and when this set it was absolutely water tight. It was in the ship, together with several more that I put in her at later dates until I left her several years later and never gave me cause to worry although I always kept a watchful eye over them.

From Cork we went to Barry Dock to load a cargo of cement in jute bags for Peterhead in Scotland, the cement came from a factory at a place called Rhws, a few miles West of Barry and was for use in the construction of the breakwater at Peterhead. I went through the Minches and Hebrides to Peterhead and enjoyed navigating through the various sounds and narrows. I have travelled through a great many of them at different times, including the Sound of Corrievrechan and Kyles of Lochalsh, some of them in the dark, long before the days of Radar and when I have made the same journeys since with the aid of Radar I still wonder how I did them.

I duly arrived at Peterhead which was not the busy port in those days that it is now with the oil rig traffic. Its greatest asset was the large fleet of steam herring drifters and kippering houses, but at that time there was a slump in the drifter trade and many were laid up and sold for breaking at give away prices, consequently many of the fishermen were unemployed. My Chief Engineer belonged to Peterhead and through him I got to know a great many of the fishermen and employed several of them at different times and found them excellent.

From Peterhead we went in ballast to Dundee where we loaded a cargo of potatoes for Dieppe, and experienced dense fog all the way. I was very relieved to arrive at Dieppe having been on the bridge most of the time and getting little or no sleep. From Dieppe we went to Le Havre where we loaded three propellors which had come off the French liner NORMANDIE and were being returned to Stowage wharfe, Deptford, close to Deadman's or Execution Dock for correction of some fault. They were made of bronze and extremely valuable and I was just able to get them into our holds by careful manipulation. I did not have a chart of the River Thames above the Nore and could not obtain one in Le Havre. Still I was not unduly worried because I was well acquainted with the Thames (I never used a Pilot) and I mused to myself when going up the Thames, did the last Master who had taken these propellors on a sea voyage do so on his 'know how'?

From Deptford we went down river to Swanscombe, a cement factory wharfe near Greenhithe where we loaded a cargo of cement in bags for Morpeth Dock, Birkenhead which we discharged with our own derricks and winches. These cement cargoes were dirty cargoes with the dust getting everywhere, also the crew had to be handy at all times to close the hatches should it start to rain. After discharging the cement cargo we went to Partington to load coal, again for Peterhead and so we had circled the whole of England, Wales and Scotland and this was more or less the pattern of our voyages for the first year or so.

After a while we started to get trouble with the boiler with the tubes leak-

ing in the back ends and occasionally leaks in the combustion chamber. On one occasion whilst on passage from Peterhead southwards, the Chief Engineer came to me and advised me to get her in somewhere as soon as possible, so I went with him to see for myself what the situation was and found the Second Engineer and the two firemen trying to maintain steam with the Starboard furnace whilst a jet of boiling water was coming through the Port furnace door which was open and striking the bulkhead; boiling water was running in a steady stream from the ash pits and they had tried to channel this into the bilges with the use of planks and ashes. I was able to look into the Port furnaces by keeping to one side of the jet of water and saw that the jet was coming from the back of the combustion chamber above the level of the bridge of firebricks where the back plate would be in the direct line of the flame. I also saw water dripping from the back of the tube plate, the steam was well down and the donkey feed pump was clattering away pumping cold water into the boiler, the extra feed from the main engine-driven pump being unable to maintain the water level. We were able to close the Port furnace door and shore it with timber from the outside. This enabled the men to pass it without being scalded, but of course we lost the use of the Port furnace.

I decided then to make for the nearest port and fortunately Blyth was only about 10 miles distant and dead to leeward, the wind being Easterly about force four, so I set a course for Blyth which I reached after about 3 hours. The main engine by this time was only maintaining steerage way and we were being helped by the wind, but to enter Blyth harbour I had to bring her on a Northerly course which would bring the wind and sea on the starboard beam and when I could really do with a little extra power to manoeuvre. However, I had to make the best of it and on arrival off Blyth I saw that the 'Block' signals were not on, that is the visual signal prohibiting entry, so I just entered unannounced without making a fuss. Had I said I was coming in with boiler trouble I would have very soon had people down making enquiries and nobody likes publicity including myself, so I put her alongside the first ship I came to and by the time we had passed our mooring lines to the shore there was not enough steam pressure to turn the windlass to heave in the slack of the ropes so it had been a near thing. We then had a closer look at the damage and found a vertical fracture about 3" long on the back plate and many smoke tubes leaking. Had it been leaking tubes only, our Engineers would have dealt with it themselves either by expanding the tube ends against the tube plate or fitting tube-stoppers and if this were not possible blocking off the tube, but the fracture required attention beyond their means.

I got into touch with the owners who told me to put the job out to tender and accept the lowest. This I did, but in the meantime the weather got very cold and a severe frost set in, we lit coal fires in the stokehold to keep the frost from the boiler, and also drained the windlass, winches and steering engine as well as the deck steam and exhaust pipes which were copper, a routine procedure in frosty weather. The boiler by now had been emptied of water but apparently it did not like the cold, for the small fracture in the combustion chamber crept and extended to about a foot long. The Insurance surveyor had by now been called in and he found several more sore spots including leaking rivets in the furnace crown plates and the crowns down below the permissible distance so that with one thing and another it had developed into a sizeable job. Eventually the Board of Trade surveyor showed up and he had a very good scrutiny of our navigation lights and life-saving equipment fortunately these were in order, but he requested that the lifeboats be swung out and lowered into the water. This we did, and he now being satisfied, we now had the job of getting them back on board again. This was an easy enough job when we had steam power to help us but now without steam it was again a case of all hands, there were only nine of us all told, to the falls to lift them up and swing them inboard again. Not a very hard or long job, but when the Engineers and firemen were busy in the engine room and we had all been occupied in pumping out the engine room and stokehold bilges, which had filled from the leaking boiler, with the emergency hand pump and with the now freezing weather and snow flurries it was a job that we could very well have done without.

78. Blyth Piers.

The weather had by now developed into a very severe frost and all the steam coasters were taking frost precautions. The deck winches in most of them were kept ticking-over and where this had been unsuccessful they were de-frosting the deck steam pipes, most of which were copper, by means of wrapping them with paraffin soaked rags and then setting fire to the rags. We were fortunate on this occasion because we had managed to get everything well-drained before the frost set in, but many others were less fortunate and a cloud of steam from the deck of one or another announced the fact that a steam pipe had burst with the frost. Still not everybody was complaining, the local copper smiths and ship repairers were having a brief bonanza. Repairs to steam pipes were not too serious and minor ones were very often dealt with by fastening a clamp around them, but if the winch or windlass cylinders got frozen up and cracked, that was an expensive job because they were made of cast iron and had to be renewed although repairs were often attempted by the inevitable cement box, and blobs of cement around the cylinders of winches were not uncommon. They were not a success and cast iron welding had not then been invented.

Eventually after a couple of weeks the repairs were completed, surveyed and passed. We had lost the original charter through the delay and we were now fixed to load a cargo of coal for Cork. The weather had by now got a little warmer, but unfortunately the hard frost had affected the coal loading due to the coal being frozen in the wagons. Loading was taking longer because the coal had to be dug out of the wagons, and consequently a large number of ships were waiting to be loaded.

However, we eventually moved under the staithes where the coal was loaded by means of chutes fed from a hopper on top of the staithes into which the wagons had been emptied, a quite quick and cheap, economical way of loading. The Northumberland coal being very light, our holds were completely full and we were in good trim and so we made a good passage to Cork averaging over nine knots which was quite a good speed at that time.

From Cork we went to Carreg-y-llam, a granite quarry in Caernarvon Bay a little to the Eastward of Nevin where we loaded granite chippings by a conveyor belt and chute alongside a short wooden jetty which extended seaward from the quarry and where we could only load in fine weather or when the wind was off the Land, but despite its remoteness a large amount of granite chippings were made and exported from there and despatch was quite good. We could load 600 tons in under two hours without any difficulty, but the ground swell which was always there, necessitated the crew being in constant attendance to the moorings during loadings and very often position had to be maintained with the assistance of the main engine. Once loaded it was a case of back off as soon as possible and away on passage before the weather deteriorated. We carried many cargoes from the Caernarvon Bay quarries mostly to the Mersey and Preston but quite often, also to London. In-between times we would run cargoes of slurry coal from Ayr in Scotland and also from Barry Dock in the Bristol Channel to Carriers Dock in Liverpool for the Clarence Dock power station for which Monroe Brothers had a contract to carry coal.

At certain times of the year there are freshets in the river at Ayr and a considerable surge is experienced which necessitates the use of 'junks' which were heavy rope moorings. During these surges the ship would range in the berth which is a sandstone quay and had to be well fendered and care had to be taken not to let the ship list away from the quay or her bilge would be exposed to the quay and severe chafing could result. Ayr was blamed for many a damaged bilge strake, as good an excuse as any I suppose! We seldom made these short journeys, more often doing longer hauls right around the United Kingdom and to and from the Continent, from the River Elbe to Brest. At this period she was a typical Home Trade tramp coaster. (See map page 96).

In due course the boiler started to give trouble again with the smoke tubes leaking and this meant that the Engineers would have to lower the steam pressure on the boiler, draw the fire, and place wood hatch boards and wet sacks on top of the fire bars. Then they would go through the furnace into the back end combustion chamber and stop the leaks by expanding the tubes with a tool called a tube expander and caulking the stay tubes when necessary. A very hot, and since this job was often done with steam pressure on the boiler, a very dangerous one. I have seen these men come out of a furnace with their clothing scorched and their faces bright red and the sweat pouring off them, and I do not doubt that it shortened their lives in many cases. The boiler continued to get worse and the Engineers were having to spend several hours in the combustion chamber every time we got into port. Only men who were desperate for work could have put up with such conditions. Eventually it got so bad that the tubes were leaking at sea and blocking up so that we had to stop at sea whilst the firemen and engineers cleared the tubes to try and raise steam. Every time I reported it I was asked to try and keep her

going until she was due for boiler cleaning which happened every three months.

Together with the recurring bouts of tube trouble we got the occasional 'weep' from the ship's sides mostly at the back of the frames where the corrosion over the years had just eaten away the plates and after my experience of the leak in the bow, I was always on the lookout for these which, by virtue of their position, were easily dealt with by fitting a cement box. Also the margin plate of the double bottom ballast tanks started to give trouble by developing fractures which allowed the tank to leak into the hold bilges and creating slack tanks and also requiring the hold bilges to be frequently pumped out with more demands on the poor old boiler. Things finally came to a head whilst on passage from Ayr to Liverpool with a cargo of slurry coal. We were due to arrive in Liverpool at about 5 a.m. on a Saturday morning in which event we would have been discharged and sailing again on Saturday night to the Caernarvon Bay quarries to load a cargo of granite chippings and would have been back again in Liverpool with a cargo of chippings ready to discharge on the Monday morning. However, after passing the Isle of Man and about half way to the Bar Light Vessel the Chief Engineer came to me to say the boiler tubes were again leaking badly and he would have to stop the engines whilst they cleared them because he could not maintain steam. So we stopped and then it was a case of 'all hands on the job'.

I came on deck for a breath of fresh air after working in the stokehold and, leaning on the rail, I noticed that the ship looked deep in the water. The weather was calm with the sea like glass so I moved along to look at her plimsoll mark and saw that the disc was out of sight! I immediately got the sounding rod and sounded the ballast tanks which were dry and then the hold bilge which showed six feet of water, so obviously we had also developed a leak. There was not sufficient steam on the boiler to work the pumps to pump the hold bilges out, so I rigged the emergency hand pump and stationed a couple of the hands pumping the bilges with it, it was not very successful. Eventually after being stopped for several hours and fitting stoppers in some tubes we were able to get steam on the boiler once more and get under way again. The boiler was still leaking very badly and the firemen were having difficulty in maintaining steam plus the fact that we now had to use the steam pump to pump out the hold bilges which were not gaining and not doing down either. We were making an additional demand on the already over-worked boiler, so I resumed my course for the Mersey and fortunately the tide was in our favour because by now we could only make about four knots in the calm weather.

We eventually arrived in Liverpool about 12 hours late. When I telephoned the manager I was greeted with "what is it this time?" I replied boiler trouble amongst other things, so I was told to instruct the Engineers to blow down the boiler forthwith and scalers had been engaged to clean it the following day, Sunday. I then told him about the leak and without the boiler to supply steam to pump the bilges we would be unable to control it, so boiler cleaning had to be postponed until the leak was located and dealt with on the Monday morning.

We duly commenced discharging by grab and when the grab had got about half way down the cargo, the leak made itself obvious, it was a longitudinal crack about a foot long in the ship's side and apparently the weight of the cargo against it had prevented it from allowing the water to gain its full force, but as soon as the cargo was clear of it there was no mistake and the water was coming in fairly steadily. The dockers made a hasty exit, but we were able to get sufficient cargo out with the grab to bring the leak above the level of the outside water and then at last pump the bilges dry. The leak was then dealt with as a temporary measure by inserting wood wedges and covering with the usual cement box. After discharging we moved across the dock to a lay-by berth where the boiler was blown down for cleaning and any necessary repairs to be carried out. Upon completion of this I was informed that we had been fixed on 'time charter' by the Cunard Line on a regular general cargo, fruit and vegetable service from France and the Channel Islands to Liverpool, and so the old girl was moving up in society!

14.

S/S "Test" joins Cunard.

81. the TEST.

Owen G. Spargo

So the 'Arm-Chair' was to be re-upholstered and be elevated in society. The time charter that had been obtained for the TEST was regarded amongst the coasting fraternity as one of the plums of the Home Trade. It had been in existence for a good many years, having been previously held by various companies, including Monks of Liverpool, Clark & Grounds of Liverpool and Robertsons of Glasgow who had their S/S BERYL chartered for several years. During the time the BERYL was on charter, the Cunard had decided to charter an additional ship, so the S/S STAGHOUND of Monroe Brothers of Liverpool was chartered. After the STAGHOUND had been on charter for a year or so, through reasons best known to themselves Cunard dispensed with the services of the BERYL and engaged the TEST to take her place. The charter was to run general cargo, fine goods, and marked garden produce between Liverpool and Jersey, Guernsey and Le Havre. It was a liner service, run to a very tight schedule and time table. Whilst allowances were made for extreme weather, the Cunard Line expected this schedule to be maintained. The ships were run to connect with the Market Garden trade, and labour was laid on in anticipation of the ships being on time.

The sequence of the ports varied with the seasonal results of the Channel Islands market gardens. As a rule either Jersey or Guernsey would be the final port before returning to Liverpool where we were expected to be in berth in Huskisson Dock, Liverpool, ready for discharging at 6 am. on the Monday morning. Everything was run to a timetable, and for the first few months the TEST behaved herself and had no difficulty in running to schedule. The old 'Arm-Chair' was getting preferential treatment, and she responded nobly. Our sailing time from the berth in Liverpool was 9 pm. on alternate Fridays. Cunard Line had everything arranged for a quick departure, all bridges were swung open without delay and the locks ready and waiting for us. We could not have had better attention if we had been the QUEEN MARY. All very un-usual for the old TEST who was more accustomed to 'keep that coaster out of the way' while the regular traders got preference.

But before all this, the ship had to have a spruce up before taking on her new duties, and as speed was to be the essence of the job she was put into dry dock for a very quick 'scrub and brush up'. Obvious essential repairs to the hull and tank top were carried out, the boiler meantime being scaled and obvious leaks attended to. The main engine cylinders were opened up, where it was found that the piston rings on the H.P. piston had rusted beyond repair. It was fitted with Lockwood and Carlisle piston rings, a patent ring which could be tightened when it wore slack, by the insertion of distance pieces, a very good and effective piece of equipment. Unfortunately in the case of the TEST the whole ring was in such a state that it had to be scrapped and whe-ther the cost of a replacement was too much or the part was obsolete I do not know, but it was decided to fit a solid H.P. piston ring in its place. This worked alright when it was new, but once it started to wear down it gave us

plenty of trouble, of which more later. In the meantime the Charterers were screaming to get hold of the ship, and the Manager and owners were eager to appease them. The Superintendent Engineer was rushed off his feet trying to get the job done in a hurry, and as customary with all half done jobs they rebounded in due course. Eventually the ship was ready, sufficiently so, to commence her charter, by leaving outstanding work to be completed during the charter whilst in port.

I was taken to the basement of the Cunard building in Liverpool which was the offices of the Mediterranean Department. Here I was introduced to the Manager and the various department heads and told what was expected of the ship during the charter. Their procedures were explained to me and I was given a stack of Cunard paperwork such as log abstracts, voyage reports, bunker reports, crew lists, expense sheets, disbursements sheets, etc. There was a Cunard house flag to be flown at the mainmast head in port and when approaching port at all times and the funnel was to be painted in the Cunard Colours. Speed was the essence of the charter and we were expected to maintain a speed of 10 knots and to arrive at our various destinations at specified times where labour was laid on. There was a very good working arrangement between the crew and the stevedores. The crew had the derricks lifted on arrival (Plate 83) and the wedges removed from the hatches, the stevedores then removed the hatches and tarpaulins to load or discharge as the case may be, and then replaced them when they had finished work for the day, leaving the crew just to replace the wedges. As this job was before 8 am. and after 5 pm. it was outside normal working hours (Cunard version). The charterers paid the crew the sum of 1/3d. an hour overtime for these hours worked and as this amounted to between 10/- and a £1 a voyage for a job they had until then been doing for nothing, and thankful to get it, they were delighted. Also with the ship trading 'foreign', I was able to get our cigarettes and a good deal of our provisions out of bond at duty free prices and save a few shillings on them. Altogether a good time was being had by everybody and by getting more time in port especially in Liverpool and knowing exactly what their movements were going to be, the local crew members were delighted, because this meant that they now knew where they were going to be and when. Also they did not have the prospect of being paid off and going on the dole, or being put on half pay every time they came to the Mersey.

Means of communication were not very good at that time, we did not have W/T or radio-telephone, so we reported at recognised signal stations such, as Lizard Point, Lands End, Smalls Lighthouse, or if going inside the Smalls, then at St. Annes Head, Milford Haven, Point Lynas and the Bar Light vessel, by international code flags by day or by Morse lamp at night. The morse lamp in itself was an interesting instrument. It used paraffin and had a prism lens glass which showed a light over an arc of about 20 degrees. It had a shutter between the actual light and the lens, which opened when a lever at the side was depressed and exposed the light for as long as was desired. They were very good and could be seen a long way. They were not as quick as the Aldis lamp but they were not slow by any means. They were generally very well looked after. I suppose because they were the only means of communication and they were the one lamp which, if they were not kept readily available and also in good working order, could bring a penalty in the way of a fine of Fifty pounds. These lamps were generally made of brass, although there was another model made in tin, probably a utility model made in the 1914/18 war. I have not come across one of these lamps since the last war and I daresay

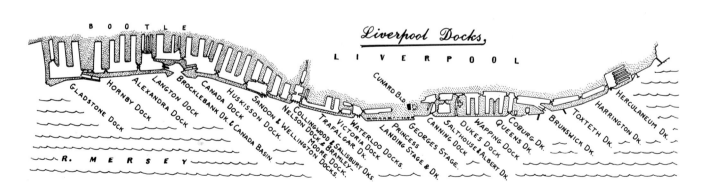

Plate 83   The TEST entering the Mersey when on charter to Cunard for their Channel Islands' service.

if some of the present antique dealers came across one it would now be a collector's item, and a very interesting one.

When arriving at St. Peter Port, Guernsey and also St. Helier, Jersey, we hoisted the Cunard house flag when about five miles off, and were very soon recognised and the Cunard house flag was hoisted on the signal station nearest to the town. The Agent and everybody with an interest in the ship and cargo were notified, a custom dating back to the old days of sail and still continued at present. The signal stations reported our passing with the time, which was of great help to all concerned in making arrangements for us. When proceeding from the Channel Islands particularly St. Helier, Jersey to Le Havre, we waited until the tide was favourable to use the inside channel and through the Race of Alderney and around Cape de la Hague where we would pick up very strong favourable tides which would boost our speed up to sometimes as much as 16 knots. In addition to saving bunkers, the distance gained when totted into our total mileage and divided by the time occupied enhanced our speed to give us a respectable average.

The tides had to be studied carefully; the wind blowing in the opposite direction to the tide, could very quickly raise up a very nasty sea in certain places such as the South Stack, off Holyhead, the Bishops and Clerks, off Milford, Cape Cornwall near Lands End, and the Channel Islands and Capes on the French coast where tidal races existed. The sea could be smooth when the wind and tide were running in the same direction but it could be like a witches cauldron when they opposed each other. When going from Jersey to Le Havre, to attempt to stem the tide in the Race off Alderney especially in bad weather, was just wasting bunkers and punishing the ship. Although we were not restricted by depth of water from sailing from either Jersey or Guernsey at any time, the ship being afloat at all times, I only twice went outside the Islands and North of the Casquets during the whole period we were on charter. One of these occasions when we left St. Helier at the top of high water during a whole gale from the W.N.W. when I would have encountered a full ebb tide in the Race of Alderney and it was more prudent to avoid the turbulence likely to be encountered there.

On this voyage, once we had got around the Casquets Lighthouse, off Guernsey we had the wind and sea behind us, and with the tide turning in our favour, we were able to make up a little for the time lost by the extra distance. On the other occasion we left Guernsey in dense fog for Le Havre when it would have been foolish to attempt the inside passage, which is mostly navigated by transit marks, which if not strictly adhered to, would very quickly result in serious trouble for it was rocky channels we were negotiating and whilst you may get away with a grounding when going astray in a channel between sand banks anything you 'touched' around the Channel Islands is rock, very often with deep water alongside of it. It would be very imprudent to say the least, not to pay very strict attention to your navigation.

To save time, we used the short cuts available when conditions were favourable, such as the Rock channel out of the Mersey, passing inside the Middle Mouse and Skerries Islands off Holyhead, close to the Bishops and South Bishop Lighthouse off the Pembroke coast and between Skokholm and Grassholm Islands, inside the Smalls and Hats and Barrels rocks and inside the Longships passing between the Longships lighthouse and Lands End. These together with the passages between the Channel Islands were about the only savings in distance we could make and we used them to fullest advantage whenever possible.

The funnel now being resplendent in the red with a black top and black bands of the Cunard Line colours, and with the masts and bridge painted, and Cunard house flag consisting of a golden lion rampant, holding a golden globe in its paws on a red background flying proudly at our main mast head, and with our bunkers completely full, and with an extra 10 tons on top of the bunker hatch, the holds being full right up with every kind of goods imaginable, and some of the ballast tanks filled for stability purposes, and what a treat for the TEST, 'fresh' water boiler feed in the after peak tank, she looked smart and ready for whatever was coming.

During the first loading, I came on board during the dinner hour, and whilst the Mate was setting out the dinner table (we did not have a cook or steward) I took the teapot to the galley to make a pot of tea. In the galley sat one of the dockers with his can of tea and putting lobster from a tin he had opened on his sandwiches. I said to him "you are doing yourself good aren't you?" He not realising who I was, replied "Aye, go to that pile over there, there is a case open at the back," indicating a heap of boxes. I slipped quietly into the shed and asked the wharfinger to come along and see the case before he put it on board. Whether he thought I was quick on the uptake I do not know, but when he saw it he exploded "the bastards" and that together with one tin of sardines, was all that ever was pilfered from the TEST during the whole of the charter.

Promptly at 7 pm. on Friday, the Cunard water clerk came on board with the manifests and bills of lading for signing. I had already entered and cleared outwards at the Custom House. I think almost every item had a separate bill of lading, and all had to be signed by me. It was a time consuming job that had to be done at each port. Then being all ready for sea, promptly at 9 pm. we set sail. No Pilots were employed since I held a Mersey Pilotage certificate which exempted the ship from compulsory pilotage whilst I was in command, neither were boatmen employed, a small gratuity being given to anybody who happened to be about the quay to throw off our ropes on the rare occasions when a crew member could not do it. We were given very preferential treatment right through the dock system, and seeing that we were now a 'foreign-going ship' and allowed bonded stores and carried our quota, the gentlemen who were responsible for our good treatment duly came along to wish us a good passage, and considering that spirits out of bond cost very little, I could afford to be generous and satisfaction was had by everybody.

The TEST responded nobly to the little bit of extra care that she had received and made several good and fast passages, maintaining her schedule without any difficulty during the first year of the charter. Small maintenance problems cropped up from time to time which we were able to deal with during loading or discharging without interrupting the programme. Everything went along very satisfactorily for all concerned.

I carried my wife and children with me during the children's school holidays, which was very good experience for them and also good company for me. Although it made me more aware of what was going on around me because I always had it at the back of my mind, what would happen in case of an accident, a collision for instance, in which case had I been alone I could probably save myself, whereas having my wife and family with me, they might all lose their lives and I in trying to save them lose my own. When a coaster was in collision she inevitably came off the worst and generally sank in a few minutes, more often than not with a loss of life. I think the seamen of that period were more collision conscious than they have been since the advent of Radar which may throw some reflections on the benefits of Radar.

At last the old TEST started to complain. She had behaved fairly well since she came on this charter, but makeshift repairs do not last for ever. First the boiler started to over feed. The steam, after passing through the main engine goes through the condenser where it is changed into water and passes into the hotwell were it is picked up by main engine feed pump and returned to the boiler. Normally very little additional extra feed water would be needed, but now the water was gaining very excessively in the boiler, indicating that we had a leak in the condenser, and salt water was getting into the boiler. This was increasing the density of the boiler water and in turn acting on the boiler tubes and furnace crowns and so we opened up the condenser and several of the tubes were found to be leaking. It had apparently been an old complaint, because many tubes were plugged with wooden plugs. We followed the example by blocking the leaking tubes with a few more wood plugs and stopped that problem. Next the coal consumption rose dramatically and then the H.P. piston, started to give trouble. Steam was getting past it and we were losing power and speed. Then the H.P. gland which was packed with U.S. patent metallic packing started to leak which increased until so much boiling water and steam were coming through the gland that the engineers could not get near it to 'swab' the piston rods. This was a system of lubricating the piston rods with a very heavy thick black oil, called cylinder oil applied with a long handled brush, called a 'swab' brush, hence the expression 'swab the rods'. Also the water coming from the gland was washing the oil from the H.P. cross head, guides and bottom end, causing these to over heat.

Then the boiler which had been behaving itself fairly well so far, started to give trouble. First with leaking tubes then with leaking rivets in the furnace crowns. This meant that the engineers had to let the steam pressure go down on the boiler when we were in port in order to go into the combustion chamber to expand the leaking tubes and caulk the leaking rivets. Because steam was needed to drive the winches for loading or discharging during the day, it was not possible to let the steam go down until after 5 or 6 pm. when the stevedores had stopped work, so while waiting to get at the boiler, the engineers had their time fully occupied during the day trying to hold the main engine together. They would then work most of the night in the boiler. Eventually, to save money, the superintendent engineer decided to repack the H.P. gland himself. He opened up the gland without much trouble and ended up with a bucketful of bits and pieces which he could not replace and had to send for the patentees agent to come and do it in the end, thereby delaying the ship for another 12 hours. We were already experiencing delays whilst the boiler was receiving periodic attention. Due to the engine and boiler trouble, the coal consumption shot up alarmingly and the average speed dropped to less than 8 knots.

By now the War had started, and we came under Naval Control orders and had to conform to routes which they laid down. As these routes were very often a much longer distance than we had hereto travelled we had an excuse for longer passages. Also on occasions the ports, especially Le Havre, would be closed for a day or two due to the presence of submarines and later mines in the vicinity.

The final blow came, I think, when the main engine air pump head valve cover came to grief whilst off Falmouth on passage to Liverpool in dense fog. We lay stopped for about 12 hours whilst the engineers made a jury-rig to get the engine going and we were able to limp into Falmouth at about 2 knots. The fog had not cleared and I had to find my way in by soundings. Fortunately it was a moonlight night and I picked up the Manacles buoy which was lit and later picked up the bottom of the land at St. Anthony's Point. The light was not working due to wartime restrictions and I should not have approached the coast during the hours of darkness. I passed close to the guard ship but he did not see me. I was able to find my way into a safe anchorage in Falmouth harbour, then the fog shut down, a real pea-souper which did not clear until noon, when the Examination vessel came alongside. The officer got very sore because I had dared to enter harbour during the hours of darkness and prophesied all kinds of punishments for me very near putting me before a firing squad. Fortunately his superiors were more understanding and were very helpful, so I put the working boat into the water, another war time offence, and with the air pump head valve cover, a round brass component about two feet in diameter with six Kinghorn valves and their covers on it and weighing about 30 lbs. in my arms, I went ashore. First I reported to the Naval Control and then the Customs who were also the Receiver of Wrecks, which I was bound to do by law because I had entered harbour in distress. All were very helpful and the Naval crowd saw the funny side of it and thought it great that I had eluded the guard ship, etc.

I took the air pump part to the local shipyard, where the manager agreed to repair it, and because we were carrying foodstuffs and probably with a bit of influence from the Cunard Line, the repairers worked on it all day and throughout the night. While these repairs were being carried out, my engineers were busy expanding and caulking boiler tubes and the two firemen, assisted by the sailors, were chiselling out encrusted salt from the furnace combustion chambers where it had formed through evaporation from the boiler leaks.

I remained at the shipyard most of the time that the repairs were being carried out, watching repairs being done to other ships to pass the time, and occasionally having a look to see how my job was progressing and was never asked my business. I had walked in and out of the main gate which was guarded, unchallenged. On my first entrance I enquired for the Manager and was directed to the manager's office who put the job in hand for me, thereafter nobody bothered. I carried the pump part back to the ship when it was repaired, and brought it back for adjustment when it did not fit at the first time. After it was finally repaired and fitted, I went back to the yard and settled my account, and only when I was finally leaving the yard was I asked "where was I going!"

Repairs being completed I resumed our voyage and after rounding Lands End set course to the Westward of the Smalls Lighthouse off the Pembroke coast (it was not possible to sail this course shortly afterwards because of a mine field). Then down came the fog again with a light Southerly wind, my course being Northerly. Not wishing to advertise my presence to a prowling submarine by using the steam whistle as prescribed by the regulations, I used the hand fog horn which was not as powerful, when on my starboard bow I heard a fog horn giving two blasts, the fog signal for a sailing ship on the port tack, I slowed the engines and gave three blasts on the fog horn, the fog signal for a sailing ship running free with the wind behind her, and the one that would have to give way had they both been sailing vessels, when out of the fog, ahead of me crossing from starboard to port there appeared a big tramp steamer of about 10,000 tons still using his fog horn and not losing any time, so it would appear we were thinking along the same lines.

We eventually arrived at Liverpool where I was told that the Cunard Line had cancelled the charter for all ships for the duration of the war. After discharging in Liverpool we went to Preston to load a cargo of coal for Ireland, which must have come as a bit of a shock to the old TEST after having carried so many posh cargoes, for her boiler started to leak like a sieve, and after loading we moved her away from the coal hoist and the superintendent engineer and his assistant with the two ships engineers started work on the boiler, and having decided that I would like something a bit more substantial under my feet I left them to it. I heard that the TEST finished her days as a block ship, and no doubt, with the amount of cement I alone put in her, she made a good one!

15. *"Stanley Force."*

87. The STANLEY FORCE entering
Preston. The A.B. on the left on the
forecastle head is the author.
Photo: John Clarkson.

At last I was going to sea; or as they used to say in my home town, "I
was going big boating". I suppose, living in a seaside town, had some influence
on my choice of careers. Perhaps, the fact that my Father and many of my
male relatives had previously 'gone to sea' may have been the deciding factor.
However, they had gone to sea in Fishing boats, whereas I was signing on in
a Cargo boat. Life in Fleetwood was very closely linked to the sea and ships.
Prior to the 1914/18 war, many schoolboys went to sea for a trip with their
fathers or brothers in a steam trawler. Some even went on the Iceland trips.
At school our lessons would be often interrupted by the sound of a ship's
whistle, as they sailed or arrived in port. Many of my class mates even
swore that they could identify the trawlers by the sound of their whistles.

During my last year at school, World War I was in its final stages. We
had by that time, become very familiar with uniforms especially naval. Most,
if not all our trawlers had a gun mounted aft. The gun crew would be fishermen who had I believe been issued with a naval uniform which had a broad
green band round one arm. We had become used to the news of German submarines, (or as we knew them, U-Boats), sinking our trawlers and other ships
in Morecambe Bay or the Irish Sea. We even lost one or two of our sailing
'Fishing Smacks' so, by and large we could not forget the sea. I suppose it
was about this period, that I began to think of being a sailor along with many
other of my class mates. As time went on, my interest grew and after very
serious consideration, my mind became 'made up' when a half cousin became
a 'Brassie' on the Belfast Mail boats. How I envied him when I saw him in
his 'bell bottom' trousers, jersey with the ship's name, 'Duke of Connaught'
across his chest, and topped with a round ribboned sailor's hat.

But I was still at school, and my Father was still in India with H.M.
Forces. My Mother was not very thrilled about my ambition to go to sea and
did not do anything to encourage me. It was May 1919 when my Father came

home from India and, after he was demobilised, resumed his pre-war occupation as a deckhand on a river dredger. I had by that time started work in a foundry. It was dusty and dirty work and with all the fumes from molten iron and lead, was I am sure very unhealthy. I disliked the job very much and longed for the wide open spaces. My Father, learning of my ambition to become a sailor, sought, and eventually found me a job on the river, in the marine department of the Lancashire and Yorkshire railway company. Thus I became half the crew of a steam launch, at the wonderful wage of twenty three shillings and four pence per week, with overtime. During the year 1919 that was a good wage for a boy, some men got little more but I had to work for my wage. Being the deck boy, I had to help and keep things shipshape, stoke the boiler, oil the engines and look after the ropes, both mooring and tow ropes as we sometimes acted as a tug boat. Also I was occasionally allowed to steer the boat, which I enjoyed very much. My nautical training had commenced. One thing I had to learn very early on was how to scull and row a boat. This was very necessary, since our moorings were in the middle of the harbour, and we needed a boat to get there and back.

I was also learning practical seamanship, as day and night with the tide, we sailed up and down the river. Sometimes we acted as the Dredging Master's tender. Other times we became a tug boat, towing fishing smacks out into the channel and towing them back on their return. We did emergency towing or acted as a diver's tender both in the harbour and on the bar. I learnt a lot and in spite of the long and irregular hours, enjoyed it. During the first two years, I progressed through the usual channel of promotion, first as a deckhand on a bigger launch (crew of three) thence down below as a fireman and engine tender. I followed that with a job as a greaser on a bucket dredger but owing to some mix up about holidays was transferred to a larger bucket dredger as a cook. This turned out to be a good thing. I was now on day work, and able to enrol as a student at the Navigation School. I attended for three evenings each week during the winter months for two years. We were taught:- Rules of the road at sea, chart work and kindred subjects, on one night. The next night was devoted to geography and arithmetic. The third night was spent learning knots, ties and splicing. Because most of the students intended to become fishermen, we were taught net mending. I found the subjects interesting, so much so, much to my surprise, I topped the class in the final examination, winning the prize as the best student. During my period at navigation school I had many talks with the Principal, Captain Ingham. He thought I was too old to start a sea career as an Apprentice or Cadet, inferring that I stood as much chance starting as an Ordinary Seaman.

In 1922, I was transferred to a sea going sand pump as an ordinary seaman. I had started my career, but not the way I had intended. However, I began to get some experience steering by compass at sea and seeing the Rules of the Road, in operation. I also learnt something about sea marks and buoyage. In fact I became very familiar with our own channel. However, being out on the bar or in the bay for most of the week I was unable to continue going to the Navigation School and I am afraid my interest in a sea going career was not quite so important. I was seemingly able to combine sea going with all the regular comforts of home, i.e. weekends off! But unknown to me, my Father had been investigating possibilities. Thus it came as a great surprise, when I arrived home one Saturday noon to find that my Father had received a letter from a friend of his who was a ship broker. The letter contained the following message:-

"Dear Jim,

The S.S. Stanley Force is alongside the quay wall and goes up river tonight's tide. She is to sail on Monday for London. If your son will go on board and see the Mate, I think he will get the vacancy. Let your son tell the Mate that Capt. Bridson asked me to send your son on board, Yours faithfully, (signed) H. Dingle.

I cannot say the letter brought me any joy, quite the reverse in fact. I had been looking forward to a weekend off and spending it with my pals. Also I suddenly realised that the even routine of my life was about to be disrupted by a loss of home comforts and security. However, not wanting to disappoint my Father, I kept the dismal thoughts to myself. First things first, I still had to get the job. After a meal, I changed into more suitable clothing, and accompanied by my Father, went down to the quay. The tide was out and we found the STANLEY FORCE lying low in the mud against the quay wall.

The only means of boarding the vessel was by a wooden ladder which had been erected from the main deck. We descended the ladder and, not seeing anyone about, approached and knocked on a door situated at main deck level aft side of the bridge. The door was opened by a rather surly individual, who we later learnt was the Mate, Mr. Harris. We introduced ourselves, and after stating our business, produced the letter from Mr. Dingle. It was only then that I learnt that the vacancy was for an A.B. which was, as far as I was

concerned, a step up. The Mate questioned me about my previous experience and did not appear favourably impressed by my answers. I do not think I would have stood any chance without the letter of introduction. Finally, apparently satisfied, he explained that the ship was to move up river on the next tide and ordered me to be on board in readiness early that evening. That was that, I had got the job, now commenced a period of hurried preparation. There was much to be done prior to my departure. My sea kit had to be assembled from scratch, not having had one before. I had to buy food to see me over the trip to London, which I later learnt would take about three or four days also I required sufficient money to see me through to the payday. With all these preparations concentrated into two days, I had no time to see my mates and bask in a period of importance. In fact it was almost like I was slipping away. There was however one major snag, being an employee of the railway company I was, according to the rules, required to work a week's notice, when about to terminate my service. This of course was not possible if I was to sail on the Monday. It was a problem, but my Father thought he could put the matter right after I had sailed. I wondered afterwards whether he was leaving an open door, in case I changed my mind.

I will always remember reporting on board that first evening, it could not have been very late, it was still daylight although the 2nd day of February, 1924. On reporting to the Mate, I was instructed to go for'ard and wait in the forecastle on the starboard side. The forecastle was divided into two compartments by a fore and aft bulkhead, firemen on the port side, sailors on the starboard, the two compartments being practically identical. The forecastle was unoccupied and I sat down to wait for my future shipmates. Thus I had ample time to survey my surroundings which were to be my new home. There was, as they say, no room to swing a cat and the dismal interior was visible only by the daylight which came through the open doorway, a small window and two small portholes above the bunks. There was a fixed but unlit oil lamp on the bulkhead situated over a fixed fore and aft table and, alongside that, was a very wobbly form. Immediately for'ard of the table was a round solid fuel stove, with its chimney sticking up through the deckhead, for'ard of that was a dark space in which one was to hang oilskins and other work clothing. Four wooden bunks, in two tiers, lay against the ship's side, with a seat attached to the bottom bunks. The space between the seat and wobbly form varied from about three to six feet. Immediately for'ard of the bunks was a column of four food lockers and for'ard of these a space to keep the coal for our stove. It was anything but a cheerful place, little did I think that it would be my home for the next six years. This was the place in which I was to eat, sleep, wash myself and do every other necessary thing. A place without any comfort or facilities. The period of waiting for my future shipmates seemed endless and with the fading daylight and not having any matches to light the lamp, I was eventually sitting in the dark. Alone with only my thoughts to pass the time, my doubts about the new venture increased with every passing minute.

I began to realise that I was exchanging the comforts and security of home life for the now doubtful and apparently dismal life at sea, living in a forecastle. I could not help feeling that I should have left things as they were and began to feel very unhappy. But after all my talk about wanting to go to sea and see the world and my great show of eagerness, I could not admit weakness now. After a while I heard, what proved to be the noisy approach of my future shipmates and awaited our meeting with some apprehension. There were three of them, and they did not appear surprised as they stepped into the forecastle. After we had exchanged names and so on, they questioned me about my previous experience and home town, etc. I tried very hard to satisfy their curiosity without resorting to untruths, but at the same time not wanting to appear too much of a 'Greenhorn' which I obviously was. Although many years have passed since that first meeting with my future shipmates, I think the occasion was such that an indelible record of events remains in my memory.

There was 'Old Bill' a whiskery old shellback from Anglesey, who said he was fifty five, (he continued to say that for the next ten years). His vocabulary being a mixture of Welsh and English, caused me to have some difficulty in understanding him during our early acquaintance. Another was known as 'Crackers', he was a fireman who came from Southern Ireland. I later learnt he could neither read nor write and had a tendency to mix his metaphors, often to his disadvantage. Finally there was Joe, he was coloured, and a few years my senior in age. He appeared to be the leader of the trio. I later discovered him to be an expert seaman and fairly well educated. After he discovered my lack of experience and the fact that I was younger than him, he tended to treat me with a certain amount of condescension. After I had proved I could hold my own, he and I, became great friends.

Eventually, with the rising tide, we were ordered to stand by ready to unmoor and move up river. It was now quite dark and I was told to light the 'masthead, side and stern lights'. This was new to me, my last ship had

Sheepshank.

electric lights. I did not even know where the lamp room was or how to ship the lights. However, 'Crackers' noticing my difficulty, offered to show me the lamp room and later how to ship the lamps. With his assistance, I performed my first job on the old STANLEY FORCE. Soon our pilot came on board with a final "let go for'ard, let go aft" we moved away from the quay side. After rounding the 'Tigers Tail' we headed up river to our loading berth at the United Alkali works jetty. This was my first trip in my new ship. I cannot recall anything special about this part of the event. I was uncertain about whether I would be allowed to go home again. But having no gear on board I was given leave.

The next day was Sunday, I returned to the ship during the morning, whether I was expected to I do not know. However, during the afternoon I went back home, there were still many things to do before I sailed. This was not a very happy time and home had suddenly become very precious. I was already finding ship board 'rough and ready' life difficult to get used to. The prospects of leaving home for an indefinite period, maybe weeks or months did not appeal to me. But as one so often hears quoted, "I'd made my bed and now must lie on it". My time away from the ship was fully occupied with preparation and I never got any time to see my pals. When returning to my new ship on Monday morning, I met the Mate of my now old ship. He seeing me going in an unexpected direction, enquired where I was going? Feeling embarrassed and not wanting to explain, I casually replied "Be seeing you" and hurried on. I often wonder what was said when I failed to turn up on my old ship, and they had subsequently learnt that I had shipped on a coaster.

After being employed for most of the day on the STANLEY FORCE I was allowed to go home again late in the afternoon to collect my gear and take leave of my family. This was not only my last night at home for some time, but turned out to be my last night in that house, as my family moved in my absence. My last evening at home was an occasion that I will never forget. The gas lit kitchen never looked so cosy. As I looked around I realised just what I was giving up. Although the prospect was to me very bleak, I did my best not to let my parents see my misery and put on a show of cheerful anticipation, but with some difficulty to maintain. My Mother, who had never agreed that I should leave home to go to sea, remarked at one stage during the evening. "Its not too late to change your mind." Little did she know how near she was in getting her wish. But after all the show I had made about being a sailor, I had to go through with it, there was no turning back. I later learnt that it had been expected that I would not stick it and would soon be back home. I am glad I proved them wrong. Although if I had known what a seasick miserable time I was to experience during the next month or so, I would most certainly have changed my mind.

Well all things come to an end and I had to take my leave of the family and catch the train back to my ship. This then was to be the real beginning of my first voyage and I wondered what the future had in store for me.

I think it was the Poet, John Masefield, who composed the poem which referred to:- "A dirty British coaster, with the salt caked funnel." This description certainly did not apply to the STANLEY FORCE. She had a yellow funnel. The hull was painted grey and divided from the red boot topping by a four inch white band. Her masts, derricks and super structure were painted orange-brown. Her boats and davits were white. All this combined to produce an outstandingly clean appearance. I later discovered how much attention was given to maintaining it. Although she was registered in Whitehaven, the owners offices were located near the Pierhead in Liverpool. I had noticed several of her sister ships in my home port from time to time and had therefore assumed that I would have plenty of opportunities to get home. Unfortunately this did not prove to be the case.

The fleet consisted of about eight vessels, all named after places in Cumberland, and varying in tonnage from 600 to 1,100 tons cargo capacity. In those days a coaster of 1,100 tons was considered a large vessel and I was told that the firm had previously owned sailing vessels. Our owners, whom we referred to as Willie and John, were located in the Liverpool office. Thus, whenever we were Liverpool bound, as much time as possible was given to sprucing the ship up, in anticipation of a visit from Willie, which was almost a certainty. Willie did not look like a ship owner. In fact the first time I met him I thought he was an interfering dockyard foreman. Willie appeared to be mainly concerned with administration, whilst John, who was an engineer, looked after Board of Trade matters, i.e. blow-downs for boiler inspection, surveys and the like. At least that was when we used to see him.

The STANLEY FORCE was about 175 feet in length, with a cargo capacity of 720 tons. Her registered tonnage was 242. Identification, Lloyd's signal manual K.F.B.D. When fully loaded her mean draft was about 12 feet 6 inches, and if properly trimmed was a good sea boat in bad weather. To get that good trim, it was usual to load 250 tons in the fore hold, with the remainder in the after hold. Careful watch was required on the fore and aft depths during the later stages of loading cargo, to obtain the required trim. Our mean draft increased by one inch with every ten tons of cargo. She carried a crew of ten comprising:- Master, Mate, Second Mate/Boatswain, Chief Engineer, Second Engineer, Two A.B.'s, Two firemen and a Cook/Steward, (often referred to as nine poor souls and the cook!). The Cook/Steward catered for the officers and looked after the midship accommodation. Sailors, Firemen, and for some reason, also the Second Engineer, catered for themselves.

The ship was of a type, quite common in coastal waters, with three masts, fore, main and mizzen, often referred to as a 'three master'. The accommodation amidships was topped by an open bridge, for'ard of this in the well deck was the fore hatch, whilst aftside on the main deck was the main hatch. Continuing aft were the bunkers, stokehold, galley, engine room and the engineers' accommodation containing two single berths, one on each side of a messroom. Above all this was the bunker hatch, two big ventilators for the stokehold and on the starboard side, a 14 foot dinghy or workboat. There was also, a port and starboard lifeboat in davits. Between these was a 200 gallon drinking water tank, galley and engine room skylights, and over the engineers' quarters was stepped the mizzen mast. The amidships accommodation contained at main and lower deck levels, a messroom, containing table and settees and a fancy square coal fired stove. On the port side, was a double berthed cabin for the Mate and Second Mate. The Cook/Steward's berth and pantry was situated on the starboard side. Access to this accommodation was via a door from the main deck and down three or four steps. The Master's accommodation was at lower bridge level with access via a door situated at the foot of the top bridge ladder. His accommodation comprised, a chart room with a single berth cabin adjoining. Aftside of the midship's accommodation was a steam operated winch, mast and derrick. (S.W.L. 25 cwt.)

Going for'ard over the lower bridge, one descended a vertical steel ladder, down into the well deck and fore hatch. For'ard of that, was another steam operated winch, mast and derrick. The fore well deck was several feet lower than the main deck, thus at sea in bad weather was often awash. Right for'ard was the crew's quarters, known as the forecastle. On the port side, were two lavatories, one for officers and the other for crew. The officers' lavatory had a flap in the pan to prevent upsurge when the ship dived into a sea, but the crew's lavatory was minus a flap, thus one developed a special technique, of standing on the seat and raising oneself every time the ship dived, thus preventing an unpleasant return. Next to the lavatory was the firemen's forecastle. The centre door led to the chain and paint/store locker. Starboard of that was the door to the seamen's forecastle and on the ship's side was the lamp room. All doors being steel did not fit very well, thus did not keep water out. Above the forecastle was the fore deck or forecastle head. On it were the mooring bitts, steam operated capstan, two small ventilators and two stove chimneys, along with mooring wire reels. I should also mention that there was a steam driven capstan right aft, for mooring purposes (plan, 131).

The navigating bridge had no overhead cover, the only protection was from a canvas dodger which could be raised and secured to a ridge wire supported by stanchions fitted on the outer boundary of the bridge. This dodger acted as a shelter from the wind and spray. Centrally situated on the foreside of the bridge was the binnacle and to the right of that, the engine room telegraph. There had been a speaking tube from the bridge to the engine room but the connecting pipe having corroded, only the mouth piece remained. Aft side of the binnacle was a large steering wheel, about four feet in diameter. When at sea the wheel was operated manually, which sometimes required two men. In confined waters, or when deemed a necessity, steering was operated by a steam engine situated in a box close behind the wheel. The warm steam engine was often a comfort to the helmsman in cold weather. During the hours of darkness, the compass was illuminated by two small oil lamps in the binnacle cover. This enabled the helmsman to see the compass points and the 'lubber line'. Lighting in the engine room was by acetylene lamps, but the rest of the lighting was provided by oil lamps. The vessel was single screw and had one main boiler fired by three furnaces, and there was also a donkey boiler. She normally carried about 50 or 60 tons of bunker coal, with an average consumption of 8 tons every 24 hours steaming. The normal speed was about 8 knots. She had three ballast tanks, one right for'ard under the fore peak. A large tank under the cargo space, with a third tank aft above the rudder. This was normally used to contain fresh water for the boiler. The ship was built in Workington and when I joined her was only four years old. This then is a general description of the old STANLEY FORCE. She was my home for over twelve years and provides a background for my coasting experiences.

92. STANLEY FORCE: Forecastle.

The First Voyage.

Thomas H. Thomason

The passage of time, now almost half a century, has done much to erase events from my mind. But some parts of my first voyage remain firmly imprinted, whilst other parts of my first voyage were so involved with being seasick that life alternated between standing up and lying down. I managed to keep my watch, but have no clear recollection of anything during the first day or so.

I had previously spent most of my working life on the sea, mainly in Morecambe Bay. Now I had become an Able Seaman on a ship which would not only take me to many ports in the British Isles but also to foreign ports as well. The only drawback was I was liable to be away from home for long periods. I little dreamt that the ship would be my home for the next dozen or more years. Also, I had not foreseen that because of seasickness, this trip would test my will-power to the extreme. If I had known what it would be like I would most probably have stayed at home.

On the night of our departure, after taking leave of my family I returned to the ship ready for sailing. Although it was early evening it was dark when I got on board. The ship was fully loaded and battened down ready for sea, therefore was clear of hatches and beams, which was just as well as I stumbled along the unfamiliar decks. I found the forecastle unoccupied and concluded that my shipmates had gone ashore for a drink. Not knowing which was to be my bunk I could only sit and wait their return. After what appeared an endless period they arrived back on board and entered the forecastle. I gathered that going ashore for a drink before sailing was the usual custom, time and money permitting. I was given the choice of an upper or lower bunk near the door, I chose the upper one. (I'm glad to say). Slinging my gear into the bunk, I began to change into sea gear. I put on my leather sea boots, that was my first mistake. I later discovered that leather boots made too much noise and contributed to an unsafe foothold on the wet steel decks.

At last with the rising tide, our river pilot came on board and we began to prepare for sailing. I, being unfamiliar with the routine, could only assist as directed. Soon it was time to go, and unmooring from the jetty we glided out into the dark river and began our journey to the sea. It had been arranged that my Father, Mother and family would watch our departure from a position near the Lower Light house. This being the usual vantage point used by people wanting to watch passing vessels. It was practically the closest that one could be to any passing ship, as they entered or left the main channel. I knew that I had about ten or fifteen minutes from leaving the jetty to passing the Lower Light, so hurried to get the jobs done as I kept an eye on the shore lights as we passed. Approaching the Ferry Landing stage we slowed down. Our river pilot climbed down the rope ladder into his boat and pushed off into the night. Now we were on our way to the London River.

As the Lower Light came in view I climbed up on to the forecastle head. I stood alone in the darkness, looking towards the Light and listening. As we got abeam I heard my Father shouting also what appeared to be the rest of my family. Because of the wind and noise of the bow wash, I had difficulty in distinguishing their shouted message but distinctly heard them shouting 'cheerio', which I acknowledged by shouting back. As we turned into the main channel towards the sea I could not resist looking back and watch the lights of my home time gradually merge and disappear from view. My mind was with my family, returning to that warm and safe house. My link had at last been broken, when I would return was in the lap of the gods.

Turning out of the main channel we headed for Lune Buoy, there Old Bill initiated me in the art of streaming the log, after which, being our watch, we went up on to the bridge. I had only been up on the bridge once before, and that was for a brief period to ship the side lights. I found it to be a dark and dismal place totally devoid of any overhead cover and exposed to the elements. It was far different from the bridge on my last ship which not only had a wheelhouse but also electric light. The only light we had, came from the binnacle which occasionally shone on the face of the man at the wheel. The Captain having gone below, the Mate was in charge, and almost as soon as I got on the bridge he ordered me to take the wheel. MY EDUCATION WAS ABOUT TO COMMENCE IN EARNEST. I was given the course of "West by South a Quarter South". My failure to repeat the course resulted in a sharp reminder from the Mate, to do so. I am afraid, due to ignorance, I was to transgress many times during the next few months.

The weather conditions had begun to deteriorate as we left the bay, soon I was having great difficulty in steering the loaded ship. This I suppose was understandable, I lacked experience and was unfamiliar with this type of vessel also night steering by compass in a rough sea. Every now and then the Mate would peer into the binnacle and more often than not find me off course. Thus I suffered an almost continuous barrage of abuse. I was very thankful when the Mate finally went below and left me to the tender mercy of Old Bill, who was in charge of the watch. The rating of Boatswain or Second Mate had not at that time been adopted. I believe Bill was signed on as a 'Lamp Trimmer'. Some years later, Bill was promoted to 'Mate' and I became the first crew member to be promoted and later signed on as 'Second Mate'.

My troubles increased with the gyrating motion of the ship, I was beginning to feel seasick. It was not long before I began to vomit, sometimes when standing at the wheel, at other times over the side. I really began to feel very ill and sorry for myself. But I got no sympathy from Old Bill, who had seen it all before. Being on four hour watches, we were due to be relieved by the Mate's watch at 4 am. (eight bells). At 3-45 am. (one bell) I was instructed by Bill to make the Mate a mug of tea and give him a call. I went below and entering the Mate's cabin, I called "Watch O". Once again I was in trouble. The Mate, whom I later discovered was usually irritable when first roused, lectured me on the proper way to call the watch. In future I was to call "One bell" and not "Watch O". As soon as I was relieved, I went for'ard to the forecastle, with the sole purpose of getting my head down. I was feeling so ill, all I wanted to do was lie down. Thus without any waste of time I turned into my bunk 'all standing' (wearing my seaboots and oilskins). Being wet did not matter, that was the least of my worries, I had not any bedding anyway. So lying on the bare boards using my kit bag and life jacket for a pillow, I covered myself with a blanket and tried to find some solace in sleep, but, as the bows rose and fell in the rough sea, I found sleep impossible. I found it necessary to lie on my side using my knees and back to jam myself in, to prevent being thrown out. Consequently my watch below was not very restful and I got little sleep. As I went back on watch at 8 am. (eight bells) I felt just as bad as ever.

It was now daylight, and as far as I can remember we had rounded the Skerries and were somewhere in the vicinity of South Stack. Some of my ship-mates had or were having a meal, and a warm drink. They tried very hard to get me to eat something, but the very thought increased my feeling of nausea and tendency to vomit. They appeared to be sympathetic to my suffer-ing, but I had a feeling they were also a little amused. They had all gone through it before. Continuing on our Southerly course we passed Bardsey and the Smalls. Although we eventually rounded the Longships and Lizard, I have no recollection of it. My watch on deck seemed to be spent retching and vomiting, from what was then, an empty stomach. Because of this, the strain was causing colic pains and my vomit was occasionally mixed with blood. All I could hope for during my watch below was to get sufficient strength for my next watch on deck. I was living in four hour periods and still turning into my bunk 'all standing'. I had not eaten, taken any fluid or undressed since I left home. Nothing mattered only getting my head down.

The Skerries.

All the food that I had brought with me as well as some sweets and chocolate, which I had bought for a treat, I gave away to my shipmates. They did not mind, it was very welcome and supplemented their food stock. My inability to eat did not bother them as long as I could stand my watch. I suppose it was due to improving weather conditions that I began to feel better. After eating something I began to take an interest in my surroundings. I remember one day on the bridge, Bill pointed to some white cliffs on the port bow, and asked me did I know what they were? Being unfamiliar with the coastline, I replied I thought it was Dover. But I was wrong, he told me that they were the 'Seven Sisters' which lay just West of Beachy Head. That was my first lesson in geography. It was, incidentally, the first bit of coastline I remember seeing after I had watched the receding lights of my home town three nights previously.

Rounding Dungeness, I had my first sight of the English Channel, and after passing Folkestone saw the 'White Cliffs of Dover'. I was very thrilled to also be able to see the coastline of France, away to starboard. It was interesting to see the numerous passing ships, of different nationalities and types. I had never seen so many ships before, at one time. My first voyage was ending as we rounded the South Foreland and entered the channel inside the Goodwin Sands. Finally after rounding the North Foreland we entered the Thames estuary, known to coastwise seamen, as the London River.

The weather was fine as we entered the estuary, it was a lovely sunny morning. The Captain came on to the bridge during our watch, this was the first time I had seen him. He was tall, gaunt looking, and appeared to feel the cold. Consequently wore much clothing and on his head a 'hard weather' hat. He appeared to be interested in my first impression of the Thames, and pointed out various lights, landmarks, light ships and buoys, as we sailed up river. Later, on reflection, I concluded that the Captain was sounding me out for intelligence and experience, also checking my eyesight. I never really got to know my Captain, as I discovered he was a very sick man, spending most of his time in his cabin, leaving many of his duties to the Mate. Shortly afterwards he went home ill and eventually died.

At last we arrived off our discharging berth at Silvertown, as soon as we had water on, we went alongside and prepared the ship for discharging. This was my first experience of arriving in a strange port. Not having been to Silvertown before, I looked forward to going ashore and seeing the place. Later, escorted by my two shipmates Bill and Joe I went ashore. Those people who were familiar with the London River in those days and places like Silvertown, Canning Town, Tidal Basin, Deptford, Woolwich and so on will remember the hustle and bustle in the shopping centres and the eager for business shop keepers. I soon discovered that window gazing often brought the shop-keeper out and one would almost be dragged into the shop. It was a bit embarrassing at times, but one had to be hard faced. My shipmates, being used to this, enjoyed watching my embarrassment. Nevertheless, I enjoyed the feeling of being a sailor ashore after a voyage, and tended to walk with an exaggerated rolling gait.

I lost no time getting a letter off to my parents. I wanted to let them know of our safe arrival, also to tell them how I had got on. Not wanting them to worry, I deliberately avoided any mention of being seasick. Now, I was beginning to learn the art of buying stores, i.e. food. As far as we were concerned, this mainly consisted of buying sufficient for day to day requirements and the duration of any pending voyage, or until we had another opportunity (and money) to replenish our food lockers. Our food purchases usually consisted of basic items, bread (although after two or three days it became very stale), sea biscuits, margarine, tea, coffee, cocoa, sugar, tinned skimmed milk, potatoes, bully beef, (often referred to as 'Harriet Lane') and perhaps some bacon and jam. If funds permitted, we would perhaps buy some easily cookable meat, a tin or two of tomatoes (these were often very cheap), some cheese (usually called 'bung') and porridge oats, (again nicknamed 'burgoo'). As time went on, and with easily cooked meals in mind, I occasionally bought a piece of brisket and by adding peas with any other vegetables, managed to make a hot meal that would last several days, reheated as required. Sometimes I made it so thick, that when cold, it was almost possible to cut it into slices.

However, all that was in the future, but I was learning that 'man does not live by bread alone'. It was after our arrival in Silvertown that I met more of my shipmates, especially 'Old John'. I had probably met them all before, but in my seasick condition, had not taken much notice. Old John was as his name implied 'old'. He was one of the ship's firemen and by the sound of his accent, a Cockney. He was not very chatty but was inclined to be friendly. My association with Old John was of short duration so I never found out much about him. He suffered from a leg ulcer and had been so troubled for some considerable time. When I saw it, I was amazed that anyone could do a job of work, suffering with such an affliction. He had not apparently sought medical attention, preferring to treat it himself. His treatment consisted of daily bath-

Sir Acton Blake
Gravesend Pilots.

ing the ulcerated leg with sea or salt water and re-applying some unhygienic bandages. This tendency towards self-treatment, I later found to be fairly common practice amongst Weekly Boat crewmen. There was often little time in port and little money to spare for medical attention. Old John was attempting the impossible, trying to cure his ulcer. During our short acquaintance the ulcerated condition deteriorated to such an extent, the wound began to give off an offensive odour, so much so, that his mate began to complain. I think someone eventually informed the Captain. Anyway, Old John went ashore, presumably for medical attention, and as far as I can remember, we never saw him again.

But I am running ahead of events, so back to Silvertown. Our stay in port was coming to an end and everyone, including myself, began to wonder about our next port of call, each hoping it would be somewhere which would provide an opportunity to visit homes. This incidentally was the only chance one would get to see their families. As long as one remained a crew member, getting home for a night was often spaced by periods of months. So, we anxiously awaited the return of our Captain, from the ship's broker, who in this case was Thomas Cook of Great Tower Street, London. Perhaps he would at least bring us some letters. At last we had our sailing orders, we were to sail for Ghent, Belgium, and load 'basic slag'. So off ashore we went to buy as much food as we could for the trip.

I was very thrilled with the prospect of going abroad and lost no time in getting a letter off to my parents to let them know. The thrill of going abroad for the first time did much to neutralise the feeling of apprehension which I had begun to experience concerning a repeat of my seasickness. The ship would be sailing light, and therefore would tend to be more lively in rough water. I had however, some consolation in the knowledge that the trip was less than 200 miles and could easily be accomplished in 24 hours. Soon we were off, down the Thames towards the sea, I found the busy river and changing scenery very interesting. When we reached open water, we found the wind had freshened from the South West and the sea was choppy. The ship began to bounce and as I had anticipated, I started to feel sick. Therefore, it was with some relief that on sighting my first foreign lightship the 'West Hinder', I learnt my misery would soon be over. It was about 10 pm. when the Dutch sea pilot boarded us, and we headed for the 'West Schelde' passing the 'Wandelaar' lightship just before midnight. By now, the wind having veered to the North West, weather conditions had improved. Towards the end of the middle watch (midnight to 4 am.) we arrived at the Dutch port of Terneuzen, this being the entrance to the Ghent canal, being low tide we moored at the dolphins to await the flood. Some hours later we entered the locks at Terneuzen, after which we commenced our journey towards Ghent.

Hitherto, these places to me had just been names on a map, now I was actually seeing them. It was only about five years since the World War ended and I was specially looking forward to seeing Belgium, also if possible, something of the 'battlefields'. Our ship stopped at the Dutch/Belgian border station and I was surprised at the apparent casual manner in which we passed from Holland into Belgium. It was about three hours after leaving Terneuzen that we arrived and berthed in Ghent. I could not get ashore fast enough to see what it was like.

In those days, discipline in a 'Weekly Boat' when on the Continent was somewhat lax. Crew members would head for the shore and bright lights as soon as they could. Shore entertainment seemed to be mainly 'Wine, women and song', which appeared to be the predominant entertainment in continental dockland areas. Cafes would remain open until dawn. Seamen would drink and dance to music which seemed to be heard in every cafe. Carousing would continue for as long as the money lasted and as one hoped, with as little trouble as possible. Drunken men tended to be easily offended especially by one who spoke a different language. I think that this was the time when English money had some value abroad, the Dutch guilder was about twelve and the Belgian franc about two hundred and twenty to the pound. English money was welcome anywhere and as a result of the good exchange rate, we appeared to be well-off.

However, back to Ghent. Old Bill and Joe, volunteered to show me the sights. I think for two reasons, first, I had more money than they had. Second, they wanted to introduce me to the local custom of 'wine, women and song'. Being a total abstainer, their efforts to get me drunk were not successful. However, I did enjoy the experience and lost no time in acquiring some souvenirs i.e. silk scarves, scent, views and so on, also I wanted to send a letter home from Ghent. I cannot remember much about our visit, but I do remember our late night, or was it early morning return to the ship. We were rather noisy and full of fun, myself included. Eventually our stay in Ghent came to an end and we sailed with a cargo of 'basic slag' for Cork, in Southern Ireland.

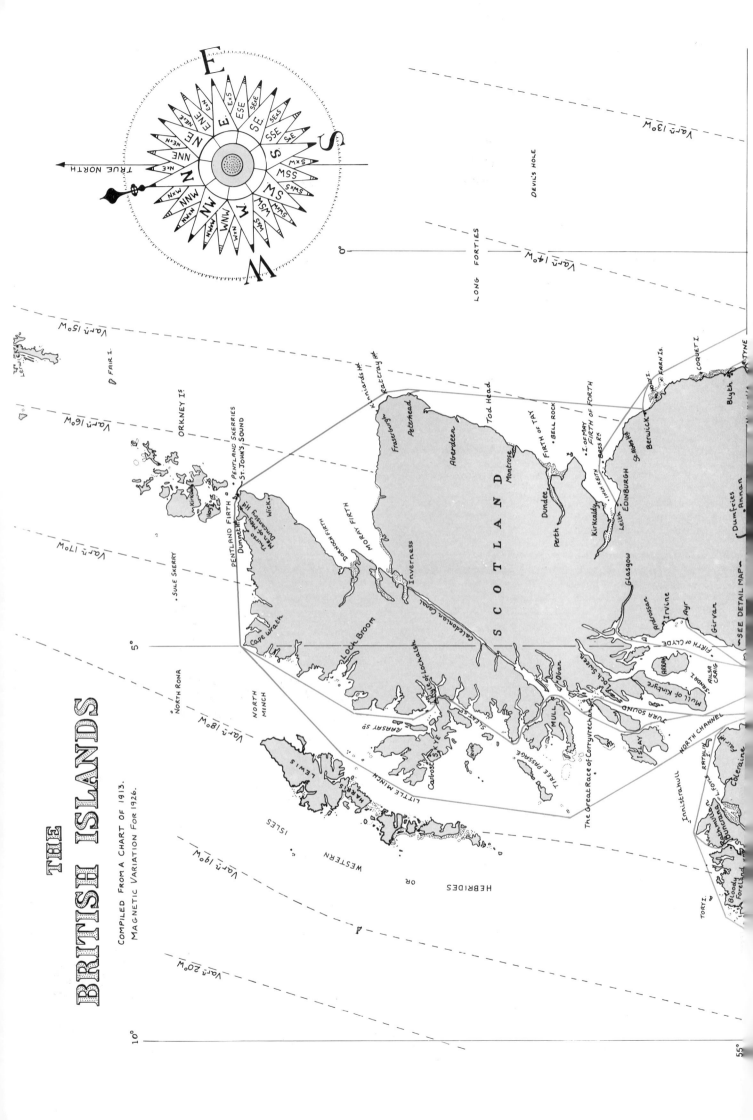

THE
BRITISH ISLANDS

COMPILED FROM A CHART OF 1913.
MAGNETIC VARIATION FOR 1926.

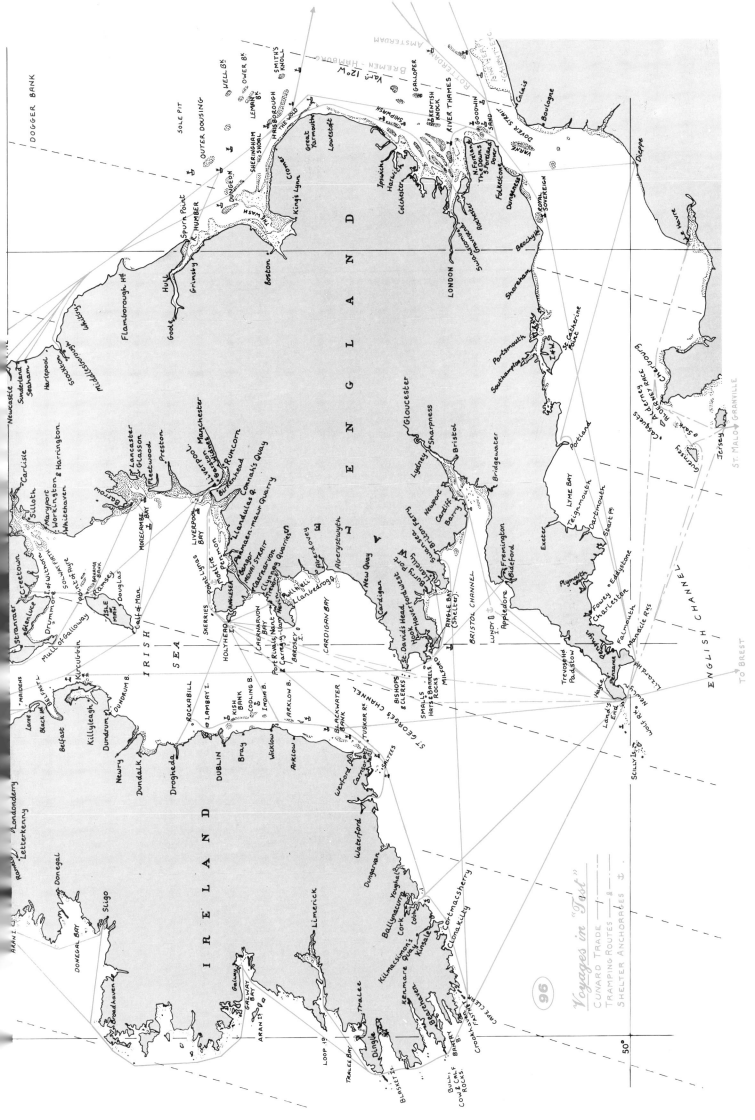

98. The photo shows, from left to right, Mr. Edwards (Mate), The Author and Joe Ward. The ship was discharging coal at Newlyn. The agent's clerk is standing on the bridge in the background.

17. *Just Routine.*

It was Saturday, 10th April 1926. We had arrived and berthed at the Brittania Pier, Middlesboro'. Our orders had been to load a cargo of steel plates, etc. for the Naval dockyards at Portsmouth and Devonport. Much to our delight, we learnt that we would be having the weekend in. This more than anything meant, we were to have two full nights in bed, or should I say, in our bunks. Nights in were always a luxury, but combined with a free weekend, more so. I cannot remember what time we started to load, but loading was discontinued at noon until Monday morning. Our loading berth was situated at the end of a long pier, therefore it was not very convenient for the shops and town. Nevertheless it was essential that we did our weekend shopping as soon as possible. We wanted sufficient food for the weekend with some extras for the forthcoming trip. Also having been paid, some of us wanted to send money home to our families. My wage was £3-4s. a week, I used to send my parents £1.10s. What was left I spent on food and other necessities. Being 'Weekly Boat' men, we were paid as near as possible every week.

I, being a total abstainer and a non-smoker, as well as being single, usually had more money to spend on my requirements and was therefore more able to indulge myself foodwise on paydays. Returning from my shopping expedition, as it was still daylight, I decided to do some 'dobying' (wash clothes). So gathering together my dirty clothes and a bar of soap, I went aft to the stokehold. Down the stokehold alongside the boiler was a tank which always contained hot water from the condensers. Because of the apparent plentiful supply of hot water we always did our washing down the stokehold and also had our occasional bath. So, sitting on a box in the quiet solitude of the stokehold I gave my socks, shirt and underclothes a birthday. The only trouble we had with using condensed water was, it tended to turn white clothes yellowish. Another problem was drying our washing which we did on the gratings over the boiler, everything got very dusty. But it was the best we could do under the circumstances. With an effort we managed to keep ourselves reasonably clean.

Anyway, after I had done my washing I had a meal, then deciding to relax, lay on my bunk reading a 'Western'. I used to read them a lot in those days. Sometimes we would get a supply of books given us by the 'Seamen's Mission'. Trying to read by the light of our one and only oil lamp was not easy when lying in my bunk, therefore, it was not surprising that I eventually dropped off to sleep. When I woke up it was Sunday morning, the weather although fine was inclined to be chilly, more so, our bogy stove had gone out and our one and only form of heat was missing. Although it was April, we found the weather a little cool on the East coast. Getting out of my bunk, I dressed and went aft to the stokehold to get a bucket of coal and some wood. It was not long before I had the comforting sound of flames roaring in the bogy stove and soon we had some warmth radiating from it. With no watches to keep and no work to do, my shipmates were naturally reluctant to leave the comfort of their bunks. It was customary to spend a free weekend relaxing in one way or another. Sometimes, we would remain in our bunks the whole of Sunday, getting something to eat as and when we felt like it. This lazy routine may seem strange to shore people, but we had no comfortable seats to sit on, and little light to read by, without having the door open. In fact our bunks were the only place of comfort we had. Thus we relaxed, yarned, smoked and dozed, enjoyto the full our temporary freedom. It was often said, "a man should stay in his bunk, for as long as he has the strength to lie down."

However, someone usually volunteered to attend to the eats, on this occasion, 'Old Will' decided to prepare his speciality, 'dry hash'. Going aft to the galley, he peeled, boiled and mashed some potatoes. Then opening a tin of bully beef he mixed it along with the mash and sliced onions. The mixture was spread out in a roasting tin and placed in the oven to brown over. This was a popular, easy to prepare and cheap meal, which we always enjoyed. A roasting tin full was usually sufficient for several men. Sometimes we had either "duff" to follow or on its own. This currant 'duff' was easy to make but took longer to cook, but it was worth the effort. Occasionally the steward would bribe us with a lump of 'duff' (black pan) for such things as, cleaning his galley fire, having his kettle boiling and so on.

With full bellies, we settled down once more in what we called "the best place in the ship" (our bunks). We often sang "Get married my Lads and have all night in, and go to sea no more". So, there we stayed until we were called on Monday morning. The Mate roused us at 7 am. It was still fine but the cool nip in the air was still with us. We hastened to put on some warm clothing as we rolled out and as usual there were one or two jobs to be done before we went to breakfast. Having bought our stores on Saturday we managed a quick fry-up of bacon, egg and dip (fried bread) followed by mugs of coffee or cocoa. Our bread was beginning to get stale, but with bacon it was not too bad. But it would have to last another three days at least. Still if it got too bad we could always fall back on sea or water biscuits and if need be, porridge. Falling back and making do was quite common practice as far as food was concerned.

After breakfast, we turned to our usual ship board work. By noon, having completed loading our cargo we began to batten down and get ready for sea. Our heavy cargo of steel plates etc, lay deep in the hold, if there is any rough weather they will act like a pendulum and we will roll our guts out especially in a beam sea. So let us hope we get a fine and smooth run. At 1-10 pm. on Monday 12th April 1926, we sailed for Portsmouth; on this trip our watch had the 'eight hours in'. (This meant we had the 8 pm. to midnight and the 4 am. to 8 am. watch below.) By the time we had got clear with everything lashed and stowed, life line rigged and the decks washed down, half our watch below had gone. So as soon as we could, we rolled into our bunks to get what was left, and have a nap before we turned out again at 'one bell' (3-45 pm.)

At 3-5 pm. we were abeam of Salt Scar buoy. The log was streamed and set. When we came on watch at 'eight bells' the course had been set at SE $\frac{1}{2}$ E. Old Will and I shared the lookout and steering, changing over every hour as was the practice. The weather being fine and the ship in good trim, she was steering easy, so apart from keeping an eye on other shipping, we spent most of our watch yarning, mainly about our homes and families, which was not unusual. However, it was necessary to keep our voices down, the 'Old Man' in his cabin underneath the bridge, might hear us talking, and come up and give us a 'rocket' for not concentrating on the job in hand. At 5-5 pm., we came abeam of Whitby Light House, the log had recorded 17 miles, which meant we were making good time, our course then was SE by S $\frac{3}{4}$ S. At eight bells (8 pm.) Will and I, went below and after a quick meal of bread, margarine and jam washed down with a mug of cocoa, we were soon in our bunks and fast asleep.

When we came back on watch at midnight, we learnt that we had passed Flamborough Head at 8-35 pm. with 47 miles recorded on the log. Our course had been altered to SE by S $\frac{1}{2}$ S and we were making for the East Dudgeon Light vessel. The weather had continued to be fine and visibility was good. As far as I can recall, there was not much shipping about. As soon as we had relieved the watch, Will and I, in turn, went aft to the galley to make our cocoa. I usually had a couple of sea biscuits well plastered with margarine and a lump of cheese. I really enjoyed this and never got tired of it. I suppose I was always hungry.

After we had our 'scran', our slang for grub, Will took the wheel for the first hour, whilst I kept the 'lookout'. During the night hours, the man on lookout would peer over the top of the canvas dodger, making the occasional visual sweep round the horizon. Standing still and staring out into the darkness was not the best way of keeping awake. But it was necessary to keep a good lookout, some ships had very poor lights or none at all (such as poaching trawlers). It was customary to signal the offender by lamp, flashing the letter 'P' (your lights are out or want trimming). There was little more scarifying than the sudden sighting of a red light on the starboard bow followed by some sharp avoiding action. Sailing ships having only sidelights could also be difficult to spot. However, jammed against the engine room telegraph, one could and sometimes did doze off for a second or two. When the knees buckled one awoke.

Sometimes, when the Mate came on the bridge or the Old Man, they would quietly approach and hold their hand in front of one's face, to see if one's

eyes were open! When I took the wheel for the second hour of our watch, Will said he would slip aft to the galley and have a look at the fire. This was normal, we always kept the fire going and the kettle filled and boiling ready for the oncoming watch, or when the cook turned out. So, after a quick look round Will left the bridge saying he would not be long. I knew from experience he would have a sit down for a few minutes on the galley locker. But when Will's absence seemed longer than usual, I began to worry. I had no means of measuring time, so could only watch and wait. As time went on I became more anxious and began to think about all sorts of calamities. I just did not know what to do and was afraid that the 'Old Man' might decide to come up. Where the hell was Will? I was both mad and afraid. I could not hear anyone moving on deck and peering for'ard over the dodger I could not see any signs of activity in the forecastle. I was afraid of waking the Old Man, he would have a fit, but what was I to do? Using the whistle lanyard to lash the wheel, I secured it long enough to go to the wing of the bridge and look aft, hoping to attract someone's attention, but no luck, it seemed hopeless.

After what seemed an eternity, I heard the sound of footsteps on the lower bridge, this proved to be one of the firemen going for'ard to call the watch. Managing to attract his attention, I asked him to go aft and find Will. He found him alright, fast asleep on the galley locker. When he was roused, he became very agitated. When he came on to the bridge, he could not apologise enough, I think he was afraid I would tell the Old Man, which I did not. It was fortunate that visibility was good and little shipping about, but most of all, that we had not had to change course during our watch. We went below at eight bells (4 am.). Will, in spite of his bonus sleep in the galley, was snoring as soon as he got his head down. April 13th, when we came back on watch at 8 am., we found that we had passed the East Dudgeon Light vessel at 4-30 am. with $13\frac{1}{2}$ miles on the log ($113\frac{1}{2}$ miles from Salt Scar buoy). The wind had remained light and Southerly, with visibility good.

Having passed off Cromer at 7 am., we were now abeam of the Haisborough Light vessel, unfortunately the weather looked like changing and visibility was not too good. Throughout the 8 am. to 12 noon watch we had hazy weather and poor visibility, we did not sight either the Newarp or Cross Sands Light vessels. Steaming across the busy area in the vicinity of the Thames estuary was not good with all the traffic about, visibility being limited. We, having to maintain a good lookout, I was not sorry to go off watch at eight bells (noon), but as always in hazy or foggy weather, our watch below was not very restful, we could not relax. At 4 pm. we were back on watch and learnt that we had passed the Shipwash Light vessel at 1-12 pm. The Sunk Light vessel had not been seen but the 'two blasts' of its fog horn had been heard, the Long Sands Light vessel having been passed at 3-25 pm. just before we came on watch. Visibility had improved slightly, but with the light Southerly wind it was still inclined to be hazy. We passed the Kentish Knock Light vessel at 4-35 pm. with the log reading 19 miles, our course was then SW by S. At 6-45 pm. we came abeam of the North Goodwin Light vessel, our log was reading 38 miles, we altered course to SW $\frac{1}{2}$ W. The area was busy with shipping and because of the haze we found difficulty in estimating distances, especially when looking for channel buoys inside the Goodwins.

By 7-20 pm. we had passed the Gull Light vessel and appeared to be making good time. But the continuous strain of maintaining a good lookout, made our watch below more than welcome, but once again one could not relax. Being in a very busy shipping area in foggy weather, it did not pay to take things for granted, but at least we could rest our eyes. This was one of the occasions when one felt sorry for the Old Man, he could not relax. It was five minutes before we went off watch that we came abeam of the South Goodwin Light vessel. Rounding the South Foreland at 8-12 pm. we altered course to SW and entered that very congested shipping lane, the Dover Straits. Fortunately, visibility whilst not good had improved somewhat, and that was most welcome. Will and I, spent a restless watch below, turning into our bunks with a feeling of apprehension. Most seafarers are like this when sailing in busy waters during foggy weather. One did not usually undress, neither would we have the door closed, especially steel doors. These had been known to jam after a collision and unfortunate occupants had been trapped and drowned. We lay in our bunks, listening and dozing.

It was 10-10 pm. when we rounded Dungeness and altered course to W by S $\frac{1}{2}$ S. Later we had to haul out to WSW to clear some 'Wreck' buoys. Fishing boats were now our main problem. I suppose they belonged to Rye and other nearby harbours. These boats, often clustered together, lay drifting on their nets or lines, the extent and direction of which we could only judge, guided by the lower or two lights which they exhibited. We often had to make wide sweeps to clear them but I am afraid we were not always successful. When Will and I came back on watch at midnight, we found that visibility had much improved, we could see the distant lights of Eastbourne.

April 14th 1-5 am. we rounded the Royal Sovereign Light vessel, and with

South Goodwin
Light Vessel

the log reading 93, altered course to W by N. Beachy Head light was in view and we passed about 1½ miles off it at 1-45 am. With the log reading 100 we altered course to W ½ N. We were now heading towards the Owers Light vessel, but the weather had become hazy again, consequently, we did not see the Light vessel, but heard the long blast of her fog signal as we passed. We did not see the Nab Tower either, but managed to locate her by the triple blast of her fog horn. Entering the Solent, we neared the end of the first stage of our voyage.

Will and I, went below at 4 am., we hoped to get the most of our watch below. We were lucky, after picking up our pilot, we berthed in Portsmouth Dockyard at 9 am. Without any waste of time, our part cargo was soon going over the side. By 5 pm., the part cargo had been discharged and soon we had unmoored and sailed for Devonport. At 7-40 pm. we dropped our pilot and at 8 pm. Will and I, still on 'eight hours in' went below at 8 pm. We were lucky we had the last watch below before arriving and the first watch below after sailing. Unfortunately, after discharging our part cargo, we were left with a slight list to starboard, but there was not anything we could do about it only hope for good weather. At 11-15 pm. when passing the Needles, we signalled name and destination, which they acknowledged. Changing course to W by S, the log was streamed and set. As we cleared the Needles we found the visibility was good, but with a Southerly wind there was some swell. Although not bad under normal conditions, nevertheless the heavy cargo of plate low in the hold, began to act as a pendulum as we feared and the ship developed a roll. This roll began to make life a bit uncomfortable.

April 15th, we passed Anvil Point at 12-50 am. and we were still rolling. Will and I, spent an uncomfortable watch on deck, especially after going aft to the galley and trying to prevent the kettle and other things being thrown off the stove. At 2-55 am. we passed well off Portland Bill, still rolling like an old tub, but at least we were making good time the log having recorded 30 miles since we passed the Needles. When we went below at eight bells (4 am.) we found the forecastle a shambles, loose gear, i.e. buckets, pans and other items moving from side to side as the ship rolled. I suppose the watch below, having tried apparently unsuccessfully to secure the loose gear, had got fed up and decided to ignore it. However, before we turned in, Will and I, managed to secure most of the gear.

Coming back on watch at 8 am. we could see the land in the vicinity of Start Point, on the starboard bow. Breakfast was very much a make do effort, it was a case of getting something to eat, because of feeling hungry, and having a hot drink to wash it down, but preparing something special was out of the question. The Cook/Steward was in a filthy temper, as this rolling motion made the preparation of the cabin breakfast difficult. Not only was it a problem keeping things on the stove, but also on the cabin table. For some reason or another he did not use 'fiddles' but was using a wet canvas table cloth, apparently the normal practice. But in spite of his precautions some of his crockery had been broken. So with all his problems, his temper did not improve, every now and again he would give vent to his feelings by directing his verbal abuse towards anyone who was at the wheel.

At 11-20 am. Start Point was abeam, we altered course to NW by W and things began to be more comfortable, the ship was not rolling quite so much. Will and I, went below at 'eight bells' (noon), we knew we would not get our full watch below, but assuming we would get a night in our bunks, decided to have a good fry up in the galley. The resultant concoction enabled us to enjoy what was left of the stale bread. Arriving in Plymouth Sound, we were boarded by our pilot at 2-15 pm. and were soon snugly berthed in the Devonport Dockyard. This was my first visit to Devonport and incidentally the last.

Devonport Dockyard, April 16th, 1926. After a restful night in our bunks, we were roused by the Mate at 6-55 am. The weather was not too good at all it was raining, and as we dressed we speculated on what job we would have to do. Usually in port, wet weather jobs other than paint washing, would be under cover. However we would soon know, one thing for sure we would not be idle. The wet weather however did not stop our discharging of cargo and later that day we shifted ship from North to the South dock. We then learnt that we were to have a weekend in, which was good news. I have often heard reference to Dockyard Maties, now seeing them in their natural habitat, I was not very impressed, perhaps I was biased. Looking back on my Devonport visit I remember very little about the place. I think my trips ashore must have been confined to shopping at the nearest convenient shops.

Devonport Dockyard, April 17th, 1926. As usual we were called by the Mate at 6-55 am. the weather was still wet with a squally wind, but we did not mind we had the comfort of a weekend in to look forward to. So, after being employed on one or two jobs, we knocked off at noon for the weekend. During the afternoon, one or two of us decided to have a clean-up and a shave. Washing and shaving, especially at sea, was not a regular event, similarly the washing

of clothing. These activities were usually left until we had plenty of time to spare, or, occasionally when anticipating a run home, a special cleaning effort would be made. This was part of what we used to call the 'Channels'. I am afraid that sailors, with the exception of firemen, did not always wash every day, consequently they tended to become rather scruffy, unshaved, untidy and unclean. But in their defence, one should remember the only fresh water was in a tank over the galley and limited. Water used for washing purposes was obtained from a tank in the stokehold. There was not any water in the forecastle.

Early on Saturday evening some of my shipmates went ashore. Joe who had previous knowledge of Devonport, acted as pilot, but I am afraid the main objective was the nearest suitable and liveliest pub. I stayed on board and made a meal. I cannot remember what I ate, but it was most likely sliced oranges sprinkled with sugar and covered with evaporated milk. This was my favourite meal, it was easy to prepare and went down well with my bread and margarine. I never got tired of it. Then, if I followed my usual routine, I most probably spent the remainder of the evening trying to read in the dim light of our one and only oil lamp, which being secured to the bulkhead did not provide a very good light. But as I have previously mentioned, the only comfortable place to relax was in one's bunk and trying to read when lying down was not easy. As a result I was inclined to get sleepy, and eventually fall fast asleep, which I must have done. I did not hear my shipmates return.

Devonport Dockyard, Sunday April 18th 1926. Being Sunday morning, and not having been roused in the usual manner, it was about 9am. when I woke up. It was wonderful to be able to stretch and anticipate another free day and night in. My shipmates were still asleep when I got out of my bunk and by the look of the disarray, they must have come back aboard in a right state. The weather was still wet and squally, but being in port the weather did not bother us much. Quickly dressing and feeling hungry, I got some bacon and a tin of tomatoes and went aft to the galley to cook myself a good breakfast. The cook, having served the cabin breakfast was sitting on the galley locker having a sandwich of some kind and at the same time preparing the vegetables ready for dinner. He did not look too good, and was probably suffering from a hangover.

The cook/steward did not have any days off, his was a seven day job. He was more often than not referred to as the 'steward' although his job was combined with cooking the cabin meals. His only benefits were, having time to eat and every night in his bunk, which I think in the winter was worth something. We suspected also he did not have to buy food for himself. However, finding a clear place on the stove, I got cracking and cooked myself a meal. When I returned to the forecastle, I found my shipmates in various stages of getting up. I think the smell of my cooked breakfast must have made them feel hungry, for they were not very long before they went aft to the galley to cook a meal. Most of us managed to have some bacon at one time or another, especially after payday. Bacon was usually cheap in those days and cooked with anything made a tasty meal. As I have already mentioned it helped with the stale bread. Our food lockers being right for'ard opposite the stove contributed little towards the maintenance of fresh food.

After breakfast, we somehow or other obtained the Sunday papers, and so we relaxed for the remainder of the day catching up on the news. I am afraid whenever we had a free Sunday in port, we would, unless there was some urgent reason to go ashore, spend most of the time lying in our bunks. It was customary to occupy the time by either reading, smoking or yarning, and if we felt industrious, stitching, patching and darning. Make do and mend was often necessary. After the cook/steward had served the cabin dinner, washed and cleared away the pans and so on, those who wished to, went aft to the galley to cook a proper dinner. These self cooked dinners were designed to be easy to prepare but also filling. We used to concoct some queer meals at times, a lot depended on what we could afford. I cannot remember what we had on this occasion, but usually when doing our cooking on our free days, we would sit in the galley yarning about many things. Often we would talk about our homes and families, which in many cases we had not seen for months, in one or two cases, for years.

Devonport Dockyard, Monday April 19th 1926. For some reason or other, the Mate was late in rousing us, he was in a bad temper when he called us at 7-30 am. The weather was still wet and squally, as a result we did a few jobs under cover. We worked until 3-30 pm. then knocked off for the day. After a meal and a wash we spent the remainder of the day, lounging about and reading.

Devonport Dockyard, Tuesday April 20th 1926. We expected to finish discharging today, as a result we began taking more notice of the weather, which was, according to my log, Westerly winds, squally. But most of all we began to think of our next port of call. There was much speculation, as there always

was on those occasions. We more or less expected that we would be going to Newlyn, being so near, and going there so often, it appeared almost a certainty. Finally we got our orders, it was Newlyn as expected. We hoped the Westerly wind would moderate before we sailed. We knew in the normal way, it would be a short trip, but head winds could prolong it, so it was best to get some extra grub. By 3-30 pm. we had completed discharging and we lost no time getting under way, the pilot being already on board. It was a bit of a dash getting our beams, hatches and tarpaulins on and everything secured before we reached open water. We dropped our pilot at 4 pm. and clearing the breakwater, began our Westerly run.

I was now in the Mate's watch and consequently again on the 'eight hours in'. So, instead of going below at 'eight bells' (4 pm.) I began a four hours watch on deck. Clearing Penlee Point, we began what proved to be a hard punch against a strong Westerly wind and rough sea. Being light ship, we began to bounce and made little headway. At 5-30 pm., the Old Man decided that the weather was too bad, we were not making much headway and wasting bunkers trying, so we might as well turn back, which we did and headed for Plymouth Sound. It was about 6-30 pm. when we entered the Sound and prepared to anchor. I had noticed a cruiser, H.M.S. ENTERPRISE, following us in, but did not pay much attention to it. But, as we swung round and prepared to drop anchor, I noticed the cruiser's semaphore signal arms were wagging away like mad, concluding that she was signalling us. I drew the Mate's attention to it. Although we could both send and receive messages in 'Morse' we were weak on semaphore. In any case the naval message speed was much too fast for us to read. This being the case, the Mate suggested we turn a blind eye and give it the Nelson touch. So we carried on and dropped our anchor. However, the ENTERPRISE would not be ignored, she called up a dockyard tug, which came alongside us with the message, "Heave up and get out", we were apparently in the cruiser's anchorage! So we, very reluctantly hove up our anchors and moved outside the breakwater. I am afraid that at the time our relationship with the Navy was a little strained. It was about 7 pm. when we anchored in Cawsand Bay, it was not very comfortable, we were feeling the Westerly swell and tended to roll. But the weather looked like it might improve, we thought the wind would shift to the Nor'ard.

Anchored in Cawsand Bay, Wednesday April 21st 1926. Coming back on watch at midnight, we noticed the wind had decreased. By 4 am. the wind, as expected, swung to the North. So, heaving up our anchors we resumed passage to Newlyn. The log was streamed and set at 4-5 am. We found the weather had improved, also visibility was good. The four to eight watch was fairly uneventful. Back on watch at 'eight bells' (8 am.) I saw we would soon be abeam of the Lizard, having apparently made good time. At 9-12 am. the Lizard was abeam and the log registered $42\frac{1}{2}$. We altered course to W by S $\frac{1}{2}$ S. The wind was still fresh from the WNW but being off the land the sea was smooth. The other watch who had gone below would be unlucky, for we would soon be in Newlyn. It was likely to be a long day for them, for we did not expect to have a night in. At 10-30 am. the log reading 53, was hauled inboard and by 11-15 am. we had picked up our pilot. It was about 11-30 am. when we berthed at the South Pier in Newlyn harbour. It was not very long before 'Charlie' the loading foreman came on board with the unwelcome but expected news that we were to load and sail that day. The only good part of his news was that we were bound for Littlehampton, which was another short run. Our cargo was to be granite chippings. We went ashore in turn, to do our shopping for stores.

We usually patronised a little shop at the top of the pier, which was kept by an old lady. Others, in need of liquid refreshment went a little further to the 'Fishermans Arms' a well known port of call. Being frequent visitors to Newlyn, we eventually became well known to many of the locals and made many friends. The future saw several of my shipmates married to local girls and later after swallowing the anchor, become domiciled in Newlyn. However, back to April 1926. We completed loading by 8-30 pm. and within a short time had backed away from the pier, turned, and headed out towards the Lizard. The wind was still WNW light and visibility good. The log was streamed at 9-5 pm. and we were on our way once more, arriving off the Lizard at 10-50 pm.

103. H.M.S. ENTERPRISE would not be ignored!

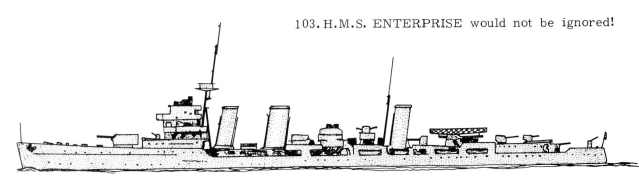

April 22nd 1926. At sea. Moderate northerly wind and good visibility. We arrived off Littlehampton at 7-45 pm. picked up the pilot at 8-30 pm. and were berthed by 9.00 pm.

April 23rd 1926. The crew were roused at 7-00 am. by the Mate and after a meal, turned to painting ship and general work, mainly of a maintenance nature. At 8-00 am. discharging of the cargo commenced using ship's gear and continued until 5 pm. in fine weather.

April 24th 1926. Roused by the Mate at 7-00 am. and after a meal continued painting ship. Cargo discharge was resumed at 8-00 am. and completed by 3.00 pm. Battened down and cleaned ship ready to sail on the tide, sailed for Newlyn in fine weather at 8-15 pm., dropped pilot at 8-25 pm., and had Owers Light vessel abeam by 10-10 pm.

April 25th 1926. At sea in fine clear weather. At 4-00 pm. entered Portland harbour and by 4-45 pm. commenced to take in bunkers from the coal hulk. By 6-15 pm. bunkering of 40 tons of coal was completed and passage resumed for Newlyn. Arrived 9-00 pm. and dropped both anchors in the harbour. I had to take a night watch on my own.

April 26th 1926. Remained at anchor, crew employed painting overside in fine weather. After being on watch, I spent the day in my bunk.

April 27th 1926. Hove up anchors and moved to loading berth at pier and 15 minutes later began to load granite chippings for London. Meanwhile, the crew went ashore to buy food. Loading completed at 3 pm., battened down and started to wash down decks, sailing 15 minutes later in fine clear weather.

April 28th 1926. At sea. Called at Portland for bunkers going alongside about 8-30 am. and resuming passage to London at 10-00 am.

April 29th 1926. At sea. By 2-30 am. Dungeness is abeam and we are entering the Dover Straits and set course to pass inside the Goodwin Sands. By 7-35 am. the N.E. Spit Buoy is reached and we are entering the mouth of the Thames. At 12-15 pm. arrived at Gravesend and picked up river pilot. Arrived off discharging berth at 1-40 pm. and went alongside Cory's Wharf at 3-20 pm. At 9-30 pm. we moved and moored to buoys. Night very foggy.

April 30th 1926. Roused at 6-00 am. (I cannot remember why, but I do remember it was very foggy). At 9-00 am. we unmoored from the buoys and anchored off Cory's Wharf and at about 2-30 pm. moved into discharging berth and commenced discharging which was completed by 7-00 pm. and we then sailed for Sunderland in wet weather and an Easterly wind. The river pilot was dropped at Gravesend. The passage northward continued uneventfully on May 1st and we arrived in Sunderland at 6-10 am. on the 2nd of May and moored to buoys in the river. When we arrived in Sunderland, we had no idea that the whole of the country had gone on strike. It was early Sunday morning when we sailed in. We thought that was the reason for the apparent lack of shore activity. Our ship not being equipped with wireless and no one having one of those (new fangled) wireless sets accounted for the fact that we had been out of touch with the news since leaving London. So, our first knowledge came with the orders to moor at the buoys in the river. The situation was later confirmed and explained, when we put the boat out and went ashore to buy Sunday papers.

Monday, May 3rd 1926. Sunderland Harbour. We remain moored to the buoys. The Skipper went ashore to the Brokers for orders, and to get the mail and we anxiously awaited his return for news. When he came back, it was with orders from our owners for the crew to be paid off and we were on 24 hours notice. However, ship work had to continue, and the Mate kept us busy painting ship. When we knocked off for the day, some of us went ashore in the small boat, to visit the railway station and enquire about trains home. We discovered that all transport was at a standstill and began to realise the seriousness of the General Strike when we discovered that our chances of transport home was nil.

Tuesday, 4th May 1926. Moored to buoys in Sunderland Harbour. Today after the Skipper had been ashore he came back with better news. The 24 hours notice to pay off, had been cancelled, we were to go on half pay instead. This was better, but not much. It meant that our pay would be just over thirty shillings a week. How the married men would manage to send money home and keep themselves in food was going to be a problem. It was not too bad for the single men, at least they could afford some food. What I did find happening was that men began sharing and that helped a bit. Being on half pay did not mean half work, the Mate kept us busy chipping and painting down the hold, whether that was to usefully occupy us, or keep us working out of sight, or both, I do not know. But there is no mistake, the owners got their money's worth out of us. Still half a loaf was better than no bread and we would not go hungry.

Wednesday, May 5th 1926. Moored to buoys in Sunderland Harbour. This day was very much like the previous day, we continued to work down the hold. The weather was fortunately fine. We were rather isolated from events a-shore, our ship being in a separate world. What news we did get was not very good, it seemed that there was trouble everywhere, We wonder how things are at home.

Thursday, May 6th 1926. Moored to buoys in Sunderland Harbour and still working down the hold. We had to go ashore to buy food. Newspapers were unobtainable. Later a single sheet news called the 'Bulletin', price one penny, was available. That was apparently the only way of getting any National news. Signed off Ships Articles at 5-15 pm. Half pay now in operation.

Friday, May 7th 1926. Moored to buoys in Sunderland Harbour. Still employed painting, etc. down the hold.

Saturday, May 8th 1926. Moored to buoys in Sunderland Harbour. Being Saturday, we tidied up for the weekend, this included washing out the fore-castle, etc.

Sunday, May 9th 1926. Moored to buoys in Sunderland Harbour. Not much activity anywhere, especially ashore. Most of our crew were either lying in their bunks, sleeping or yarning. Some were hanging around the galley hoping for some 'Blackpan'. Others were sewing, mending or washing their clothing and so on. Money being short, there was a shortage of cigarettes and tobacco, also something to read. To pass the time, I took the small boat up river for a sail, it was very pleasant.

Monday and Tuesday, 10th and 11th May 1926. Moored to buoys in Sunderland Harbour. We are still employed, painting, etc. down the hold.

Wednesday, May 12th 1926. Moored to buoys in Sunderland Harbour. We had some good news today, the General Strike is over, and better still we are to sail for Rotterdam. We will be back on full pay tomorrow.

The scrap log was a voluntary effort on my part, and was part of an endeavour towards increasing my knowledge of Home Trade navigation. Many years have passed since then and many changes have taken place, expecially concerning methods. Before I forget, the word 'log' can mean either of two things. One:- The book in which 'Events' are recorded i.e. progress, weather, change of course, unusual happenings and so on; like a diary. Crew members are said to have signed 'on the log', when they join the ship. This is the time when their particulars are recorded and they sign or make their mark. When they leave the ship they are said to have 'signed off the log'. The reference to 'log' in my scrap log refers to the instrument which records distance run, a measure of miles between two known times. The instrument was fitted in a bracket right aft on the port quarter. It was permanently connected to a wheel by a woven rope, which was about a yard long. The wheel, about a foot in diameter, acted as a balance wheel. When in use this was connected to a three-triangular-bladed float by a thin woven cotton line, made fast to an eye on the free side of the balance wheel. The cotton line being about eight or ten fathoms long, made it possible to tow the 'three bladed float' well clear of the propellor wash. As the ship moved through the water, the bladed float would revolve and twist the long thin rope, which would in turn cause the balance wheel to revolve and the instrument to operate. The mileage would be shown by a finger on a dial. The dial face was calibrated from 'one to one hundred'.

Courses are recorded as points of the compass. In my early days at Navigation School we were taught:- "A compass card is a circular piece of cardboard or mica, graduated to points, half and quarter points and sometimes degrees." etc. Now courses are given in degrees and the compass card is graduated into 360 degrees. Therefore, North by East would be given as 'Eleven' degrees, East as 'Ninety', South East as 'one Hundred and Thirty Five' degrees and so on increasing in degrees through compass points South and East towards the North. In 1932, helm orders became international. Prior to then, the order 'Port your helm' meant pulling the wheel to Starboard. This is best illustrated by a rhyme published in an old 'Reeds Seamanship' manual. When three lights I see ahead. (i.e. masthead and both sidelights), I 'Port' my helm, and show my red. (i.e. I cause my vessel to incline towards the right and thus hide my Starboard (Green) light.) After the change, Port meant 'Wheel to Port' and Starboard, 'Wheel to Starboard'. Needless to say, the change caused confusion and mistakes were not unknown in the early days immediately following the change. By the way, this was life at sea in a 'Weekly Boat' which differs in many ways to life in a 'Monthly Boat'. When reading my log entries, I was inclined to, using the entries as a base, either elaborate or condense the account of daily happenings. But I finally decided that, if I gave the details exactly as I wrote them at the time, it would help to provide a clearer picture of the daily routine in a typical 'weekly boat'.

(For further log extracts, see Appendix).

Walker's
'Cherub' log.

18. Voyage with Variations.

Thomas H. Thomason

Although it was way back in the late 1920s, I will never forget a voyage which could so easily have been our last. It was a dark and stormy night when we left the Bristol Channel port of Swansea bound for the London River. The STANLEY FORCE lay deep in the water with her holds full of 'anthracite peas'. Seamen familiar with this type of cargo will know, that like grain, it tends to shift in bad weather, especially when the holds are not filled to capacity. As we sailed out into the dark night, looking back at the receding lights of Swansea and the Mumbles, I could not help but envy the people whom I imagined were sitting by their comfortable and warm firesides. Heading on our South Westerly course, we found weather conditions deteriorating with every mile. The wind was increasing and sea rising. It was with some feeling of relief that we learnt that the 'Old Man' had decided that we should anchor under the lee of Lundy until the weather improved. We later learnt that a vessel which had continued on the South Westerly course, foundered off Hartland Point with all hands, a crew of twenty one.

We spent the remainder of that night and the following morning, lying snug under Lundy. When daylight came, we saw we had plenty of company. All like us, apparently waiting for the weather to moderate. Many ships did not carry radio or as we knew it in those days 'wireless'. Consequently they did not have the benefit of an up to date weather forecast. So, as was customary, we kept an eye on the other vessels, if any hove up their anchor and moved off, the 'Old Man' was told immediately. The Masters of Home Trade vessels were driven hard by their owners, quick passages, speedy loading and discharge of cargo was considered imperative. Therefore, ships only became weather bound when it was impossible to do otherwise. The movement of any ship from a windbound anchorage usually initiated a general scramble. This state of affairs was dangerous and was probably one of the reasons why ships were lost, because of being driven too hard for too long and perhaps to the point of no return. We, having already experienced such occasions, would no doubt do so again. So it was, with what appeared to be an improvement in the weather, we, along with other ships, hove up and resumed our South Westerly passage towards the Longships.

Clearing Lundy, we found that weather conditions had improved but the sea was still rough. However, with no apparent reason to turn back we continued on course for the Longships. Some hours later, when about 30 miles SW of Lundy, the weather began to deteriorate. The Westerly wind was increasing and the sea building up into Atlantic rollers. Occasionally some of the wave tops were level with the lower bridge. Unfortunately being deep in the water with a cargo liable to shift, also a large expanse of vulnerable canvas-covered hatchways, shipping heavy seas was a problem. We had arrived at the stage when 'putting about' was too hazardous. We just could not risk getting broad side to the heavy seas. We could end up with a shifted cargo or stove in hatches, the risk was too terrible to contemplate. We had reeved thick ropes through the scupper doors in the high bulwarks of the fore well deck. This was to keep the doors from closing. The weight of a temporary load of sea water in the fore well deck could have seriously interfered with our buoyancy. As turning back was too risky, we just had to ride it out. We had what might be considered a little consolation. There were other ships in the vicinity also in the same predicament, making heavy weather of it. All we could do was watch one another but if any help had been required in the situation it would have been impossible, so all we could do was nurse our ships. This was one of the occasions when experience and seamanship becomes invaluable. Our 'Old Man' was experienced, enough to know when to accept prevailing conditions rather than fight them. So began, what was to be a slow hard slog towards the Longships. After spending some time watching the seas, the 'Old Man' decided we might ride easier if we met the oncoming seas with the bluff of our bow. So, with sufficient speed to maintain steerage way, we eased the ship a little to port. There was no doubt about it, the ship not only rode the seas easier, but seemed to ship less water. The bows would rise to the oncoming waves and after a momentary pause, slide down into the trough. Occasionally one would think the ship would not recover and rise again. This went on hour after hour and every once in a while those on the unprotected bridge would get drenched with spray.

The large steering wheel, manually operated when at sea, kicked as the helmsman, standing braced with feet apart, worked hard to retain control and keep the ship on course. The watches continued to be changed every four hours but for the deck crowd this mainly consisted of being relieved from the wheel and lookout. Getting for'ard was difficult, also there was no comfort in the cold wet forecastle, being shaken about like a 'Jack in a box'. Lookout consisted of mainly observing the other hard pressed vessels, and watching a depressing succession of large and ugly Atlantic rollers as they swept towards us. Throughout the day, the 'Old Man' stood jammed against the telegraph (no doubt to take the weight off his tired and aching legs and feet) gazing silently at the sea, over the top of the canvas dodger. Now and again he broke his silence with a remark about the weather or to give a sharp reminder to the man at the wheel to watch his steering. The cook appeared on the bridge from time to time, bringing the 'Old Man' a mug of tea and a sandwich. No doubt it was very welcome.

Life in the ship had become disorganised in one way or another. Down in the engine room, an engineer stood by the main steam valve, ready to reduce steam when the stern lifted and the propellor raced. All chances of a hot meal had gone after we had shipped a sea through the galley. The only means of getting a hot drink was by boiling water on the cabin stove. The cabin being situated amidships was fairly steady in comparison to the rest of the ship. Meals, such as they were, we had sitting on the cabin floor, holding on to our food and drink so as not to lose them. Life in the forecastle as I have already mentioned was practically impossible. It was like being in a lift, rising and falling at such a rate one was almost thrown against the deck head as she dropped into a sea. The place was littered with loose gear and all this, along with the cold and wet discouraged any attempt to stay. Consequently, we began to spend our 'watches below' on either the stokehold or engine room gratings. It was a bit dusty on the stokehold grating but at least it was warm and dry, excepting when the occasional shower of water came through an overhead grating. Sleeping was impossible, but we did manage to doze now and again.

Illumination in the engine room was by acetylene lamps, all other lighting was provided by oil lamps, including the navigation lamps. These lamps had to be cleaned and trimmed daily, and the lamp room being right for'ard caused cleaning, trimming and lighting to be a difficult operation. Every now and again when a sea came over the forecastle head, a shower of water would pour over the lamp room door, usually wetting any occupant. Because of the approaching sunset, I was given the job of lighting the navigation lamps and placing them into position. This would require me to make several journeys between the lamp room and other parts of the ship. Not very difficult in good weather, but now it would be a prolonged and dangerous occupation, which included two visits on to the exposed forecastle head. So, after lighting the mast head lamp, I stood under the shelter of the forecastle head, to watch and wait for a suitable opportunity. As the bows began to rise, I made a dash for the ladder

leading up on to the forecastle head, placing the lamp in its bracket, and dashed down to haul the lamp up before the ship dived into a sea. I had one other job to do before that was complete, this was to check if the lamp was still alight. This required me to return to the forecastle head, go as far for'ard as I dare, so that I could see the light. Again, watching my opportunity, I returned to the forecastle head, went for'ard, and holding on to the fore stay, had a quick glance upwards. Yes, the lamp was still alight. Now came the side lights, these were heavy brass lamps which I could only carry one at a time. So, once again, waiting for a suitable opportunity, I climbed on to the fore hatch and made a bee line for the lower bridge using the lifeline we had rigged fore and aft across the fore hatch on the port side, leading to the lower bridge ladder. Two journeys up on to the bridge and I had the side lights in position. Now came the stern light, this was a smaller lantern, but I had further to carry it, along a wet and heaving main deck, then up on to the after housing. Last came the binnacle lights, these were only small, apart from crossing the fore hatch, there was not any problem. I was glad when the job was completed, we should be all right as long as the lamps remained alight. As the night got darker, it was easier to see the light beam from our mast head and sidelights, this was occasionally visible, reflected from the spray or wave tops.

The night hours dragged, it was wet and miserable, the seas were still large, occasionally the wave tops would show up in the beam of our side lights. The only light on the bridge came from the binnacle, which frequently illuminated the muffled face of the man at the wheel. There was an occasional glow from a pipe or cigarette or the beam from an electric torch held by someone on the lower bridge carrying out a distant visual inspection of the fore and main hatch covers. This was necessary in bad weather during the hours of darkness, to check wedges, battens and canvas covers. There was a constant click of machine cogs in the steering gear box at the rear of the bridge, accompanied by the rattle of steering gear chains on the main steel deck, as her stern flopped into the sea. An hour at the wheel was long enough without a spell as the helmsman required all his strength and skill to control the wheel as it kicked. Throughout the night, the 'Old Man' remained on the bridge, silently watching the sea. There was not anything that one could do, only watch and hope. However, it was a comfort to have the 'Old Man' on the bridge, we felt safer, I wonder how he felt?

When daylight came, there was not a ship in sight, and we began to wonder what had happened to them. Later we learnt that there had been some loss and damage. Weather conditions appeared to be similar to the previous day, but there did look like a possibility of improvement, at least the sky gave that indication. It was, if I remember correctly, sometime during the late afternoon when we sighted Pendeen off the port bow. Although our troubles were far from over, with the sighting, conditions became more bearable. We began to look forward to rounding the Longships and running before the bad weather. This we eventually did, and later after rounding the Lizard we found the weather conditions had improved quite a bit, although we had the problem of steering the ship in a heavy following sea. It was a job to keep her from broaching to. After we had rounded Lizard, the 'Old Man' decided we should put into Plymouth Sound. I think he wanted to contact our owners and the people who were waiting for our cargo. Also I suspect he wanted a rest, he had had very little since we left Lundy.

It was early morning and still quite dark as we entered the Sound. When we came abeam of the Lighthouse on the breakwater, we appeared to poop a sea. Although it was quite dark we felt it come aboard. The ship appeared to lie sluggish in the water for a little while until she had lost the deck load of water through the scuppers. We eventually anchored in quiet water and life became peaceful again. After the 'Old Man' had finished with engines he gave us the usual instructions about lights, bearings, etc. then went to leave the bridge. I saw him open the small gate at the top of the bridge ladder and step out. I did not see what happened next, but heard him cry out. Going to investigate, I saw the bridge ladder was missing and he was lying on the lower bridge deck about eight feet below. I presumed he had fallen down. Anyway, he was apparently fully conscious, which was obvious as he was loudly expressing his feelings in language, which for him, was stronger than usual. I concluded that with all the noise he was making, he could not be badly hurt. Luckily my surmise proved correct. Later the bridge ladder was located nearby. It had apparently been displaced by the sea as it came inboard. One thing for sure, I am glad I was not the first to leave the bridge.

Life at sea was tough, there was little sympathy for anyone suffering misfortune. No one was considered injured or disabled unless they were unconscious or dead. It was as simple as that. Ship board requirements had to be fulfilled, therefore, leadswinging or scrimshanking was not popular with one's shipmates who would be required to carry out any extra duties. There was an occasion in Blyth when the cook fell down the fore hold. I heard someone say, "If he's fallen on his head he won't have hurt himself". He came out bruised

Bowline.

but otherwise none the worse. There was another time when in Liverpool docks, a fireman and myself had been ashore, returning to the ship with our arms full of fish and chips, the fireman, instead of going aft to the gangway, jumped from the dockside into the fore rigging. I foolishly followed him, but in the darkness missed the ship and fell into the water. I splashed about in the darkness, totally invisible to the fireman on the ship's rail. He shouted, he was coming down. I did not think that was a good idea, so shouted back, "throw me a rope" which he did. Luckily I soon located the floating rope and in no time at all, had a bow line round my waist. I knew then I would not sink. Being February, it was cold in the water, we both kept on shouting for help but it seemed ages before anyone came. At last my shipmates came out of the forecastle and they were soon joined by the 'Old Man' who had come out to see what all the noise was about. After he was told, the following dialogue took place:-

Captain Hughes, leaning over the rail,	"Who is that down there?"
Me, splashing about in the water,	"Tommy, Sir."
Captain Hughes,	"Have you been drinking?"
Me, having swallowed much dock water,	"No Sir".
Captain Hughes,	"Haul him aboard."

I often wonder what his reaction would have been if I had said I had been drinking. Now, I will never know. I have known several occasions when men, ill or injured enough to require medical attention, have had to continue duty. Indeed I have had first hand experience of that situation several times during my life at sea. We were treated rough and we acted tough.

However, back to our anchorage in Plymouth Sound. In the morning, after we had breakfast, I was told I would be taking the boat ashore, to get a message off to the owners and to enable the cook and others to buy more food, etc. I have mentioned earlier that we did not carry wireless, therefore, our only means of contacting the owners was either by signal lamp or flags, via one of Lloyds Signal Stations. Although we had an oil Morse lamp, we never used it. One or two of us had electric torches, which we used instead. But sending and receiving messages by morse was often a difficult and prolonged operation. During the day, when using flags, general vocabulary messages were limited. Therefore, on this occasion, it was considered more appropriate to use the telephone. In spite of a statutory life boat drill requirement, getting the boats out was not easy, it usually required much pushing and hauling before we got a boat swung out. All this accompanied by outbursts of swearing with reference to the boat's origin and antiquated gear.

Finally, getting the boat into the water, we slid down the falls and made ready to push off. After some last minute instructions we were away. There were five of us in the boat, two sailors, a fireman, the cook and myself. I, being in charge, and conscious of the fact that we were under observation, tried to get some kind of order in the boat. But, alas, my youthful appearance did not help. However, concentrating on the job in hand, I steered the boat towards the Barbican. That is where I made my first mistake, I should have headed to windward to offset the drift. After a while I noticed we were making too much leeway towards white water and a rocky shore. I suggested that the lads lay back on their oars and pull harder. That is when things started to go wrong. First, the cook's oar fouled another, causing some disorganisation and a general exchange of uncomplimentary remarks. This was soon followed by another oarsman catching a crab and being pushed off his thwart by the fourteen foot oar. Once again there was confusion in the boat. By this time I was becoming increasingly apprehensive, not only about our dangerous drift on a lee shore, but also because I felt we were the subject of much criticism from watchers on the ship and shore. I decided to exchange my place at the tiller for that of stroke oar, after first vehemently expressing strong criticism of our seamanship in general, using strong language which was for me totally out of character, much to the surprise of my shipmates!

Sitting down on the thwart, I commenced to pull hard on the stroke oar, bawling out my time like an Oxford cox. Now I thought, we are beginning to look like sailors. But, I was soon to be disillusioned, snap went my oar, over I went, backwards into the bottom of the boat, again disorganisation accompanied by much laughter. The calamity rendered me speechless, without comment I picked up another oar and, resuming my place as the stroke oar, pulled with a vigour no doubt energised by temper. But again disaster, my rowlock broke, over I went again, backwards into the bottom of the boat. This was too much, especially the laughing comments being made as I sat soaking

Plate 110

STANLEY FORCE in which
Mr. Thomason sailed for 12
years

my posterior in the bilge water. Keeping my thoughts to myself, I shipped a fresh rowlock and resumed my efforts on the oar, with a quick glance to leeward I laid back on my oar thinking, surely nothing else could go wrong. But I was mistaken, the man at the tiller began to have trouble steering. Investigating, we found the rudder had broken away from the pintles and was hanging loose. Shipping a steering oar, we resumed our journey and without further mishap arrived in the Barbican, to be greeted by some good natured banter from some of the locals and some Cornish Fishermen, whose boats lay windbound in the harbour. They had been watching our progress, I could imagine their comments!

I was not too happy, being mainly concerned with the reception I expected when we returned to our ship. The display of seamanship and the damage, how would I explain it? Going ashore, I managed to get the message off to the owners. Cook and the rest of my shipmates did their shopping, after which we all returned to the Barbican. Again we met some of the Cornish Fishermen, some of whom we knew. They invited us aboard one of their boats and gave us tea and sandwiches. After a bit of a yarn about the weather and other things we began to make a move. Before leaving, they suggested we row well to windward after we cleared the Barbican. This we did, then squaring away towards our ship, arrived back on board without further incident. My feeling of apprehension was groundless. Surprisingly the 'Old Man' had little to say about our show of bad seamanship and the boat damage. I suppose he had more important things to worry about.

Later that day, the weather having improved, we hove up anchor and steaming seaward out of the Sound, resumed our passage to the London River. Four hours later after rounding Start Point we began an Easterly run up channel. The weather had, as far as I can remember, continued to improve. Approximately twenty four hours later after rounding Dungeness we entered the Dover Straits. With the weather still improving we rounded South Foreland and entered the Gull Channel inside the Goodwins. Passing the North Foreland and rounding the Elbow buoy with the Girdler Light vessel in sight, we finally entered the London River. It was about 8 am. when we arrived off our discharging berth but had to anchor. Sometime later we went alongside and commenced to discharge our cargo. Later that day after we had been paid, the lads went ashore to buy stores, and celebrated their safe arrival by getting drunk, at least that was their excuse.

I have never before or since had the experience of attending a semi-religious drunken, thanksgiving meeting. It developed from a remark made by one of us, which was something like this:- "Well lads, I suppose we should be thankful to be here" (there was not any doubt about that, we all were). Anyway, this remark seemed to generate a sanctimonious atmosphere, with several men trying in their own way to express their appreciation on our safe deliverance. Most seamen do not openly profess to be religious or believe in the Almighty, but often when things are rough they tend to acknowledge a Superior being. However, being thankful to something was the general tone of the lads. The next day it was forgotten, which was just as well. Life at sea was a mixture of good and bad. Fortunately one tended to remember the good. So life went on, and as we often said, "another day, another dollar."

111. Two pictures of Captain Williams taken with a 'box' camera aboard the STANLEY FORCE in 1926. He is standing by the fore hatch (right) with to his left, Joe Ward making a print using daylight paper. Below, at sea, the Skipper holds a mug of tea on the bridge. The binnacle is in the foreground.

19

112. Looking aft from the bridge of the STANLEY FORCE at sea in 1926. The photo shows the Cook Steward, Charlie Johnson standing on the bunker hatch. The photo was taken by the author, processed and printed on board.

Jokes, Ignorance & Consequences.

Thomas H. Thomason

Occasionally, when people live together in a closely knit community, one becomes the target for some leg pull. The victim may have a known weakness which is played upon to provide amusement, sometimes unkindly. I once had a shipmate who could neither read or write, he was a great big chap who could best be described as 'strong in the arm and weak in the head'. He was not simple, but for want of a suitable descripton, was considered gullible. He had a problem, which concerned writing letters to his girl friend. He thought his problem had been solved when one of his shipmates volunteered to write his letters for him and read any replies. He did not seem to mind the general interest shown by his mates, whenever he was dictating a letter or having one read out to him. But there was not any doubt, his shipmates found those occasions very amusing. What our illiterate shipmate did not seem to realise was that he was providing amusement, also, some of what he dictated was altered in meaning by the addition of innuendoes. When any letter was read out to him, occasionally a deliberate change in the phraseology would be made to raise a laugh from the audience. It was not until he had a trip home that he discovered how he had been fooled. He went to visit his girl, she was so angry she would not let him into her house. I am pleased to say, she later learned how he had been tricked and all was well again. Needless to say, our shipmate was more careful about his future choice of letter writers.

Another of my shipmates was also unable to read or write, but no-one could fool him on money matters. He was a native of Southern Ireland and according to some of the stories he told, had played a part in the Irish rebellion. He used to tell how they ambushed British Army patrols and afterwards hid out in the hills. I got the impression that he had taken some part in the killings, which now played on his mind. He was very nervous in the dark and this provided a little amusement from time to time. Ship's firemen, even when in port, had to tend the fires in the stokehold, and each night in turn, they would bank the fires so that they would last until morning. In port, the stokehole was a dark and lonely place. The only means of illumination was provided by an oil ducklamp, which would be supplemented by the glow from a furnace whenever a door was opened.

To get through to the stokehole one could go via the engine room, or by a more direct route descending a steep vertical ladder from the gratings. Occasionally, when our nervous shipmate was engaged in banking the fires, one of the men would creep quietly on to the gratings and start to make some queer noises, the gratings being invisible in the overhead darkness, enabled anyone to stand unseen. If the noises were repeated our shipmate, suspecting some trick, would be seen to peer upwards in an effort to see anyone on the gratings. He would probably shout; "who dat?" he having a natural difficulty in pronouncing 'th'. Naturally his tormentors would not reply, but would gleefully watch his behaviour as they continued to torment him. Not being sure about the cause of the noise he would commence to show signs of rage by throwing things about and cursing loudly. I suppose it was a means of fighting his apprehensions. The tormenting would usually end when the man on the grating became unable to contain his laughter.

Double bend.

I remember an occasion, when the Irishman and I, sat in the circle of a Sunderland cinema. Suddenly he jumped up, crying "There's some body behind me." When I looked round there was not anyone near, but I could not convince him. At one stage I had to practically hold him down. Firemen and sailors were accommodated right for'ard in the bows, at well deck level. The forecastle was divided into two compartments by a wooden fore and aft partition. The partition extended for'ard almost to the bow, and upwards to about a foot from the deck head. It was possible to squeeze round the fore end or by standing on the table, see over the top. The firemen lived on the port side and sailors on the starboard. There was an occasion, when intending to play a trick on our nervous shipmate, we passed a length of black cotton round the fore end of the dividing wooden partition and secured the end between his top bunk and the ship's side. To this we tied several tin lids. The other end of the thread was secured between our top bunks and the ship's side, convenient for us to operate when lying in our bunks. When all had turned in and everyone was quiet, we gave a little tug on our end of the thread, which caused the tin lids to rattle. At first there was not any reaction from the occupants of the port side, so we repeated the operation several times. We eventually heard movement, the mysterious noise had begun to puzzle and irritate the Irishman. We could hear him muttering. Finally his reaction was as we had anticipated, he jumped on to the table and peered over the dividing partition to see what we were up to. But we were lying in our bunks pretending to be asleep. Eventually we, being unable to contain our laughter, gave the game away. Wasn't he mad, he could have murdered us!

Joking and skylarking played a very necessary part in our lives, during those far off days. We had to make our own fun which helped us to put up with the discomforts of our confined and dismal accommodation. There were no entertainment facilities i.e wireless or a gramophone, we could not afford one anyway. Yarning and reading was the usual pastime, not everyone wanted to read. So we yarned and improvised our fun. There was an outstanding occasion when playing tricks almost had serious consequences.

It was a Sunday morning, our ship lay snug alongside a wharfe in the London River. Our crew was enjoying one of those few weekends in port. Going ashore was not an attractive proposition, for two reasons, we had not much money and the wharfe was a long way from town. So, we were spending the time doing what we usually did on these occasions, washing our clothes also mending, sewing and darning. Eventually lying in our bunks trying to read or falling off to sleep. We had, if I remember, reached a stage of general lethargy. Thinking to liven things up a bit I decided to torment the firemen by playing a trick on them.

Going next door I started to have a yarn with one of the firemen called George Murdoch. He was a West Indian and always full of fun. Whilst I talked I surreptitiously eased open the top flap of their coal burning bogy stove and dropped a firework in. It was a big one, which I think was called a "Thunder Flash". We seldom let our stoves go out, it was our only means of warmth, but at night or during quiet hours we would bank them with slack to make them slow burning. The firemen's stove had been banked, it was black on top of the fire, so I knew that some time would elapse before the firework ignited. Knowing this, I was able to spend a few minutes yarning with George before returning to our forecastle. I turned into my bunk to patiently await the excitement. I would not have been so happy if I had known what would eventually happen. It was only in later years that I was able to realise what I had done. I had unknowingly created a bomb. The slowly heating slack was giving off an inflammable and explosive gas and it was in a confined space. The sudden ignition by an explosive firework had dangerous possibilities. But I did not know that then, in common with most seafarers my education on such matters was practically nil.

However, I lay in my bunk awaiting the bang with gleeful anticipation. Time passed, and still no bang. I began to think my joke had misfired, and was becoming very sleepy. All at once I was startled into wakefulness by a terrific bang next door, this was followed by a short period of silence then pandemonium. We turned out and went next door to see what had happened. Nobody seemed to know, but the stove lid was missing and part of the stove back was damaged. Fortunately no one was hurt, but everyone had had a fright. Luckily the stove had been saved from complete destruction by the pressure released through the easily displaced loose lid. Everyone speculated on what had happened. It was something in the stove, that was obvious, but what was it? It was a mystery to everyone but myself, who was by now wishing that I had not been so foolish. Supposing someone had been injured, what would I have done? I did not feel very happy. I was in a quandary about telling everyone what I had done, I just did not know what to do. If I told the Skipper, I would have most probably been signed off or at least have to pay for a new stove. In the end, not to my credit, I decided to say nothing, and was not very

Firing irons.

proud of myself. One thing I did do was, make a decision not to play risky tricks again.

As I said earlier on, our knowledge of chemical hazards was practically none. We eventually learned the hazards of various cargoes especially combustion in coal cargoes and such like, but our knowledge was very limited. This was illustrated by another incident, which occurred at sea. We used acetylene lighting in the engine room, so naturally our engineers had some knowledge of acetylene gas and its generation from carbide. One cold and wet day at sea, the Skipper came on to the bridge and started to comment about the queer smell. We had noticed it earlier on, but not considering it of any importance had decided to ignore it. But the Skipper persisted to sniff round. He finally located the source, it was coming from a cannister which was attached to one of our lifebuoys. These lifebuoys were held by a retaining pin, in shutes located externally on the port and starboard wing of the bridge. A small canister was secured by a ring to the shute. If the buoys were released the accompanying canister would be snatched from its securing ring which would cause the canister to be perforated. The buoy and its attached canister would then be left astern in the first instance, and under normal conditions become difficult to locate. But, water leaking into the perforated canister would react with the carbide contents and generate acetylene. Thus the buoy would be easily located by:- in the first instance white vapour, quickly followed by a flare and black smoke. So, the Skipper had located an acetylene leak. He instructed me to take the canister to the engine room and ask the Second to solder the leak. Our Second was a big hairy man with a bushy moustache. He was a good all round engineer, but more used to fishing boats than merchant ships.

I left the canister with him and returned to the bridge. I had not been on the bridge very long when we heard a hell of a bang in the engine room. When I went to investigate, I met the Second coming out, he looked rather shaken. His whiskers were singed and he had bits of solder sticking to his moustache. He later told me that, when I left him he put the canister on the work bench ready for soldering. As soon as he put the hot soldering iron near the canister, it exploded and practically blew itself to bits. He had a very lucky escape, but once again this was failure to anticipate a danger, apparently due to lack of knowledge. He was a very lucky man, he could so easily have been blinded. In retrospect, I now realise many dangerous things must have been done due to lack of knowledge.

For instance when working by the ship in drydock, we often had to do what could be termed as risky jobs. One I remember in particular was having to climb up and down ropes to work from a single plank suspended outside the hull, sometimes with a thirty or forty foot drop to the dry dock bottom, this was taken as a normal routine job. Several occasions when in drydock, we were given the very dirty job of cleaning out the main ballast tank. This tank was situated in the ship's bottom underneath the cargo hold. It was a large shallow tank about two foot six inches in depth with fore and aft partitions at about three or four foot intervals. These partitions helped to prevent water surge when sailing in ballast. Access to the ballast tank was by means of small manholes spaced at intervals above the channels. To work in the tank, one had to squeeze through one of the manholes and crawl through the muddy deposit on one's belly to the desired position. There we would scrape and ladle the mud into a bucket then crawl and manhandle the full bucket to the nearest manhole to be emptied. It was quite dark in the tank and sometimes very cold. The only light we had was supplied by candles, which when lit were stood in a large nut to keep them upright.

No one seemed to attach much importance to the possibility of dangerous fumes which could be liberated from the muddy deposit. The only instruction I can remember was:- "if the candle goes out, come out", which in some cases probably required a few minutes of crawling before reaching a manhole. I should mention that when we worked by the ship in drydock, it was occasionally for half our normal pay. We usually had a twenty four hour notice to either accept being paid off or work by at half pay. In spite of the hardship caused, we always chose half pay because jobs were not all that plentiful.

20.
Robbed in our Sleep.

Thomas H. Thomason

"So you still have it then?" remarked my old shipmate, Joe, as he stepped into the forecastle. He was referring to an 'English Lever' watch, which was hanging on a bracket, rather prominently at the head of my bunk. I had bought the watch some months earlier in Swansea, and Joe had always admired it. When in major British and Continental ports, we were frequently boarded by men (and women), who would be selling all kinds of things, i.e. clothing, (often feminine underwear), watches, clocks, soap, bottles of scent, silks, rubber goods, Spanish Fly, knives and even guns. They would display their goods which would often dazzle the crew men. They would be tempted to spend their hard earned money, only to find in some cases they had been swindled. I remember an occasion when lying in the London River, a man came on board selling what he claimed to be:- Gold Cased Hunter Watches with Platinum Chains, price Twelve Shillings and Six Pence. We ought to have known, but they looked so attractive in their 'chamois' leather bag. A number of us bought a watch, including the Skipper. It was not long before the Gold turned to Brass and the time piece developed faults. The Skipper was so mad he threw his watch at someone and I think most of the others had the same ending. Funnily enough, the salesman was boarding us again some months later. One of the men remarked, "You've been here before." The man immediately vanished.

When visiting Rotterdam, we often had a visit from a man who was, as he said selling fox furs. He carried them in a draw string bag and claimed they had come from another ship. We never encouraged him, but he often called, using the same story. Whether he had real fox furs I never tried to find out. Another salesman I remember sold things like 'Dutch Drops'. What it was for I never knew. But my shipmate Joe explained that they were good for us. So I, muggins, used to buy a bottle now and again and drink it in small doses. Whether I had any benefit from it I do not know.

However, back to my 'English Lever Watch'. By experience, we had learnt to be more cautious in our buying, occasionally even attempting to barter. That is how I acquired my 'English Lever' watch. During one of our occasional visits to Swansea Docks, a man came on board selling amongst other things 'the watch'. Having a watch already, I was not really interested, but casually began to barter with him. I was very much surprised when he eventually agreed to accept my watch (which was not very reliable) and Ten Shillings for the 'English Lever' watch. I was so pleased with my watch I made a special bracket for it at the head of my bunk. However, back to my visitor old shipmate 'Joe'. It was Saturday evening and we were moored in one of the town docks of Antwerp. He was now a member of the crew of one of our sister ships, berthed in a nearby dock. Learning of our close proximity, he had decided to pay us a visit. His purpose no doubt being twofold, to renew contact with old shipmates and join them for a night ashore amongst the bright lights.

As was normal, when on the Continent, ships' crews tended to go ashore and enjoy the facilities whenever an opportunity presented itself and as long as they had money to spend. The dockland areas of the large continental seaports contained many attractions for visiting seafarers. Old timers, will I am sure remember, the world wide known areas of vice, the cafes and other places, which never seemed to close. To call them 'cafes' was a misnomer, the last thing they sold was food. Many cafes had names which were mainly to attract the various nationalities. For the attention of the British, I remember a cafe called, 'The Old Cork Fender'. There was also a 'Cafe Blighty' and other names with British associations such as Cafe London. Some of my old shipmates spent much of their hard earned wages in these places. But as far as I could see it was the usual custom for seafarers to carouse as long as they could find the money to spend. I suppose this was a way of forgetting temporarily at least, the hard life at sea. Yes, I think the occasional binge acted as a safety valve. As one walked down the street in one of these areas, one would often hear a continuous sound of music, overlapping, as one moved along from one establishment to another. The music would often be provided by a mechanically operated instrument or by musicians. This would be continuous during the late and early hours accompanied by singing and dancing.

The girls who worked in the cafes, were like the seafaring patrons, of many nationalities. I was informed by my shipmates that the girls did not receive any wages but relied on tips and any other method of acquiring money. Therefore, it was not surprising that many were prostitutes, arranging business with any willing customers whilst serving the drinks. Being cautious, I only

Carrick bend.

drank what I knew to be 'lemonade' contenting myself to sit and watch their antics. Especially as they grew sillier and sillier with every drink.

After much washing and shaving, we went ashore, and in no time at all were entering the nearby 'Cafe Blighty'. This was a place well known to our crewmen, they visited it almost every time they came to Antwerp. Consequently they were well acquainted with the proprietor. Once inside the men commenced to enjoy themselves, drinking, dancing, singing and flirting with the girls. As the night wore on, the dancing became more rowdy, more like hugging and wrestling. Indeed on several occasions, some of the participants became laughing, struggling heaps on the floor. By the look of it, the girls appeared to enjoy the scramble as much as the men. The antics got crazier and crazier, some of the men had begun to put flowers in their hair. One man had sat down at the keyboard of a mechanical piano, pretending to play it. He got a surprise, when 'The Madame' switched it on, from behind the bar. The would be musician had great fun trying to accompany the moving keys. I think he was drunk enough to think he was actually playing the piano.

It was approaching midnight, when I, feeling tired and knowing that the fun and games would continue for a few more hours, decided to leave them and return to my ship. I knew that dockland area was not a safe place to venture in alone after dark. However, because the ship was fairly close by, I decided to risk it. Soon I was back on board, as I expected, both forecastles were unoccupied. I decided that this would be a good opportunity, whilst I had some peace and quiet, to write a letter home. I sat down at the forecastle table and within the limited illumination provided by the oil lamp, commenced to write my letter. I had not been writing very long when I began to feel very sleepy. No matter how much I tried to keep awake, I kept falling forward across the table unable to stay awake. I began to think of getting into my bunk, but realised in my semi-conscious mind, there was a problem. Should I lock the forecastle door or leave it unlocked? If I locked the door and fell fast asleep, I would probably not hear my returning shipmates, and they, no doubt being very drunk, being unable to get in, would probably become very nasty. I had seen that happen before, and I did not want to be the victim of any quarrel. My sleepy condition overcoming my common sense caused me to follow the line of least resistance, and turning into my bunk I was soon asleep. I did not wake when my shipmates returned.

In those days, the dockland area of Antwerp was the haunt of people who lived by crime. Anything movable, whether on ship or on shore, was, if worth anything at all, stolen. The mugging and robbing of seamen after dark in dockland was commonplace, as was stealing from ships. Whenever ships arrived in Antwerp it was usual to issue the crew members with cautionary leaflets, advising them to close and secure all portholes and windows especially on the shore side. Also to lock all doors when leaving cabins, forecastles and other compartments unattended or unoccupied. Masters of ships were advised to engage a watchman from the Maritime Watching Company. However, with the passage of time and absence of any trouble precautions and vigilance tended to become lax. We began to take chances.

It was almost noon when I woke up, from a deep sleep. Being Sunday, it did not matter, we had the day to ourselves. As I lay, dreamily enjoying my lie in, I sleepily listened to my shipmates as they awoke from their drunken slumber. I could hear them noisily complaining about the difficulty of finding their clothing, thinking to myself, they must have been in a right state when they came aboard. As I lay and listened I casually glanced towards the shelf over my bunk on which I kept a suitcase containing my best go-ashore clothing. It was not there, neither were my best shoes, or my watch. I was instantly awake and sitting up, enquiring if anyone had seen my suitcase. They had; one chap said when he woke up it was on his bed, but was empty. I was out of my bunk in a jiffy, joining the others searching for our belongings but our search was fruitless; we had been robbed. But when we did not know. It must have been sometime during the early hours. Suspicion was immediately focussed on the watchman, and the lads went aft to find him, but he had gone, which was fortunate for him. My shipmates being in an angry mood would probably have either done him a physical injury or thrown him overboard. There is no doubt about it he would have been a very unfortunate man had they caught him. We never saw him again.

The robbery took place sometime in the morning, and we must have been doped in some way, so that we remained unconscious whilst the thief or thieves went through our gear. I have a slight recollection of someone leaning over me whilst I was asleep, but could not be sure. Perhaps it was just as well I did not wake up at the time. However, I was more fortunate than my shipmates, they lost most of their gear, whilst I only lost my best go-ashore gear and watch. I had a tin trunk underneath the bunks which contained some gifts I intended to take home, this had not been disturbed. One thing for sure, we resumed our security precautions,

21.

A Change of Status

Thomas H. Thomason

I am now (1931) acting Second Mate and in charge of a watch, also I have assumed the responsibility for keeping the official ship's log. Therefore it is understandable, that what was once my scrap log is now beginning to look like a diary. This was an unsettled period in my life. I was seriously contemplating marriage. I was engaged to a girl I had known for several years having met her on my first visit to Shoreham in the ship, on Sunday January 16th, 1927.

In the afternoon a man from the Seaman's Mission came on board to invite us to the Evening Service. Some of us half-promised to go, but eventually it was only a man from SKELWITH FORCE, also in at Shoreham, who accompanied me to the little Mission Hall near the canal locks at Southwick. We sat sucking sweets and doing our best to join in with the hymn singing, the words of which were projected on to a screen by means of a lantern. When we came out of the Mission Hall we caught up with two girls and, with their permission, walked with them and chatted for a while. We told them we were sailors and they promised to see us off from the locks the following night, which they did when we sailed for Methil. But having obtained her name and address, I started to correspond with one of the girls as a friend. Over the years we continued to exchange letters and from time to time I managed to see her at Shoreham. We grew fond of one another, so much so that I arranged for her and her friend to spend a holiday at my home during my leave. After which my girl and I had become engaged to be married.

On becoming acting second mate I exchanged my life in the forecastle for one amidships, and was sharing a room, located on the port side under the lower bridge, with the mate. This was a great change in many ways, I was to eat in the cabin and share a table with the Skipper, Mate, and Chief Engineer. It was the practice for those living amidships to pay the Cook/Steward the sum of 14 shillings each week. He would then cater, cook and serve our meals. It was normal to have breakfast at 8 am, dinner at noon, tea at 4 pm. and supper at 8 pm. When at sea, all these times being 'eight bells' and corresponding to the change of watch. Consequently, the mate and second mate, when at sea, had to relieve each other at meal times. Under this system, I was spared the worry of catering for myself. We expected to sign on a new cook at our next port of call. This we did at Blyth and he started on 20th June, 1931 by making us a good breakfast. That same day I had my first dinner in the saloon with the other officers and felt rather out of place at first.

My diary shows that from June 1931 to September 1931 we were following much the same pattern of voyages as we had been in 1926. Mainly carrying granite from Newlyn to London and Ipswich and then returning to Newlyn in ballast or loading coal in Goole or Blyth for South Western ports such as Falmouth. We had orders to load coal at Goole for Teignmouth and as I had not visited there before I was looking forward to going. We sailed for Teignmouth at 2.30 pm. on 25th July and met a strong SSW wind and a rough sea on clearing the Humber which slowed our progress southwards. We passed the Royal Sovereign Lightship at 1.30 am. on the 27th in very bad weather, with a WSW gale blowing. The old ship was labouring heavily, listing to the weather and shipping plenty of water and so we got a soaking on the bridge. We dropped anchor off Teignmouth at 2 am. and berthed at 6 am. on the 28th and they started to discharge our cargo right away. We sailed at 7 pm. on the 29th for Newlyn. It was a rush to catch the tide out, as a result we sailed with our hatches uncovered. When we got outside there was a bit of a roll. It was whilst putting on the hatch beams that I had an accident. My fingers

became trapped by a beam and I narrowly escaped amputation of three fingers. It was very painful and I must have looked foolish lying on the galley floor, but I was in agony and did not know what to do to ease the pain. I was unable to sleep during my watch below and had to steer 'one-handed' during my watch on deck. On arrival at Newlyn I did not go to the doctor's, I could not cotton on to the idea. The Skipper did not either, he said they might send me home and I did not want to go home that way. The lads let me off easy but it was some time before my fingers recovered. A tough life!

If we were returning from London directly to Newlyn we often bunkered at Gravesend. We did this when we sailed for Penzance on 15th July, 1931. We left Deptford at 2 pm. Just on leaving, one of the boiler tubes gave out. Efforts to fix it were made as we lay at the coal hulk in Gravesend taking in bunker coal. The tide at Penzance on Friday was 7-11 am. and if the tube was not fixed soon the tide would be missed. The repairs were not successful and so we anchored again at 9.0 pm. and did not get away until 5.0 am., the following morning, the tubes now being O.K. We soon found ourselves punching into a gale. If the tubes gave out now, what a mess we would be in; fortunately we had no more trouble on that occasion. We finally got into Penzance at 6 am. on the 18th and began loading china clay. I was glad when we finished loading on Monday and we could get everything clean again.

One usually expects bad weather to be associated with the winter, but after years of experience at sea, one eventually learns never to take things for granted, especially the weather. Therefore, it was routine, when going to sea, for certain precautions to be taken. If sailing light ship, i.e. without cargo, it was customary to cover the hatches with only one tarpaulin. Mooring ropes would be left on the forecastle head and after-grating, secured by lashings. Anchor chain pipe covers for the windlass and ventilator covers would not be used. Also the life line which is normally attached to the lower bridge ladder, (from the well deck) across the hatch to the forecastle head ladder, on the port side, would not be rigged. These are the main differences between light and loaded ship precautions. Light or loaded, derricks would be lowered and secured. When the ship was loaded, especially in the winter, the hatches would be covered by three tarpaulins, the top two secured in the cleats by battens and wedges. The hatch in the fore well deck was considerably lower than the main hatch and therefore more likely to be damaged by incoming sea. Because of this, the covered hatch was further strengthened by wire strops across the hatchway, hooked into rings on the coamings and tightened by box screws. Stanchions were stepped into their fittings on the port side of the hatch-coamings and a life line rigged. I should mention that in those days we had no deck lights, the only illumination came from opened doors and uncovered portholes. It was necessary to restrict the escape of light beams forward of the bridge, so as not to interfere with visibility.

Moving around a darkened ship, especially in bad weather could be hazardous and one had to remember the location of secure handholds. We often used to say, "Remember, two hands for yourself and one for the owner." In addition to the above mentioned precautions, mooring ropes would be taken down from the forecastle head and lashed down across the hatch behind the fore winch. All fenders and other loose gear would be stowed in the winch. All openings including ventilators would be covered with canvas. Anchor chains hanging parallel in the locker, would be lashed together to stop them from banging about. The after mooring ropes, usually coiled on the grating over the rudder quadrant, would normally be taken and secured on the top of the engineer's quarters. These then were our standard precautions, each time we left port. The owners only provided hurricane or duck lamps even our Morse lamp was oil with a thumb operated shutter. Some of us purchased torches and having a button on could be used for signalling, we got no reimbursement for them from the owners, but we would have been lost without them.

However, back to the subject of 'bad weather'. When the ship is labouring in bad weather, and possibly shipping heavy seas, the experienced seaman would be able to anticipate possible sources of danger and thus maintain the necessary vigilance. Most seamen have experienced the hazard of a shifting cargo or insecure deck cargo. Some cargoes by their very nature, are inclined to shift if stowed in the hold with plenty of ullage. I have in mind, grain, anthracite peas, granite chippings and bog ore, which tends to puddle when shaken about. We lost one of our sister ships, AYSGARTH FORCE, with a cargo of bog ore. After leaving a Dutch port in March 1925 she encountered heavy weather. The cargo of ore began to puddle, and the ship developed a list. Apparently the Skipper decided to expose the listed side to weather, in the hope that she would wash back on to an even keel. But instead, the hatchway was damaged and she began to take in water, consequently listing more. Eventually the crew had to abandon ship and unfortunately one of the crew was lost.

This kind of hazard was fairly straight forward, it was the unexpected that caused the most trouble. I remember an occasion in the North Sea on a South-

erly passage. The sea was not unusually rough and was not causing any problems. But, all at once we were hit by a sea which seemed to come from nowhere. It caught us aft on the port side. The wave appeared to wash over the after housing and carried the small boat out of its chocks on the starboard side. The boat was left hanging outboard swinging from its davits. We got it back and secured inboard, but the sudden big sea certainly caught us by surprise. By the way this happened in daylight, it could have been worse in the dark. Therefore, during bad or uncertain weather it was wise not to leave too much to chance, so that if trouble was detected immediate action could put things right. When shipping heavy water, we always kept an eye on the hatchways and any other deck gear. During the hours of darkness in those conditions, it was usual to carry out frequent inspections. From the bridge aft it was not too bad, but for'ard of the bridge, being lower in the well deck, inspection could be tricky. During the dark hours we would usually stand on the lower bridge and with the aid of an electric torch, carry out systematic remote inspection of the hatch coverings, etc. As I said before the after deck had little problems in daylight, but during the dark hours, one had to remember the location of secure handholds if they were required. Anyway, one soon learnt the art of self-preservation. I remember one occasion when we were crossing from the West of Ireland and heading for the Longships. The weather was bad with wind and sea from the West. It was hard keeping her on course as the sea tossed her about. She was making heavy weather of it, and everything that could rattle and bang about, did so. It was dark when I went down from the bridge, it was my intention to have a look at the steering gear amongst other things. When I got aft I found that the grating over the rudder quadrant had been broken. We must have pooped a sea at some time. However, to make matters worse, the after mooring ropes had for some reason been left secured to the grating. I do not know why we had not taken them aloft, it was my end of the ship. But the most important thing requiring attention was getting the ropes off the grating and secured aloft as soon as possible. The weight of the ropes was causing the grating to rest on the quadrant and if this jammed, we would soon be in serious trouble. By the way, the area was illuminated by the beam from the stern light which was situated above the after deck housing. So, I could see what was to be done, but the trouble was, getting aft had taken a bit of time, therefore, returning to the bridge and coming aft again might lose valuable time the way things looked, so I decided to try to move the ropes myself. Bending down to examine the underside of the grating, I sensed danger and looking up saw a large wave curling over my head, with its foaming top glittering in the beam of the stern light. I instinctively turned, back to the sea, and grabbing the sides of a metal ladder, protecting my head I waited for the weight of water to fall on me, which it subsequently did. It all happened so quickly that my actions were not premeditated, they were instinctive. I could have tried to climb the ladder, but my hand hold would have then been less secure. Men have been temporarily stunned by incoming heavy seas and in consequence gone overboard. However, back to my story, I struggled with the rope and it was a slow job working on my own, but eventually I managed to get it coiled and secured. When I got back to the bridge I told the Old Man, but as far as I can remember he made no unusual comments. It was all part of the job.

"We're not going to Calcutta" said one of my shipmates as we left the North East coast at Blyth. We were bound for an Irish port and our passage lay Northwards round Cape Wrath. It was late in the day and although the weather was fine, I was paying special attention to the mooring rope lashings on the fore hatch. I did not pay too much attention to his sarcastic comments, they were not unusual. He was a man with a permanent chip on his shoulder as far as I was concerned. I suppose this was understandable, he had at one time been Skipper of his own ship, but for some reason which I do not know, he was sailing with us as an A.B. I suppose that I, being a young Second Mate irritated him.

For the next twenty four hours we plodded our way Northwards, and the weather began to deteriorate as we neared the Pentlands. Those people who are familiar with that area will know that it can be a dodgy place in bad weather. But before we had reached the Pentlands, the weather had really turned sour on us. It was sometime during the midnight to four a.m. watch that our troubles began. Our speed was much reduced as we laboured our way against the heavy seas. Every now and then we would ship a sea over the forecastle head which would fill the fore well deck and send a shower of spray over the open bridge. We had no wheelhouse, therefore all we could do was duck under the shelter of the canvas dodger every time the spray came over, all that is, except the man at the wheel who being in an exposed position holding on to a kicking wheel could do nothing but suffer, not always in silence. It was a black night with little to break the blackness excepting the white tops of the waves. The Old Man had been standing watching silently the rough seas. To steady himself, and no doubt to take the weight off his feet, he had jammed himself against the telegraph. We all did this from time to time,

especially when feeling tired, it was possible to relax but at the same time remain upright. From time to time, I carried out the usual remote hatch inspection. It was not difficult with the main hatch, I could stand at the back of the bridge and with the beam from my torch manage a systematic inspection. But the fore hatch was more difficult, it was necessary to descend to the lower bridge and shine my torch from there.

It was during one of the fore hatch inspections that I missed the mooring ropes that had been previously lashed on the hatch. I went on to the bridge and told the Old Man. His comments were quite brief and to the point, "You'd better find them" he said, which is what I expected, anyhow. So, down I went to carry out a difficult, wet and hazardous search of the well deck area. I had to watch my opportunity as the seas occasionally swept over the well deck. It was to be expected that I would get wet, but I did not want to get drowned. We had no deck lights, therefore, the only useful light came from my hand torch and an occasional beam of light from one of the cabin portholes as it was temporarily uncovered by the swaying curtain. Eventually, the missing ropes were located under the lower bridge ladder in the well deck scuppers on the starboard side. Most of the time the ropes were awash as the seas continued to come inboard. But there was an additional snag, part of one rope had gone through the scuppers and was streaming aft. I did not know how much was overboard, but one thing for sure, if it was long enough, it could foul the propellor. If that happened, we would would really be in trouble, especially in these waters. Any loss of power and we would either broach to or hit the rocks, or something equally as bad. Anyway, I lost no time in letting the Old Man know, he ordered me to call out the watch below and get the rope inboard as soon as possible. Remembering the sarcastic comments of my shipmate as we left Blyth, I must confess I experienced a feeling of satisfaction as I roused him out of his bunk!

It did not take long to turn out and get dressed. In the normal way, we would jump out of our bunks, get dressed and be relieving the watch in five minutes. In an emergency, as now, it was managed even quicker and soon we were standing under the lee of the forecastle head waiting for a chance to get to the after end of the well deck. The ship appeared to be shipping less water, we must have eased down, nevertheless we had to maintain steerage way, which was sufficient for us to ship a sea now and again. We started our struggle in the dark, it was not possible to see each other all the time, so we shouted at one another just to make sure where everyone was. Eventually, we got the trailing rope inboard and started to recoil it on the fore hatch. This was a long drawn out operation, mainly because every now and again a sea would come inboard and sweeping across the fore hatch carry us and the rope aft against the bridge bulkhead. Luckily we had the lowered derrick and guys to hang on to, which was necessary from time to time. We did not coil the rope below in the fore peak as that would have meant having the door open and perhaps an inrush of sea water as the well deck filled. In any case, when the ropes were lashed across the hatch it provided some protection to the tarpaulin covers. It was during one of our attempts to coil the rope that, after being scattered by a sea, we lost a man. As we called to one another, he did not answer and we feared the worst. However, we finally located him, half drowned in the surging water underneath the lower bridge ladder, very shaken by the experience. To cut a long story short, we eventually managed to get everything secured, and continued our plod towards Cape Wrath.

However, our half drowned shipmate, having apparently had enough, decided to leave us at the first suitable opportunity. This he did the next time we visited his home port. He had decided to resume his previous occupation as a home water fisherman. The Pentland Firth incident must however have left a mark on his memory, because some thirty years later, when I met him again, he reminded me of it. He had however, resumed a life at sea in yachts and a salvage tug in which he had even more hazardous experiences.

The bad weather episodes I have mentioned are not particular to us, most seafarers had similar or even worse experiences than we did. But it is funny, one often does not fully appreciate the seriousness of the situation at the time. That realisation seems to come in retrospect. In April 1932, I spent my leave in Fishersgate (Shoreham) when my wife and I were married at the church in Church Road, Portslade. My wife came to sea with me once or twice, and she had her experience of bad weather. I remember one time when I had to jam her into her bunk to keep her from falling out. On another occasion, we had rounded the Longships and headed Northwards. The weather was bad and we had amongst other things, a deck cargo of large metal drums, they were fortunately empty. The incoming seas had loosened the lashings, and some of the drums were washing about and banging against the bridge bulkhead. Every now and again they would bang like drums, which my wife found almost unbearable as she was feeling seasick. We had to go down and try to secure them, but it was hopeless, so we conveniently eased the troublesome drums overboard to solve our problem. Much to my wife's relief!

22.

The Chief Engineer.

Thomas H. Thomason

Although I was shipmates with him for some eight or ten years, he was always addressed as 'Chief' or referred to, as 'The Chief'. I can recollect few occasions when he was addressed by his first name. Now and again the Skipper would call him 'Davie' or the Second Engineer would call him 'Dave'. But generally he was known to all the crew as 'The Chief'. I knew very little about his background, he was in the ship when I joined her. Our ship was then about three years old. I got the impression that he had been with the Company for a number of years. Although he lived in Liverpool, he originally came from Workington, which apparently had some connection with our owners. He seemed to know them fairly well and always referred to them as 'Willie and John'. The Chief was a man with little religious belief, but I gathered from conversation that his home in Liverpool was basically Catholic. I met his wife later, when she had a few trips with us. She was a small but dominant person. There was no doubt she was the boss! The Chief was one of the old time engineers, whether he had served his time ashore or got a ticket, I never knew, it was never referred to.

Prior to the 1914/18 war, much of the coastwise trade had been done in sailing ships. With the advent of steam, boats began a practice of manning the engine rooms with experienced, rather than certified engineers, bearing in mind I am only referring to Home Trade vessels. But these engineers had to be good to hold their job, certified or not. They were responsible for all mechanically operated machinery and steam raising plant as well as the men involved. Mechanical failures, breakdowns, etc. had to be attended to and rectified, whether at sea or in port. Therefore, a good experienced man was necessary to direct operations. Our Chief was in that category. He always wore a clean brown boiler suit and a school boy type peak cap. This seemed to be the popular rig of most coastwise engineers. I seldom saw our Chief dressed any other way, even in port. He was a sturdily built man about five foot eight inches in height and to the best of my recollection, almost bald. His reddish face was adorned with a bushy moustache closely trimmed level with the top lip. Facially, he resembled the well-known television actor, Alf Garnett. He had a rasping voice and a laugh which would start like a strangled cough. His pleasure in life was mainly confined to booze. He often used to say:- "If all the sea was beer, and I was a little duck, I'd dive to the bottom and never come up". Yes! he certainly liked his beer. When under the influence of booze he could be temperamental. He had a tendency to boast now and again. He once challenged me to a race along the dock side and, although he was about twice my age, I only just managed to beat him.

We had been loading coal in Goole and were about to sail, when the Chief came on board rather the worse for drink. For those who do not know Goole Docks, I should explain that the water level in the docks was rather high. Also the flood tide in the river was strong, and as far as I can remember it was our intention to go out through the locks, stern first, so that we would be ready swung to meet the flood. We unmoored and proceeded to move stern first to the junction. A stern wire had been run from the port quarter to the dock wall corner and it was the intention by going slow astern and checking with the mooring wire to guide the ship round the corner into the next length. We had done this operation many times before, therefore were quite familiar with what was required. As we went astern I began to have difficulty in holding the check wire. I shouted to the bridge to stop engines, but we continued to go astern. The wire was paying out too fast to belay and all we could do was stand clear. The ship continued gaining stern way across the dock crashing into the dock wall causing damage to her rudder and stern post. As a result we were unable to sail because the full extent of the damage was not known. Arrangements had to be made for us to go into drydock, which was not such a good idea with a loaded ship. However, we drydocked the next day, for survey and repair.

I was not involved in the subsequent investigation, so do not know what the explanation was concerning the apparent excessive and uncontrollable stern way prior to the collision. But I do know that the Chief was replaced and sent home. Talking to the Second Engineer after the incident, I learnt that as we sailed, the Chief went down to the engine room rather drunk. He decided to take over the main engine controls from the Second. He being the boss, the Second found it difficult to refuse the takeover. As the Second said, "What could I do? The Chief was the boss". I do not know what happened to the Chief after he was sent home, we often wondered but never found out. But we did not expect to see him again. However, some months later he rejoined us, but he was a changed man, very much subdued and as far as I can remember drank very little booze.

It was perhaps a year or two later when bound for Goole we had to anchor in Hull Roads to await the tide. I was on anchor watch and just after midnight I stood at the galley door talking to one of the firemen. As we talked the Chief passed us and went into the engine room doorway. After a minute or two the fireman said "I'd better go, or the Chief will be after me". Then he too went down the engine room ladder. Within minutes he was back up again, rather agitated, saying "You'd better come and have a look at the Chief, there's something wrong with him." I went below, and found the Chief lying on his back on the engine room plates, as I approached him, he made a bubbling noise then stopped breathing. I tried to revive him by artificial respiration without any success and eventually had to conclude he was dead. I made all the usual tests but as far as I could ascertain both pulse and respiration had stopped. The Skipper was informed, and he instructed me to signal the shore and get assistance. After some minutes flashing my morse lamp, I eventually received an acknowledgement. I sent a message, "We have a man dead." This was a mistake, I should have sent the message, "We need medical assistance." As a result, because of my wrong message, there was apparently deemed to be no urgency. Eventually we received instructions to heave up and go alongside the pier. This we did and found an ambulance waiting. After we got the Chief's body ashore, the Skipper instructed me to go with it to the Mortuary, which was not a pleasant journey. It is so long ago now, and the details of what took place before I left the Chief have faded with passing years. But on reflection I could not help but think how easily death was accepted with minimal investigation. Also, I could not help but think that Goole was an unlucky port for the Chief, or was it? Anyway, he passed out of our lives without causing a ripple, it was a case of, "The Chief is dead, long live the Chief". Who would it be?

Another incident which involved a casualty came about in a rather different way. The first visit to a foreign country, for many people, is usually an occasion which one remembers for a long time. Most people's idea of life in a foreign country is influenced by such things as films and books. Seamen in their forecastle yarns tend to exaggerate their experiences in foreign ports. It is true that many major foreign ports contained many features enjoyed by seafaring men, of all nations, who visit the ports. During the night hours, men could be seen drifting from one dive or cafe to another, seeking the best entertainment they could find, while they had money to spend. So, it is understandable, many young men (or boys) starting a sea career, would look forward to their first trip abroad.

It was sometime during the late 20s that we received orders to sail for Morlaix in Brittany. We had been there before and knew Morlaix to be pleasant place with the harbour quay close to the town and a huge railway viaduct spanning the river. The town was small at that time, but it contained the usual cafes, as well as a 'brothel' which was, at that time, a normal institution in French towns. So, for visiting seafarers, the basic ingredients for a good night ashore existed. Thus most of the crew planned to get ashore as soon as it was possible and enjoy the amenities. I remember during one of our previous visits to Morlaix, we heard about some trouble in the 'brothel', a girl had been robbed.

A seaman had been blamed, but the money was not found. Later that morning when our men returned aboard, one of them had a limp. As soon as he got on board, he took off his boots and removed a roll of notes from his toecap. He was the thief. He had apparently pretended to be helplessly drunk whilst the search for the missing money had been going on. We had amongst our crew, a young fireman who had never been abroad before. He had looked forward to our Morlaix visit with much anticipation, especially after his shipmates told him of their previous visits. After we had docked, preparations for a night ashore began. This consisted of having sufficient money, by either getting a sub or borrowing from one's mates. Then washing, shaving and dressing up in one's go-ashore clothes. The night ashore would start as soon as they got ashore and most probably last until the early hours or until they had spent all their money.

The young fireman was soon ready and waiting impatiently for his mates. At last all were ready and they trooped along the main deck towards the gangway. But not the fireman, he was so excited, he started to tightrope walk

'PRICKER'

Firing iron.

along the top of the bulwarks, showing off. As he was stepping from the bulwarks to the head of the gangway he lost his balance. As he fell, luckily inboard, he must have caught his body on either the top of the bulwarks or the
gangway. It was probably then that he injured his ribs. When we assisted him
to his feet he was obviously in pain in his chest. Now he had lost all interest
in going ashore, so we assisted him back to the forecastle and helped him
into his bunk. By this time the pain in his chest had become worse, so we
decided to tell the 'Old Man'. He requested some information about the extent
of the injury. I, being the only qualified 'first aider' in our crew, was asked
to examine the fireman and give an opinion.

After I had examined the man, I explained that according to the signs and
symptoms, there was a possibility of a fractured rib. This did not please the
'Old Man' one bit. Accidents and injuries in foreign ports caused more than
the usual problems. Nevertheless, a doctor was called, I think this was done
through the shipping agent. However, after the doctor had examined the man,
he more or less confirmed my diagnosis. But he stated the man was fit to
travel back with us to England and there get any further necessary treatment.

When the young fireman was told he could return to England with us, he
became very upset and demanded that he should be put ashore into hospital.
This was what the 'Old Man' had been trying to avoid, leaving a man ashore
in a foreign port was a complicated affair, requiring the assistance of a
Consul and so on.

In due course the ambulance arrived and the injured fireman helped into it.
After it moved off he perked up expecting pretty nurses. His mate on returning said the hospital looked more like a workhouse and when they got inside,
found male orderlies. At this the fireman suggested returning to the ship but
arrangements had been made and so he had to stay.

Another form of disillusionment lay in store for deck hands who expected
free time in port or at least easy painting jobs since they could find themselves tallying cargoes or working winches, or both. I have no recollection of
driving winches to load cargo, but plenty of driving winches to discharge.
Fifty/sixty years ago, crew loading and discharging cargo was fairly common
in schooners and small steamers, especially in places where cargo shore
handling facilities did not exist. I remember schooners on the brick trade
between the continent and London River. They usually carried about 150 tons,
which were loaded and unloaded by the crew. If I recollect correctly the
freightage was about Ten Shillings a ton, so they had to work to make it pay.
Perhaps the crew were paid tonnage but I cannot say. However, our driving
winches were a relic of the old days. We hated it but were unable to refuse.
It took away any free time we might get when in port, working practically
watch and watch on the winches, that of course involved the firemen maintaining steam pressure, too.

Driving winches on those occasions was supposed to be part of the freight
agreement, but we often felt that someone got some 'Cumshaw' for our labour,
we never got a penny extra. It was a case of 'do the job' or else. The worst
of it was, we had to work as long as the shore gang worked, who may, being
paid tonnage, want to finish the discharge. If that was so, it meant a long
stretch for us. After they had finished we may have to sweep the hold, batten
down ready for sea, clean the ship as much as possible before sailing. Washing down in port was in the main prohibited, especially if any solids were
washed through the scuppers.

Coaling herring drifters out of the ship in Lerwick was a typical case of
crew driving winches. During the herring season in the Shetlands (about May)
it would practically be daylight all the time. Lerwick used to be a hive of
industry involving the goings and comings of drifters from all round the mainland and Shetlands. The fleet used to follow the herring from North to South
of the British Isles. They worked all hours that God sent, and those involved
with the industry had to work accordingly. For religious reasons they did not
work Sundays, but as soon as it was midnight, off they went to sea. And so it
went on all week, in with a catch, unload, perhaps bunker, then out again.

All the drifters were coal burners and bunkering went on, in spasms all
day. Bunker coal was transhipped direct from a ship to the drifters. There
was a firm in Lowestoft who had a coal hulk called the 'King Coal'. This was
used in the bunkering operations. However, whenever we carried coal to
Lerwick for the drifters, we would moor off the harbour and the drifters would
come alongside us to bunker, and we had to drive the winches. The days were
long, being almost constant daylight, they could come alongside us sometimes
about five in the morning and we would continue on the winches until they
stopped coming. I can only remember getting ashore once in Lerwick, so
hardly know what the place looked like. Once we had completed discharging
our cargo, it would be 'batten down ready for sea,' and off we would go to
our next port of call. One would be almost too tired to keep awake during the
first watch on deck. Sometimes we were almost glad to get to sea.

23. *The Completed Story.*

Thomas H. Thomason

A newspaper cutting taken from a newspaper called 'The Irish Independent', which I had long ago pasted in my scrap book, reminds me of an incident that occurred during the early days of January 1933, when on passage from Londonderry to the Bristol Channel. I have at some time or other, sailed into and out of most major ports in the British Isles, but my visit to Londonderry was a 'one off' occasion. Thus I remember little about the City itself, but recall much of the events which concerned our departure.

Our arrival in Londonderry was just too late for the Christmas holidays, not that Christmas made much difference to us, only that being a holiday it would enable us to enjoy a night or two of untroubled sleep in our bunks. We ate the same food as always, which depended mainly on what was available. Several vessels like us had arrived late. Referring to my newspaper cuttings, I see they include the S.S. NEPHRITE, the STARFINCH, the ACHILL, ENDA, ISLESMAN and my own ship the STANLEY FORCE.

Miss Houston, the lady in charge of the Sailors Rest, was determined that the ships' crews would have some enjoyment to celebrate Christmas. She, along with her many helpers, arranged a Christmas Dinner and Social evening for our benefit. Many of us accepted her invitation. After what was to us a wonderful Xmas Dinner we joined in, rather self-consciously, the party games initiated by Miss Houston and her helpers. Needless to say we all enjoyed the evening and on our behalf Mr. Muir, S.S. STARFINCH, proposed a vote of thanks. Before we left the Sailors Rest that night, each man received a Christmas present, each parcel containing either handkerchiefs, socks, sweets, cigarettes, writing pads, woollens or other articles. This was a nice conclusion to what had been a very wonderful evening. Miss Houston and her helpers will never know just how much we appreciated their kindness to us all.

Towards the end of 1932, we received orders to sail for the Bristol Channel. The weather was fine when we sailed in ballast out of Lough Foyle towards the open sea on an Easterly run to Rathlin Island. We had no idea of the trials and tribulations in store as like many coasters, we had no radio. Therefore, we did not have the advantage of an up to date weather forecast. It was my first watch on deck and when we got clear, the Old Man after giving the usual instructions, went below to his cabin. I was a pipe smoker and seldom if ever went on watch without my pipe and tobacco.

However, on this occasion I had left my pipe below in my cabin. So, waiting until I thought the Old Man had got settled, I had a quick look round the horizon then after telling the man at the wheel I would not be long, I quietly descended to my cabin beneath the lower bridge. I could only have been off the bridge for a few minutes but when I got back fog had closed in and visibility was down to nil. I lost no time in calling the Old Man. This was done by removing a canvas cover from his ventilator at deck level and shouting down it. I told him about the fog and he gave me the usual instructions, "Keep a good lookout - if you hear any whistles, bells, or fog signals of any kind, blow your whistle and I'll come up." As far as I can remember, nothing of any importance occurred during the rest of our watch on deck.

Back on watch some hours later, I found that the fog had gone and we had cleared Fair Head. We were now on a Southerly course down the East coast of Ireland. But, there was a freshening Southerly wind and a rising sea, which did not seem too promising. Our speed was obviously much reduced, instead of the usual 9/10 knots when light ship, making headway was becoming a laborious slowing progress with life on board becoming more uncomfortable due to the lively motion of the ship, which got worse with every passing hour. The bows were beginning to lift steeply on the oncoming seas then fall like a stone into the following troughs. The suddenness made lying in a bunk in the forecastle anything but restful and conditions amidships were little better.

I believe it was sometime during the 'eight to twelve midnight' watch that we had our first knowledge of trouble down below. This was when the Chief Engineer suddenly appeared on the bridge, which was a very unusual occasion, and informed the Skipper that the boiler tubes had begun to leak. By the way this was the only way of verbal contact with the engine room because the piping on the speaking tube had corroded away. It seemed that the ship's heavy labouring and consequential vibrations had resulted in the boiler tubes beginning to leak in the backends. This was serious, but not a new experience, it meant that we had to think of a safe anchorage to carry out repairs. The last time we had been off the Lizard and been fortunate to find suitable anchorage in Mounts Bay, but this time we were facing heavy weather from the South on the East coast of Ireland.

It was not very long before the Chief came back on the bridge and told the Skipper that the leak was getting worse and they would soon have to draw the fires. I remember the Skipper saying "Keep her going as long as you can, Chief." We were still in the open sea and the desirable safe anchorage was a problem. Meanwhile we were edging our way to the West in the hope of finding some smoother water and a secure anchorage. But time was running out fast, it was not very long before the Chief reported that the boiler water had disappeared from the gauge glasses and now the fires were being drawn. This was dismal news. Luckily there was noticeable smoothing from Lambay Island which lay unseen ahead. We were now somewhere between Lambay and Rockabill which lay astern. Anyway, with power almost gone we let go the port anchor and giving her plenty of chain, hoped for the best. We did not feel very happy as the ship bounced and tugged at her cable and spent anxious hours occasionally feeling the cable to see if she was dragging the anchor. So, throughout the hours of darkness, we watched, waited and hoped that the anchor would hold long enough for repairs to be made and steam to be raised.

Meanwhile in the stokehold, engineers and firemen working within the limited illumination provided by oil and duck lamps, and the inconvenience of limited space, continued unceasingly to get the leaks stopped. They knew as we did, time was important and what time there was depended on the anchor holding. It is almost impossible to describe the operation of caulking leaking tubes in the hot dusty backend of a furnace from which the fire has recently been removed. But as soon as it was considered humanly possible, someone had to crawl into the furnace space and through to the backend, and, with the aid of a hammer and caulking tool, get to work on the ends of the tubes and seal the leaks. This was an engineer's job, and in this case it was the Chief. First he had to wrap himself in sacking and other material to insulate himself from contact with the hot metal. One could only stay inside for a very limited time, but during the time a man was inside, another man was stationed outside ready to pull the inside man out if he looked to be in trouble. Needless to say, the caulking operation depended very much on the limit of human endurance, but the job had to be done, if at all possible.

Meanwhile on deck we waited and watched, now and again we would look down into the stokehold in the hope that we would see the job completed, but we could not see much. When daylight came we saw Lambay Island ahead and Rockabill astern, also we could see low lying land to the West, some miles off. Later, looking at a chart of 1928, we appeared to be anchored in the vicinity of the old three mile limit line, in about 13 fathoms m.l.s.

Sometime during the morning we learnt that the tubes had been successfully caulked and they had begun to raise steam. We knew that we would have to wait some time before sufficient steam pressure was available. In the meantime we continued to watch our anchorage and hope. It was sometime during the fore noon watch that the anchor chain parted. The sea was still rough, and we began to roll and drift to leeward, towards the now menacing Rockabill. The situation had now taken a turn for the worse, we began to think we had 'had it'. The Skipper ordered the distress signal to be hoisted. This

was the two flag international Distress Signal N.C. It was soon flying from a hoist on the foremast. We were also ordered to clear the boats and get them ready for swinging out. Meanwhile on the bridge, the Skipper was watching developments and, with the cook at the practically useless wheel, appeared to be trying to steer the ship inshore and inside Rockabill. Being light ship, our hull caught the wind and we tended to behave like a sailing ship. Nevertheless, our leeward drift appeared to be bringing us dangerously close to Rockabill and the sight of the rough seas breaking on the rocks made us think that if we did not get clear and struck, chances of getting away in our boats were pretty slim.

Naturally we kept an eye on our drift but I cannot say that I saw anyone showing signs of fear. What I did see was a man collecting his personal gear and another tying his cap on with a rope yarn. I think we tried to find something to take our minds off the nearing Rockabill. Eventually, after what seemed a lifetime, we cleared Rockabill and continued our drift towards the Skerries. In the meantime, the lightkeepers on Rockabill having seen our distress signals had begun to fire a gun to alert the lifeboat station on the mainland. Having drifted into smoother water, we let go the starboard anchor, but as soon as it began to hold the chain parted, now we were without a readily available anchor. The Skipper ordered that as much anchor chain as possible should be paid out so that it would drag on the bottom and holding us head to wind help to reduce the drift.

We were still hoping there would be time to raise the necessary steam pressure to operate the main engines but the situation was not too promising. The mainland could be seen quite clearly. With our anchor chains dragging on the bottom we were being held head to wind, consequently our drift had been considerably reduced. Although the sea was still rough it was not too bad inshore of Rockabill. In spite of our distress signals and the firing of a gun from Rockabill, there did not appear to be any response from the mainland. We saw two trawlers away to the North but nothing else. Eventually with the approaching darkness our distress signal flags were hauled down, they did not appear to be now serving any useful purpose.

At last our Chief gave us the news we had been waiting for, we now had sufficient steam to operate the main engines. I forgot to mention we had steam on the donkey boiler which worked the anchor windlass. We hove up our dragging anchor chains and slowly turning our ship began to edge her out towards the North East away from the land. Power was limited by low pressure steam but with the aid of wind on our quarter we managed to maintain steerage way and make progress, barely rotating the log. I do not know what it was like down below, but I got the idea that we were still nursing the boiler tubes.

With the increasing darkness, the range of visibility became uncertain, therefore, we were keeping a good lookout for the sight of any lights or ships. Home Trade navigation in those days relied very much on a known point of departure, thence by compass and log, sometimes supplemented by the lead, when in doubt, experience being the basic requirement. Neither had we a wheelhouse or in fact any overhead cover on the bridge. Thus anyone on the bridge had practically an all round view of the horizon. So, with four men, which included the Skipper and man at the wheel, staring out into the darkness, we inched our way towards the open sea. We were not exactly sure of our position and needed confirmation from some source, either lights ashore or on vessels.

We knew that somewhere ahead on the Irish mainland lay St. John's Point with the off-shore South Rock. Also the Isle of Man with the Chicken Rocks off its Southern tip. There was a gap between the mainland and the Island of about 30 miles which in the normal way was not any problem, but we not being too sure of our position had to give it some special thought. It appeared that our repaired boiler tubes were holding and steam pressure was back to normal, which was something to be thankful for.

People who have experienced long hours on lookout will agree that after a while imagination plays tricks with the eyesight. Sometimes during a very dark night one can find difficulty in fixing one's vision above or below the horizon, so there is a tendency to stare wide eyed in the hope of catching something. I saw, or thought I saw, a glow in the sky, just for a second. No-one else saw it apparently, so I put it down to imagination. Continuing my lookout I saw the glow again on the horizon. I said nothing, thinking "I'll make sure before I say anything." Eventually I took a compass bearing and reported the sighting to the Skipper. Everyone concentrated on the area of my compass bearing, but could not see the glow. Naturally, with three people out of four (one of whom was supposed to have eyes like a hawk) unable to pick up my glow, they began to doubt me. To satisfy them, I began to count off the interval between each glow, I established that it was regular and practically convinced the others.

The Skipper went down to the chart room to have a look at the chart and an almanac. When he came back on the bridge he said he was unable to idenfify the glow. But I could still see the glow, the fact that the others could not puzzled me. Nevertheless, I continued to count off the light durations, so much so the Skipper decided to go back to the chart room and check again. When he came up he said he had at last identified the glow, saying it was the flash from the fog gun on the South Rock Light Vessel. Now we had a fix on our position and I am sure the skipper was as relieved as we were. I was able to see the glow much clearer now, but none of the others could, neither could we hear the sound of the gun. I do not know when anyone else saw the gun flash, an odd experience. Although the light vessel had a double flashing light it was not seen in my watch. Later I heard the South Rock gun as we passed it.

Thinking back, I cannot remember any pre-knowledge of being bound for Belfast. It appears to be, as far as I was concerned something taken for granted. When I came on watch again it was getting daylight and we had entered Belfast Lough. Being in smooth water we began to rig the spare anchor. This was secured to brackets on a bulkhead in the fore well deck. In over a dozen years this was the first and only time I had seen it moved. Now it was necessary. After we had fished the end of the anchor chain from the hosepipe we hauled it round the bow and inboard over the rail into the well deck, securing it with a shackle to the now free spare anchor. Using the for' ard winch and derrick, we lifted the anchor outboard and gradually eased it for'ard at the same time taking in the slack chain using the windlass on the forecastle head. Finally we had the anchor safely housed in the hawsepipe

After docking in Belfast the Skipper went ashore, but before he did, he instructed us not to talk to anyone about our escapade. Why? I do not know. However, later on buying a newspaper, we found our incident had made the headlines. The paper stated that North and South of Ireland and various parts of Britain suffered havoc in communications through continued gales. Several vessels were either reported lost or in trouble. I believe a newspaper reporter boarded us after we docked but whether he got any information I cannot say.

The newspaper headline in the 'Irish Independent' was as follows:- "Life boats go out in search of ship, but no trace of vessel found."

"For hours yesterday, lifeboats from Howthe and Clogherhead, gallantly fought in mountainous seas to bring aid to a three-masted ship, supposedly of Belfast, that had flown distress signals. They returned at nightfall baffled by her disappearance, but concluded that she finally made safety in a Northern port." the newspaper report continued.

After reading the newspaper report, there was no doubt in our minds that we were the missing vessel referred to in the incident. We had certainly made headlines, but most important, we were lucky enough to be able to read it. I still cannot understand, why the lifeboats could not find us. As I previously stated, we could see the land and what appeared to be trawlers to the Nor'ard but I suppose the sea was so big and our boat was so small! Anyway, safely in Belfast, we wondered what our next orders would be. When the Skipper returned, we learned that replacement anchors and chain were being dispatched from Liverpool on the overnight mail boat.

The next morning was spent taking on board the anchors and chain and after stowing the chain in the lockers and anchors in the hawsepipes we unmoored and sailed for the Mersey. As far as the crew was concerned that is all the information we had. However, when we picked up the Liverpool pilot at the bar we learnt that we were going to Cammel Lairds, Birkenhead. Shortly after our arrival we moved into one of the dry docks.

It seemed no one attached any importance to our recent escapade, neither it seemed was there any show of appreciation concerning our success in getting the ship back home. In fact it was quite the opposite, as soon as we had berthed in dry dock, no time was lost by our owners in giving us 24 hours notice to go on half pay. This was not the first time we had experienced this so we knew what was entailed. We could of course request to be paid off, but that meant uncertainty in being signed on again. I remember the last job I did on full pay, I sat up half the night bringing the ship's official log up to date. Later I was told to take it to the owners' office in Water Street, Liverpool. Why me? I'll never know. Perhaps I was being secretly vetted by the owners. I do not know but only a few days later I was offered a Mate's berth in one of their bigger boats, which I turned down for reasons best known to myself.

None of our crew signed off and we began the uncomfortable period of living in a cold ship with all the inconvenience of amongst other things having to use the crude dockyard toilets. We worked dockyard hours, chipping, painting, cleaning out ballast tanks and bilges, etc. For this the sailors and firemen received about thirty shillings a week to buy their own food and necessities. If married they had to send what they could to their wives and families.

24.

The

Best Laid

Schemes.

E

CERTIFICATE OF DISCHARGE

OF A SEAMAN NOT DISCHARGED
BEFORE A SUPERINTENDENT OF A
MERCANTILE MARINE OFFICE.

Name of Ship and Official Number, Port of Registry and Gross Tonnage.	Horse Power.	Description of Voyage or Employment.
S/S STANLEY FORCE. OF WHITEHAVEN OFF. 134944 Gross. 586	61.9	HOME TRADE

Name of Seaman.	Year of Birth.	Place of Birth.
THOMAS H. THOMASON Rank or Rating.	1904	Fleetwood
Second-mate	Numbers of Certificates (if any). Dis.A. No. —	Any other Cert.
Date of Engagement.		Place of Engagement.
2. 2. 24		FLEETWOOD
Date of Discharge.		Place of Discharge.
26. 3. 36		LONDON

I Certify that the above particulars are correct and that the above-named Seaman was discharged accordingly.

Dated this 26 day of MARCH 1936

Signature of Seaman :

T. H. Thomason

Signature of Master. William S Williams

Signature of Witness. Wm Matthews

Occupation Mate

Address On Board

NOTE.—Any person who forges or fraudulently alters any Certificate of Discharge, or who makes use of any such Certificate, which is forged or altered or does not belong to him, is guilty of a misdemeanour, and may be fined or imprisoned.

N.B.—Should this Certificate come into the possession of any person to whom it does not belong, it should be handed to the Superintendent of the nearest Mercantile Marine Office, or be transmitted to the Registrar General of Shipping and Seamen, Tower Hill, London, E.C. 3.

Price 4d. per quire.

*5102. Wt.30887/2239. 75M. 3/35. Wy.P.C. 613. (4)

Thomas H. Thomason

Luck does exist; good or bad, it plays a part in all our lives. To depend on luck is dangerous, like the turn of a card, it could go either way. Some incident could, as in my case, cause a complete breakdown in planning, and a totally unexpected end product. In my own experience, luck has been in our favour, although at times it did not look that way. Looking back we could not, my Wife and I, have arranged things better, in spite of the apparent setbacks. We had been married for a few years and had begun to give some serious thought to the future. Whilst I had been single, the carefree roaming way of life at sea was accepted as part of the life I had chosen. Now we were beginning to realise that in the years ahead our time together could be measured in days and our separations in months.

I had for some time been giving serious consideration to having a job ashore and investigating possible channels. The trouble was the country was suffering from a period of depression and jobs ashore were few and far between. Another thing was, I had spent a lifetime making the sea my career and had no shore job experience. Therefore, it was most probable, if I got a job ashore it would be unskilled or possibly of a labouring nature. However, I was prepared to tackle that if it was necessary. Towards the end of 1935, during one of my rare visits home, my Wife and I, after a long discussion about the future, made a decision. We agreed that we save as much as we could during 1936 and at the end of that year I would sign off my ship and get down to the object of finding a job ashore.

It was towards the end of March 1936 that an incident occurred in Falmouth which caused damage to the ship's bulwarks, aft on the port side. I cannot remember the details, but it runs in my mind that due to weather conditions, we fouled one of the piers and stoved the bulwarks in. The damage was not

sufficient to prevent our sailing, but was nevertheless unsightly. We left Falmouth for the London River, and I think we had a rough passage. It was not until we entered the Thames estuary that we had some smooth water. The 'Old Man' came on to the bridge when we were somewhere off Shoeburyness. He suggested that we should have a go at tidying up the damaged bulwarks. After changing the steering wheel from manual operation to steam assisted, the 'Old Man' took over the wheel and the Mate, an A.B. and myself went aft to see what we could do. Borrowing some planks, a jack and a seven pound hammer from the Chief, we got to work. After a while we had succeeded in pushing the damaged bulwarks upright, but the supporting stanchions remained buckled and detached at the top end. Going back on the bridge I gave the 'Old Man' a report on what we had done. He was inclined to let that do until we got into our discharging berth. But, thinking we could straighten out the buckled stanchions, I suggested we carried on to see if this was possible. After some hesitation he agreed, and I went back to the repair job. It was our intention to punch out the broken rivets and using long bolts, pull the stanchions straight. Not having a suitable punch, we decided to use a long bolt as a punch. Leaning outboard over the bulwarks, I held the substitute punch in my left hand and with the hammer in my right thumped away, without any success. Finally I lost the hammer when it slipped out of my hand and disappeared into the sea. We could not continue without a hammer, so back I went to the Chief. He naturally was not too pleased about me losing his hammer, but lent me another one. Before we resumed, the Mate suggested that we might manage better if I held the punch for him to hit it with the hammer. I did not agree with that, saying something about the possibility of him missing the punch and hitting my hand. But he assured me that would not happen, and I like a fool, believed him.

Once more I leaned outboard over the bulwarks, holding the punch in my left hand and gripping the bulwarks with my right. The Mate swung the hammer, I do not know how many times he hit the punch but eventually the expected happened, he missed the punch and hit my hand. Things went a little hazy after that, I do know I was in agony, and was unable to release my hand from the punch as I rolled about the deck, not knowing what to do with myself, My hand had been crushed at the base of the left thumb and was bleeding quite freely. After a while, the steward came along and put a dressing on, but I was still feeling very shaky, and had no clear recollection of what was going on. I do not know if anyone had told the 'Old Man', but when I went on to the bridge he asked me what had happened, then seeing I had one hand available, he told me to take the wheel, which being steam steering I could manage.

I stayed on the bridge for much of the way up river. When we arrived off our discharging berth in Deptford Creek, we had to anchor and await sufficient water in. Whilst anchoring, we started to clear the hatchways for discharging. This means hoisting the derricks, taking off and rolling up tarpaulins, finally removing the heavy wooden hatch covers and lifting out the beams. All this I had to assist with, using one hand. It was awkward and I was having some pain from my injured hand. On one occasion I stumbled and instinctively put my left hand out to grab the hatch coaming. My injured thumb was knocked backwards, which may have worsened my injury, I do not know. However, the increased pain was almost as bad as when I first received the injury. The pain had eased a bit before we got alongside. After we had berthed the 'Old Man' examined my hand after which he expressed the opinion that it would be all right in a day or two. Whether he really believed that I do not know. Much to my surprise he said I could go home if I wanted to. It was a surprise sure enough, I normally had to ask him, could I go? Under normal conditions, I would have been thinking about a possible night home, but the accident had put all such thoughts out of my mind.

I lost no time getting ready for off. I had to wash down, shave and put my go-ashore gear on. It was a bit awkward one-handed, but with some assistance I finally managed and away I went. It was quite a journey to my home. By train from Deptford to London Bridge, another train to Hayes, Kent and finally a short bus ride, then after about a quarter of a hour's walk I arrived home. My Wife was now living with her sister in Kent. It was dark when I arrived my Wife was pleased to see me, she did not know about our arrival in London. But when she saw my, by now, bloody and bandaged hand, she was a little upset and wanted to know what I had been doing. I had to show her the injury, it was ready for bathing anyway. When my Wife's sister, who is a trained nurse saw it, she advised me to let a doctor see it. My Wife and I went up the road to see a local doctor, who examined my hand and after applying a fresh dressing advised me to go to the hospital.

The next morning I returned to my ship, I was not very early, my hand was very painful and I did not feel like hurrying. When I got back on board, I saw the 'Old Man' and told him what the doctor had said, he agreed, and I immediately made my way to Greenwich Seamens Hospital. There I was exam-

ined and X-rayed. My injured hand was dressed. I think it was stitched but cannot remember clearly. However, a nurse put my arm in a sling and before I left I was told to come back the next day. I said I could not, I would be at sea. The doctor said I could not, my hand was fractured and it would take a few days to see how the wound would heal before they could set the fractured bone and put my hand in plaster. I was both glad and sorry, a decision had been made for me against which I had no argument. I was a little apprehensive about the future and I was not ready. I wondered what my Wife would say.

When I got back on board I told the 'Old Man' what the doctor had said. He naturally was not very pleased about it. I do not know what sort of a report he would have to make out about the accident, but he would have to replace me before he sailed and getting used to another Second Mate would be to say the least, a bit of a bind. On learning that the ship would not be finished discharging until the next day, I decided that I would pack up my personal gear and collect it on the following day, after I had been to the hospital. When I got back home I told my Wife what the doctor had said. I think she was pleased that I would be staying home for a while, but like me was a bit worried about our financial position. We did not really know what, if any, our income would be. It would most certainly be less than normal, that is for sure.

The following day I returned to the hospital for a check up, and afterwards went back to my ship to collect my gear. I signed off articles and received my Second Mate's discharge certificate (which I still have). I packed as much of my personal gear as I could carry, and the remainder I put in to my big seabag and a biscuit tin. I stowed them in a cupboard, it was my intention at that time to rejoin my ship as soon as I was medically fit. But this was not to be, although that had been my intention, I had in fact made my last trip in the old ship, which had been practically my home for over a dozen years. The ship was due to sail in the early afternoon, so I hung about waiting to see her off. It is funny, now I was beginning to feel left out of things, especially when I saw the crew getting ready for sea and it did not involve me. Before I went ashore I said cheerio to the 'Old Man' and my shipmates, then stood on the quayside to see them off. At last she was moving and as the gap widened between the ship and quay I felt a little sad as I watched the gradual breaking link. Following the cry of "let go aft" I threw the stern rope free and could not resist the habit of years of crying "all gone aft". Then I stood and watched her sail out of my life. I never saw her again and although I had several letters from the 'Old Man' I never saw him again, either. He was to change ship soon after, and after surviving the war finally died of cancer. By the way I never did get the rest of my sea gear, I guess somebody was lucky.

After my ship had sailed I returned home, feeling a little apprehensive and insecure, wondering what the future had in store for me. I was naturally glad to be going home, but it was the shortage of funds that worried me. I mentioned previously about the hospital nurse putting my arm in a sling. This began to be somewhat of an embarrassment, especially when people began to help me in and out of the tram and train. As soon as I could I surreptitiously dispensed with the sling, putting it into my pocket. I did not wear it again, only when returning to the hospital or doctor. There was a funny sequel to this. Shortly afterwards, when returning to London to see the Shipping Office doctor, I saw a man sitting near me in the tram, who also had a bandaged hand. We got talking and I found that he was also going to see the Shipping Office doctor. Naturally we got off the tram and walked along together. But before we got to the Shipping Office, we dodged round a corner to put our arm slings on. I bet if anyone saw us they thought we were a couple of lead-swingers.

During the first fortnight ashore I had to make fairly frequent visits to the hospital and this was proving very costly in our depreciated financial condition. Although I now had some idea of what my income would be, it was not enough to allow for any extras. Therefore, I decided to apply for some financial assistance towards my travelling expenses. I went to the Shipping Office in Dock Street, London E.1., and made an application for monetary aid. I was advised that I could either come to some arrangements with some driver of a commercial vehicle, in other words to hitch a lift, or I could stay in hospital. They were not very helpful, but then sailors in those days had few benefits that they were entitled to. My income was now:- £1-10s (£1-50p) per week, National Insurance, or as it was then known 'Lloyd George'. There was an additional sum of 15/- (75p) per week from a club. So we had to manage on an income totalling £2-5s (£2-25p). We were a bit better off when my Wife got a part time job, which increased our income by 10/- (50p) a week.

Three months went by before I was considered medically fit. During that time I had been investigating the possibility of a job ashore. I had been ashore so long and got used to the comforts of home. I did not relish going back to sea again. Eventually I did get a job ashore. That blow from a seven pound hammer suddenly changed my lifestyle but in the end it was all for the best.

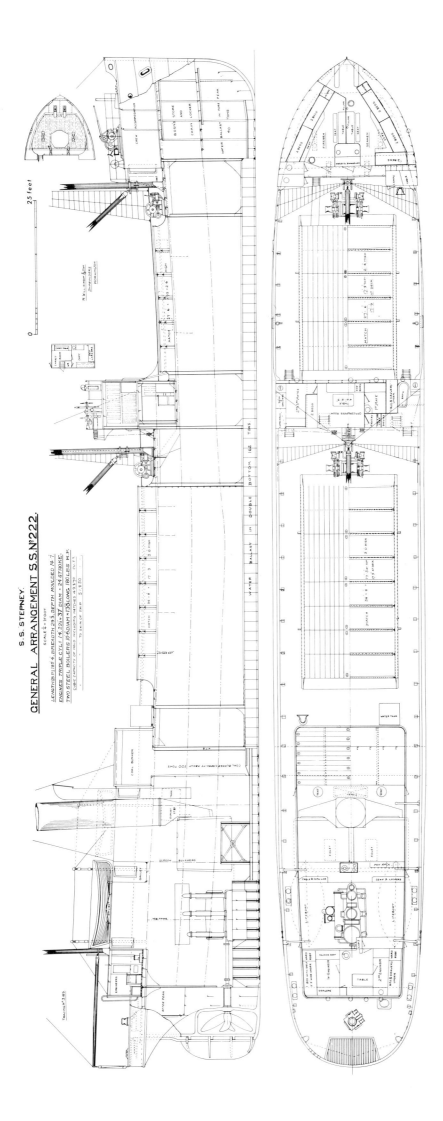

S.S. STEPNEY.

GENERAL ARRANGEMENT S.S. N°222.

SCALE ⅛ = 1 FOOT

LENGTH (B.P.) 185·4, BREADTH 29·3, DEPTH MOULDED 14·7.
ENGINES TRIPLE CYL: 14.22½×37 DIAM:×24 STROKE.
TWO STEEL BOILERS 10·6 DIAM:×10·5 LONG 180 LBS W.P.

CUBIC CAPACITY OF HOLD INCLUDING HATCHES 49.9 TO CU.FT.
TO SKIN OF SHIP 51,450

R.WILLIAMSON & SON
WORKINGTON.

(131) S.S. STEPNEY. No plans of the STANLEY FORCE have survived apparently and the plan above is that of the STEPNEY which though some 21 feet longer than the STANLEY FORCE, was also built by Williamson of Workington to a similar design. The main differences in the STANLEY FORCE were as follows: The forecastle layout was similar, except that there were only four bunks in the seamen's quarters and the division between seamen and firemen was straight. The smaller STANLEY FORCE was narrower amidships so there was not space for the bath shown on this plan and the pantry and cabin (for the steward) were against the ship's starboard side. The cabin on the port side was the same in both ships except that in the STANLEY FORCE it was occupied by the First and Second Mates. The Master's cabin on the lower bridge was the same in both ships. Aft, the engineer's accommodation and galley were closely similar. Unlike the STANLEY FORCE, the STEPNEY had the more expensive arrangement of twin boilers.

25.

132. The EDEN FORCE.

Reminiscences.

Thomas H. Thomason

I have been ashore now for many years but, living as I do near the sea, accounts for the regular reminder of ships, shipmates and my association with that life of long ago. I still have the tendency to use nautical terms and expressions.

While on articles the ship was our home, indeed for many men it was the only home they ever had. The ship was our world and the Almighty was the 'Old Man'. Those who earned their living on the sea had little respect for any shore authority, whom we often referred to as 'pen pushers' etc. I am glad not only to have spent some time at sea but also to have been shipmates with many good men. So, now and again, my memory is stirred by some sight, sound or saying and I am reminded of ships and shipmates, sometimes one in particular. They are scattered and if alive, old like me. Some years ago I decided to trace some of them but found only three. Some I know are having that long 'watch below' either ashore or with 'Davy Jones'.

There is no doubt, the old sailing ship men were often superior in practical seamanship. Seamen in large ships were often referred to as 'Soogy Moogy' sailors, in other words, paint washers. This of course mainly applied to passenger boats. Part of an A.B.'s qualifications was stated to be:- to be able to reef, splice and steer, but with the decline of sail, reefing was not often required. However, in both sail and steam, boat handling was a must and efficiency was essential.

Seamen were still required to use a palm and needle for the purpose of repair or making canvas items. Some vessels still used tri-sails on the main and mizzen, to add a knot or two to their speed, when the wind was suitable. Also it was necessary to be able to splice wire and rope, rig tackle for lifting and other purposes, make fenders, wash, chip and paint anywhere from truck to keel and mix our own paints. (The author holds a palm in the photo, 98).

Sea lanes round the British Isles were becoming increasingly populated by vessels of all kinds, shapes and sizes as well as many nationalities. Occasionally, the way ahead would be obstructed by fishing vessels of one sort or another, singly or in fleets, drifting on nets or lines, or perhaps with a trawl down. This would often mean a change of course to avoid them or their gear. During the hours of darkness, avoiding drift nets or lines required some complicated manoeuvres, unfortunately at times not completely successful.

During the 1914/18 post-war years, there was a noticeable reduction in the number of sailing vessels, large, small, cargo and fishing. Also it was becoming apparent that there was a growing demand for bigger and faster vessels, suitable for quick loading and discharge. The freight trade was becoming more competitive with foreign owners chasing us for cargoes. By the mid-1920s sighting a sailing vessel was a rare event, especially a 'Square Rigger'. This usually brought all hands on deck, it was such a rare occasion.

We did over the years sight one of the square riggers, participating in the annual Australia grain race and my personal scrap log for June 18th 1926 notes that at 5 pm. 'Sighted ARCHIBALD RUSSELL in full sail off Dungeness.'

When on the Continent we did not receive our pay in the normal way, but anyone who wished could ask for a 'sub', which we had to more often than not to buy food. But some of the men could not resist spending their money on other things and as a result when they sailed there would be insufficient food for the voyage. This I am afraid happened all too often and the men concerned would scrounge food from their shipmates or hang round the galley for any 'Blackpan' from the cook. Blackpan was usually surplus or waste from the cabin table and very often consisted of stew, hash or duff. Many cooks used the Blackpan as a bribe, a payment for some service i.e. filling the galley bunker, cleaning the galley fire ready for the cook in the mornings and having the kettle boiling when he turned out.

One was never in a good mood when called to go on watch, especially if the weather was bad. It was irritating to be roused by an apparently cheerful person, with the cry of:- "One bell you sleepers rise and shine". (One bell being a quarter hour before 'eight bells' when the watch was relieved). Lack of response from the sleepers usually resulted in an extra call:- "Come on my sons, you know what sons I mean". Sometimes, the cheerful attitude of the caller combined with the thought of leaving one's bunk, especially if it was to be a cold and wet watch on deck, would stretch one's goodwill to the limit, and the newly roused sleeper often made some verbal response concerning the doubtful parentage of the caller. This would usually be followed by a query. "What's the weather like?" the answer "seaboots and oilskins" would mean it would be a wet watch on deck. The only consolation one had was, that in four hours time the apparently cheerful callers would be reversed.

Seafarers, usually gave priority to the needs existing at any one time, and when at sea, especially in winter, being warm and dry was very important. Consequently, the forecastle door would be kept closed, to keep the water out and the heat in. When at sea in a loaded ship, the ventilator covers would be on, to prevent a flood whenever the ship buried her bows into a sea. With every hole bunged up, the bogy stove going full blast and an oil lamp burning, it was no wonder that the forecastle atmosphere became deficient in oxygen. It was sometimes difficult to keep the oil lamp burning, in spite, of turning the wick up, even then we could barely maintain a flame, all this plus the smell of unwashed men, drying clothes, stale tobacco and food, not forgetting the oily smell from oilskins to which we used to give a coat of boiled oil occasionally. So it was not any wonder with all these sources contributing their various smells, the internal atmosphere became foul and unhealthy. To most people the fug would have been intolerable, but to the regular occupants it was part of keeping warm. No wonder some seamen had chest complaints. By the way, whenever the forecastle door was opened, the flame on the wick in the oil lamp would flare up, and if not turned down quickly the lamp glass could be broken. One of the most important things about sea-going clothing was weather protection. In the winter, long-johns under two pairs of trousers was not unusual, neither was two jerseys over the shirt. A woollen scarf (often a gift from a Seamen's Mission) wound round the neck over the head and ears, was worn, topped by a sou'wester or hard weather hat. All these along with rubber thigh boots and a waterproof coat helped one to keep warm and as dry as possible. The waterproof coat would usually be kept in place by a body and soul lashing, as we more often than not lost the buttons. In the winter, gloves or mitts were necessary when at the wheel, occasionally men would use 'old socks'. This could cause the spokes of the wheel to smell of sweaty feet and the spokes passed close to the nose, therefore, wearing socks for mitts was not popular! For additional comfort, we would sometimes put a firebrick in the galley oven, later, when going off watch, we would wrap, it in a cloth or towel and put it into our bunks, it was great.

Occasionally the forecastle would become infested with bugs. Fleas we did not seem to mind, but bugs were different. With a changing crew, organised hygiene was difficult. To control the infestation one mainly relied on personal effort, which was mainly applied to one's bunk, clothing and food locker. I suppose we could have complained to the sanitary officials when they boarded us in some ports, but we were afraid to do so. Sending money home was a personal matter. This was normally done by postal order in a registered envelope from the nearest post office. Weekly boat crew signed articles when they joined the ship, and would continue to re-sign every six months whilst they remained a member of the crew. Once they had signed on, they lost all their rights; they had signed for seven days a week and twenty four hours in every day, anything over and above that was overtime. We used to say:- "Six days shalt thou labour and on the seventh, do twice as much." We could not call any time our own, day or night. Any time-off depended on conditions, or the whim of the 'Old Man' or Mate, and nothing could be done about it.

Archibald Russell

When at sea, we kept four hour watches and still used the old terminology of 'One Bell' when the watch was called, and 'Eight Bells' when the watches changed. Each trip, one watch would get what was referred to as 'eight hours in', this meant that the watch concerned would be below during the 8 pm. to midnight and 4 am. to 8 am. Occasionally, for one reason or another we would lose our watch below, this was usually during the daytime, and was, I believe called keeping 'calashy watches'. Doing a continuous 12 hour watch was not popular, and we sometimes thought it was not necessary. But we could not refuse to do it.

I often think of some of the hard slogs we had, labouring our way towards the Longships, from either the Smalls, Bristol Channel, Fastnet and so on. Once or twice, I recollect we came close to disaster. There was one occasion when attempting to round the Lizard. The night was as black as pitch, the only light to be seen was the quick flash of the Lizard light and the phosphorescence of the wave tops as they broke on our hull. We had been hours trying to round Lizard and appeared to be making no headway. After a while, the Old Man decided to turn and run for Falmouth, but turning was not only a problem it was dangerous in the rough sea. After watching the sea for a while the Old Man made up his mind to try it. But first he sent me aft to warn the engineer and to close all doors including the galley, stokehold and engine room doors. As soon as the Old Man thought it suitable to do so, we commenced our turn. We spent a few anxious moments as we watched the seas, they appeared bigger than ever. We, with our big canvas covered hatchways offered little protection against the weight of water from any incoming sea of that size. Eventually, after what appeared to be a lifetime, we got her round and headed for Falmouth and some peace. There were many similar occasions. It was very disappointing to go below with Cape Wrath near abeam and come back on watch four hours later and find the Cape just abaft the beam. I can only recollect one occasion when we failed to round the Cape, and we finally went South about. The long passage meant some food rationing.

Occasionally, I think of the time when we have had to leave the safety of some harbour and put out to sea in very bad weather. We used to wish that something would happen to postpone our departure. Now and again we would sail on the last of the tide without waiting to batten down. Then we would have to work as fast as possible to get secured before we reached rough water. It was no joke lifting heavy beams and hatches as the ship got lively. Sometimes the distance between rough and smooth water was not very far. I was thinking for example of Blyth on the N.E. coast. We would drive the ship at full speed between the sheltering piers emerging into rough water. It was not so bad 'light ship' but if loaded we would most likely start shipping water. We used to take many risks. The owners drove the old man and he kept driving us.

"Old Bill" must be dead by now. He remained "55" for as long as I was with him and that was about 13 years. He was a tough old salt and had started his sea career in the old topsail schooners, which used to sail round our coast and occasionally over to America. During all the time we were shipmates he only managed to get home to Anglesey once a year; practically a stranger to his family. Many officers and crew men in our firm were natives of North Wales or Anglesey. Their chance of getting a visit home was very remote. If one lived in a seaport the odds were more in favour, such as myself, living in Fleetwood. In those days, leave either with or without pay was not a right whilst we were signed on, even in one's home port. Several times in my home port I have been only minutes away from my home, with no guarantee that I would eventually get leave. I remember one occasion after an absence of about twelve months I got six hours at home. So it is understandable that men took advantage of any opportunity to visit their folks. I recollect a shipmate jumping at the chance of walking from Bangor to Llangefni and back, to get a night home. We were anchored in the Menai Straits weather bound, and getting repairs to our windlass.

There were occasions when we were bound for Liverpool and with plenty of time to spare for tide, we would pay a call to Red Wharfe Bay. This was when we had Captain Roberts and others who lived locally, as crew members. As far as I can remember, our call was always made during the hours of darkness but our arrival would always be noticed by those on shore. As we steamed into the bay, morse lamps would be flashing all over the place, calling us up. When we answered, the enquiry would always be "What ship?" I could imagine the bush telegraph at work ashore. Anyway, we would drop anchor and lower the small boat, Captain Roberts and others would head for shore and pay a flying visit to their homes and families. These quick visits would often be brief breaks in months of absence.

I served under several captains during my time in the Stanley Force. Those which come to mind are Captain Bridson, Captain Wilson, Captain Hughes, Captain Harris, Captain Williams, Captain Roberts and another Captain Williams. Captain Elliott was one of our Skippers for a period during the late 1920s. He was, I believe a Manxman, but he lived in Connah's Quay,

South Stack.

He was a stout cheerful man with protruding eyes and a very gravelly voice.

Our first Captain Williams looked every inch a Skipper and was usually neat in appearance. He was not with us very long, but I do remember him especially for his love of singing. This was common to most North Welshmen, and I had several as shipmates. Captain Williams seemed to delight in arranging a vocal picnic on the fore hatch occasionally when in port. He would somehow gather us together and start a sing song. Some, myself included, did not want to be involved, but found it very difficult to chance risking the Old Man's displeasure. So, we had to join in and let it rip with the rest of them. The tunes we sang were mostly hymn tunes with a good chorus, I must confess, once we got going we generally enjoyed it, sometimes we put in our own words but no one seemed to mind as long as we kept the tune.

Among the mates I remember were Mr. Harris (later Captain), Mr. Williams and Mr. Matthews of Llangefni, Anglesey who was the second mate/boatswain when I joined the ship. Of Chief Engineers there was Mr. Dawson and Mr. Aitkin who had a heart attack and died on board in Hull roads. Both came from Liverpool. Second engineers included Mr. Munday of Teignmouth and Mr. Cole of Newlyn.

The STANLEY FORCE survived the 1939/45 war and continued to sail the sea lanes round the British Isles for many years afterwards. Her end came on the 14th of February 1953 when she foundered after striking submerged wreckage south west of Cap La Hague on passage Guernsey to London with granite. So now I'll never see her. Unfortunately, one man was lost with her. I got very attached to the old ship and had a chance to change ships once. I think it was early in 1933 when in dry dock at Birkenhead. I was offered the job as mate in one of her sister ships, the EDEN FORCE but for several reasons, turned it down.

My souvenirs include some of my own scrap logs, photographs, cargo plans, charts and a nautical almanack dated 1936. I have also, the speaking tube mouthpiece (previously mentioned), two old 'Red Dusters' which should have been used as brass rags. Often with links like these I am able to go back in time and re-live my days (and nights) aboard the old 'Stanfo'. To me she is almost like the 'Flying Dutchman'.

135. Some of the crew of the STANLEY FORCE photographed at Blyth while waiting to load coal. Standing (from left to right), the Author, Thomas Thomason and Joe Ward, both Seamen and Mr. Edwards, the Mate. The two men sitting down are Paddy Mulcahy and Tom Cleary, both Firemen.

Appendix

Extracts of the Log of STANLEY FORCE
Thomas H. Thomason.

October 8th 1926. Garston, Liverpool.

6-00 am. Raining heavily.

Noon. Sailed for Penmaenmawr. Wind Westerly, weather fine.

6-10 pm. Arrived and anchored off Penmanemawr.

9-00 pm. Commenced to heave up anchor, but the piston of the windlass broke and we could not continue. Weather deteriorating, strong Westerly wind increasing, sea rising.

October 9th 1926. At Sea (Menai Straits).

12-15 am. Using the fore winch, we fleeted the anchor chain inboard (30 fathoms).

1-00 am. Alongside loading pier, Penmaenmawr. Weather bad, sea rough, in danger of damaging ship hitting the bottom. Decided to come off again. Gale worsened from the West and big sea running. Ship would not steer properly.

8-30 am. Anchored off Bangor. Put small boat in the water and rowed ashore with piston for repairs. Great difficulty rowing against wind. Repairs to be finished by 1-0 pm, so rowed back to ship leaving Skipper and Chief Engineer ashore. Westerly gale still blowing, rain showers.

4-15 pm. Went ashore again in boat to pick up Chief and Skipper.

5-45 pm. Landed 'Old Bill' on Anglesey side to walk to his home in Llangefni. On returning in the boat we hooked it on the davits and hoisted it to rail level for the night. Crew on anchor watches, four on and four off. Both anchors out. Weather improving?

October 10th 1926. Anchored in Menai Straits. The day commenced with a dead calm. The ship lay across the tide for about 3 hours. At daybreak it began to blow again from the Westward.

Noon. Took boat ashore to fetch 'Old Bill' aboard.

1-30 pm. Took Skipper to Bangor Pier to telephone the owners.

3-30 pm. Hove up both anchors and proceeded to the mouth of Menai Straits.

4-00 pm. Anchored off Penmon Quarries. Weather showery, signs of more wind. But it remained calm for the night. Anchor watches.

October 11th 1926. Anchored in Menai Straits. The day commenced fine, light Westerly wind, showery. Later wind began to blow hard from SW with showers of rain.

11-00 am. Hove up anchor and made another attempt to get alongside the loading pier at Penmaenmawr. Weather too bad, came off.

2-00 pm. Anchored off Bangor Pier. Boat sent ashore for food supplies and fresh orders.

4-00 pm. We got fresh orders, proceed to Newlyn.

4-15 pm. Hove up anchor and proceeded to Newlyn. The weather is still bad, wind about WNW.

5-45 pm. Anchored in Red Wharf Bay, (45 fathoms of chain out). Weather looks promising.

October 12th 1926. At Sea.

6-50 am. Hove up anchor and resumed passage. Wind about WSW. We are not making much progress.

7-55 am. Point Lynas abeam. Weather conditions seem to be improving. We cannot see any ships sheltering in Holyhead.

11-25 am. South Stack abeam, course SW$\frac{1}{4}$S. Commenced heavy rain, weather getting worse, SWly wind increasing. Considering putting ship about.

4-45 pm. 'Bout ship, running for Holyhead. Course NE$\frac{1}{2}$N. Sea building up.

8-10 pm. South Stack abeam.

8-45 pm. Anchored in Holyhead Harbour, both anchors, each 45 fathoms of chain.

Midnight Westerly gale, ship sheering and swinging, heavy strain on anchor chains. Holyhead Breakwater light bearing, NExE.

October 13th 1926. Windbound Holyhead Harbour. The day commenced with a Westerly gale.

6-00 am. Anchors dragging, hove up and steamed further in and let go both anchors.

3-30 pm. Put boat out. Skipper telephoned the owners. Skerries bears NExN$\frac{1}{2}$N. Holyhead Breakwater light bears ENE and the White and Green Light bears SSE.

6-00 pm. Weather still bad, inclined to showers.

October 14th 1926. Windbound Holyhead Harbour. Day commenced Westerly gale and heavy rain.

1-30 am. Rain has stopped and wind is easing. After about half an hour wind increased blowing harder than before from the West.

4-00 am. No vessels have left the anchorage.

Noon. Wind decreasing.

4-00 pm. During the afternoon three vessels left the anchorage, but one had returned. The wind appears to be decreasing, swinging NW.

9-00 pm. Hove up anchors and resumed passage, not much sea, better than we expected.

9-50 pm. South Stack abeam, Course SW$\frac{1}{2}$S. Log not streamed.

October 15th 1926. At Sea.

2-35 am. Bardsey abeam, course SW$\frac{1}{2}$S. Log still not streamed. Strumble Head. Light Westerly wind, weather very clear.

10-45 am. Smalls abeam, course SxW$\frac{1}{2}$W. Weather hazy and wet.

10-45 pm. Pendeen abeam. Course SWxW$\frac{1}{2}$W. Wet.

Midnight. Longships abeam. Weather clear.

October 16th 1926. At Sea.

2-00 am. Arrived and berthed in Newlyn. Weather wet. GALACUM alongside pier.

2-30 pm. Commenced loading granite for London.

9-10 pm. Finished loading.

10-10 pm. Sailed for London.

10-20 pm. Log set at buoy, course SExS. Wind Easterly. Wet and hazy.

October 17th 1926. At Sea.

12-40 am. Lizard abeam, log 17. Course East.

6-20 am. Eddystone abeam, log 56. Course East.

10-00 am. Start Point abeam, log 85. Course ExN.

3-50 pm. Log hauled 30.

4-20 pm. Portland Bill abeam, course not recorded.

5-40 pm. Moored alongside coal hulk in Portland Harbour, to take in 15tons bunker coal.

5-55 pm. Commenced bunkering.

6-45 pm. Finished bunkering.

6-50 pm. Unmoored and resumed passage.

7-30 pm. Log streamed and set.

9-52 pm. Anvil Point abeam, log 18. Course ExS$\frac{1}{2}$S. Wind NE. Clear.

October 18th 1926. At Sea.

2-30 am. St. Catherines, I. o. W. abeam, log 50. Course East.

5-20 am. Owers Light vessel abeam, log 69. Course ExN. Wind NE. Moderately clear.

10-35 am. Beachy Head abeam, log 7. Course ExN$\frac{1}{2}$N.

11-50 am. Royal Sovereign Light Vessel abeam, log 17 and course ExN$\frac{1}{2}$N.

3-50 pm. Dungness abeam, log 46. Course NExE$\frac{1}{2}$E.

6-55 pm. Dover Piers abeam, log 68. Course NExE.

7-10 pm. South Foreland abeam, log hauled 71. Course NE.

9-50 pm. NE Spit Buoy abeam, course N$\frac{1}{2}$W.

10-20 pm. East Tonge Buoy abeam,

11-37 pm. Girdler Light vessel abeam. course WxN. Weather very clear, cold NNE wind.

October 19th 1926. At Sea. Heading up the Thames.

4-50 am. Anchored in Lower Reach, off Gravesend. Thick fog.

8-10 am. Hove up anchor, fouled by a steamer, no damage done.

8-40 am. River pilot came aboard, headed up-river at full speed.

4-00 pm. Berthed at Albert Dock Hoists.

October 20th 1926. Albert Dock Hoists, London River.

4-30 am. Shifted ship to discharge part cargo.

10-00 am. Finished discharging, unmoored and sailed for Fry's Wharf.

11-45 am. Berthed Fry's Wharf, resumed discharging.

5-00 pm. Finished discharging for the day.

October 21st 1926. Fry's Wharfe (London River).

6-00 am. Resumed discharging.

11-00 am. All finished discharging. Weather wet.

Noon. Sailed for Antwerp. River Pilot aboard.

2-45 pm. Dropped Pilot at Gravesend. Weather fine strong Easterly wind.

4-45 pm. Nore Light Vessel abeam.

5-25 pm. Girdler Light Vessel abeam. Course ExS.

6-30 pm. North Foreland abeam, log streamed and set. Course ExS. Wind about NE. Fine and clear.

October 22nd 1926. At Sea.

12-10 am. West Hinder Light vessel abeam, log hauled.

12-20 am. Picked up the pilot. Slight NEly swell. Course now, ExS$\frac{1}{2}$S.

3-10 am. Terschelling Bank Light abeam, course E$\frac{1}{2}$S.

6-50 am. Flushing, changed pilots.

12-30 pm. Arrived and anchored in the river off Antwerp Docks.

2-30 pm. Hove up anchor and entered docks.

3-45 pm. Moored in the basin.

9-10 pm. Berthed in Siberia Docks. Weather fine.

October 23rd 1926. Antwerp, Belgium. Weather fine and very cold, awaiting cargo.

October 24th 1926. Antwerp, Belgium. Sunday not much activity ashore or aboard.

October 25th 1926. Antwerp, Belgium.

8-00 am. Commenced loading coal for Belfast.

4-00 pm. Finished loading for day. Have about 300 tons aboard. No more available.

October 26th 1926. Antwerp, Belgium.

Mid-day Resumed loading cargo.

4-00 pm. All finished loading, awaiting bunker coal. Weather South East winds, wet.

October 27th 1926. Antwerp, Belgium. Still awaiting bunker coal, crew all at work painting. Weather fine, very warm.

October 28th 1926. Antwerp, Belgium.

8-00 am. Commenced to take in bunker coal.

11-00 am. Finished bunkering, about 100 tons. Stacked on top and on deck between main hatch and bunker hatch (extra bunkers were still being taken because of the coal strike in Britain).

3-15 pm. Sailed for Belfast. Pilot on board.

6-45 pm. Anchored in the Schelde, fog bound.

October 29th 1926. Anchored in the Schelde.

7-45 am. On our second attempt we were able to heave up and resume passage.

? Flushing. Changed Pilots. Weather hazy.

Noon. Dropped sea Pilot near Wandelaar Light Vessel. Weather fine, wind NEly. Big sea running. Resumed passage on course WNW.

2-30 pm. West Hinder Light Vessel abeam, log streamed and set. Course W$\frac{1}{2}$S.

5-25 pm. Sandettie Light Vessel abeam, log 23. Course West, wind NNE.

7-45 pm. South Goodwin Light Vessel abeam, log 40. Course WxS$\frac{1}{2}$S. (Entering Dover Straits).

10-35 pm. Dungeness abeam, log 61. Course WxS$\frac{1}{2}$S. Wind NE, fine and clear.

October 30th 1926. At Sea.

1-20 am. Royal Sovereign Light Vessel abeam, log 83. Course W$\frac{1}{2}$N. Wind now NNW.

2-28 am. Beachy Head abeam, log 91. Course W$\frac{1}{2}$N.

7-15 am. Owers Light Vessel abeam, log 28. Course WxN. Wind now NEly.

10-00 am. St. Catherine abeam, log 49. Course WxN. Course WxN$\frac{1}{2}$M.

1-30 pm. Anvil Point abeam, log 77. Course WxN$\frac{1}{2}$N. Weather showery.

3-55 pm. Portland Bill abeam, log 96. Course West. Wind NEly. Clear. During the afternoon, we had to about ship to get clear of seven minesweepers engaged in sweeping manoeuvres and about 30 other H. M. ships.

10-00 pm. Start Point abeam, log 45. Course W$\frac{1}{2}$N. Wind ENE. Fine and clear. We reported ship at Prawle Point Signal Station.

October 31st 1926. At Sea.

1-15 am. Eddystone Light abeam, log 67. Course W$\frac{1}{2}$N.

6-05 am. Lizard abeam, log 6. Course NWxW.

9-10 am. Longships abeam, log 29. Course NxE$\frac{1}{2}$E.

10-00 am. Pendeen abeam, log 35. Course NExN$\frac{1}{2}$N. Heavy NEly swell.

? Smalls.

November 1st 1926. At Sea.

1-50 am. South Bishops abeam, log 45. Course NExN.

4-00 am. Fresh ESE wind, heavy overcast.

8-00 am. Bardsey abeam, log 91. Course NExN.

12-55 pm. South Stack abeam, log 30. Course North. Southerly gale, heavy sea.

4-00 pm. Weather similar, visibility not good.

6-30 pm. Chickens abeam, log 75. Course N$\frac{1}{2}$E. Southerly gale, wet.

10-00 pm. Sighted Mull of Galloway.

November 2nd 1926. At Sea.

12-45 am. Mew Island abeam, log hauled 22.

3-30 am. Arrived and berthed, Queens Quay, Belfast.

9-00 am. Shifted ship, commenced discharging.

5-00 pm. Discharging stopped and shifted ship to Albert Quay, resumed discharging.

November 3rd 1926. Belfast. Crew worked all night cleaning out holds.

8-00 am. After cleaning holds shifted ship to berth alongside steamer in York Dock, and commenced loading maize for Glasgow.

6-00 pm. Finished loading and sailed for Glasgow. Pilot on board.

7-00 pm. Dropped Pilot. Weather fine and clear, wind SWly.

7-45 pm. Black Head abeam, log streamed and set. Course NE$\frac{1}{2}$E. Weather fine and clear.

? Ailsa Craig.

1-55 am. Pladda Island abeam, log 47. Course NExN.

2-40 am. Holy Island abeam, log 54. CourseNExN$\frac{1}{2}$N.

4-25 am. Cumbrae Island abeam, log hauled 68. Greenock, Pilot boarded.

9-00 am. Berthed in Glasgow, commenced discharge.

6-20 pm. All finished discharging.

7-15 pm. Sailed for Fleetwood. Weather slight rain hazy.

9-50 pm. Greenock, dropped Pilot.

11-40 pm. Cumbrae Island, log streamed and set. Weather, strong southerly gale, heavy rain.

November 5th 1926. At Sea.

12-15 am. Turned back, difficulty steering ship in the bad conditions.

2-35 am. Anchored off Greenock (65 fathoms of chain and starboard anchor).

4-00 am. Southerly gale and rain.

8-00 am. No change. Crew employed washing holds.

Noon. Wind changed to the West. We have both anchors out and are dragging on both.

12-30 pm. Hove up anchors and proceeded to Rothesay Roads. Westerly gale.

3-30 pm. Anchored in Rothesay Roads.

4-00 pm. Westerly gale and showers.

8-00 pm. No change.

Midnight. Still Westerly gale and heavy showers.

November 6th 1926. Anchored in Rothesay Roads.

7-30 am. Hove up anchors and resumed passage.

8-15 am. Cumbrae Island abeam. Wind moderating SWly, sea choppy.

10-00 am. Anchored off Lamlash. Wind strong WSW.

3-30 pm. Hove up and resumed passage.

4-30 pm. Pladda Island abeam. Course not recorded.

8-00 pm. Moderating SW wind, clear.

8-45 pm. Black Head abeam, Course South.

10-50 pm. Mull of Galloway abeam, Course SE$\frac{1}{2}$S. Moderate SW wind, sea fair.

November 7th 1926. At Sea.

? Point of Ayre. Course South.

4-00 am. Fresh WSW wind and sea rough.

7-00 am. Morecambe Bay Light Vessel abeam. Course E$\frac{1}{2}$S.

8-30 am. Lune Buoy abeam. Log hauled?

10-50 am. Fleetwood Pilot came on board.

11-30 am. Berthed at Burn Naze Jetty.

4-00 pm. Strong Westerly winds and heavy showers.

6-00 pm. Commenced loading a cargo of soda ash. Loading continued throughout the night.

November 8th 1926. Burn Naze Jetty, Fleetwood. Day commenced with a fresh Easterly wind, sky heavily overcast. Crew working all day painting the funnel. Loading continues. Day ended with fresh NW wind.

November 9th 1926. Burn Naze Jetty, Fleetwood.

1-00 am. Sailed for Bristol, Pilot on board.

1-20 am. Dropped pilot opposite Ferry Dock at Fleetwood.

2-20 am. Lune Buoy, log streamed and set. Course WxS. Fine and clear.

3-40 am. Morecambe Bay Light vessel abeam, log 10. Course WxS.

10-30 am. Skerries. Passed inside.

11-30 am. South Stack abeam, log 71. Course SWxS$\frac{1}{2}$S.

3-45 pm. Bardsey abeam. Course SW$\frac{1}{2}$S. Weather fine and clear.

November 10th 1926. At Sea.

12-07 am. South Bishops abeam, log 67. Course SxW.

1-35 am. Skokholm Island abeam, log 79.

2-00 am. St. Annes Point abeam, log 82. Course SExE$\frac{1}{2}$E.

3-25 am. St. Govan's Light Vessel abeam, log 92.

\- ? ?

10-30 pm. Arrived and berthed in Bristol.

November 11th 1926. Bristol.

8-00 am. Commenced discharge of cargo. Weather inclined to be wet.

5-00 pm. Finished discharging for the day. Weather fine.

November 12th 1926. Bristol.

8-00 am. Resumed discharging. Weather hazy, but cleared towards noon.

2-15 pm. All finished discharging.

3-00 pm. Shifted ship to basin locks, awaiting tide.

? Sailed for Newlyn. Pilot on board.

11-40 pm. Dropped pilot at Pill.

November 13th 1926. At Sea.

3-30 am. SW gale increasing. Making no headway.

4-15 am. Weather too bad, 'bout ship for Penarth.

6-45 am. Let go port anchor in Penarth Roads. Weather SW gale, heavy rain showers with thunder towards evening.

November 14th 1926. At Sea.

November 14th 1926. Anchored Weather Bound. Day commenced Westerly gale and showers, heavy at times.

8-00 am. Weather, no change.

Noon. Weather, no change.

8-00 pm. Gale moderating, clear. The day ended with fresh SW wind.

November 15th 1926. Anchored Weather Bound.

1-00 am. Hove up anchor and resumed passage.

3-20 am. Nash Point abeam.

7-00 am. Ship making no headway,

Index

*names of ships

Index